Marvels of Science

Marvels of Science

50 Fascinating 5-Minute Reads

Kendall Haven

1994
Libraries Unlimited, Inc.
Englewood, Colorado

LIBRARIES UNLIMITED, INC.
P.O. Box 6633
Englewood, CO 80155-6633
1-800-237-6124

Project editor: Tama J. Serfoss
Electronic production editor: Stephen Haenel
Copy editor: Tama J. Serfoss
Proofreader: Lori Kranz
Indexer: David V. Loertscher
Design and layout: Judy Gay Matthews

Library of Congress Cataloging-in-Publication Data

Haven, Kendall F.
   Marvels of science : 50 fascinating 5-minute reads / Kendall Haven.
   xxii, 238 p. 17x25 cm.
   Includes bibliographical references and index.
   ISBN 1-56308-159-8
   1. Discoveries in science--History. 2. Science--History.
3. Science--History--Miscellanea. I. Title.
Q180.55.D57H38 1994
509--dc20   93-44610
                                        CIP

Contents

Physical Sciences

Life Sciences

Introduction

Two eighth-graders sat on the shaded, stone steps of a local junior high school shortly after the bell rang ending the first day of school in September. One, a thoughtful, black-haired girl, tried to console her friend, a lanky, blond boy wearing a letterman sweater.

"Come on. It can't be *that* bad . . ."

"Did you look at this? Two science classes. I'm gonna die of boredom this semester!"

Why do so many of us turn our noses up at science and think it's boring? You might well think it's difficult, and that there are a lot of formulas to learn and math to unravel. That can be true. But boring? No way!

I hold a master's of science in oceanography and worked in applied science research for six years before finding my real love, storytelling and writing. Still, I grew up with this same, deeply ingrained belief that science is as boring a subject as any in school. I didn't just think the *study* of science was boring. I believed the *doing* of science was also boring, that everything about science was boring. Why did I believe that? Because no one told me about, or showed me the drama, the intrigue, and the passion, that are very real parts of science investigations.

I remember thinking that Sir Isaac Newton must have awakened one day, stretched, and muttered, "Ho, hum. It's been a while since I've been in the spotlight. Guess I better invent gravity today." Then he got dressed and wandered outside looking for something symbolic. And, bam! There dangled a conveniently poised apple just waiting for an opportune moment to drop.

Wrong! It didn't happen that way at all. Newton was plagued for years by nagging questions. Nothing made sense. Apples fell. Rain fell. Trees fell. People fell. Why didn't the moon fall? Why didn't the stars fall? Why didn't the earth fall into the sun? Then came a moment of euphoric, joy-filled insight. Gravity! What a moment that must have been when the lights finally lit, the pieces fell together, and the universe suddenly made sense!

The history of science is stuffed with such moments of glorious epiphany. Not just the gaudy, famous ones; there have been thousands of such moments ranging from earth-shaking breakthroughs to insignificant but personally satisfying moments of realization. These are the moments when understanding triumphs over confusion and doubt. Maybe it comes in one big bang at the end; maybe as a thousand little tremors along the way. But it comes. And it is oh so sweet and satisfying. Whatever else science may be, it is certainly not boring.

I jumped at the chance to write this book of stories because I think science has gotten a bum rap. Science is a world of mystery, doubt, risk, struggle, courage, frustration, intuition, imagination, winner-take-all races, and magnanimous teamwork. Science has all the elements of rich human drama. By its very nature, science is a continual leap of blind faith into the unknown. That is always exciting.

Why don't we ever hear about this excitement, or see it, or think about it, or teach it? I believe it is because these very human and most interesting elements of science don't show up in the discoveries, concepts, and teachings of science themselves. Rather, they live in the process of *doing* science. And that, it seems, is the last thing we think of when teaching science to our children.

I fully realize that class time is precious and that covering mandated science curricula leaves little room for creative diversions. Yet, I believe deeply that stories of the people and process of science are, or should be, an essential element of science teaching. Why? Because they are a more effective and efficient way to teach. When a teacher uses stories to make scientists real, dynamic people with interesting, compelling dilemmas, and to make the process of doing science intriguing, then students will teach themselves the theorems and concepts.

It's true. I have conducted hundreds of teacher workshops all over the country on the in-class uses of storytelling. At virtually every one of them, teachers have reaffirmed the validity of this concept. The experience of a California high school biology teacher I know is typical. For one day during his basic biology class, he would walk into class dressed as Charles Darwin. For 53 minutes, he regaled the class with the rhythm and feel of life aboard the *Beagle*: stories of adventures, gossip about shipmates, and he would speak of Darwin's hopes, fears, and dreams.

On both chapter and semester final exams, students consistently scored higher on the Darwin section than on any other, semester after semester, year after year. This teacher always figured it was because everybody liked Darwin, just as he did.

Then he took a storytelling course from me and realized that, for that one day, he told a story of the process and people of science. For that one day he made science come alive. And his students learned. Why? Because these stories provide context, perspective, and relevance for the scientific concepts. Stories excite students, focus their attention and interest, and create enthusiasm and empathy. Once so motivated, students are eager to teach themselves.

That teacher has now added Gregor Mendel to his repertoire, and is looking for three or four more good candidates to sprinkle throughout the course. He has come to believe that stories of the process and people of science are the most powerful teaching tool he has.

We tend to look at stories and storytelling as entertainment, or at least as supplementary material that you get when and if time permits. But more and more teachers are finding that stories are a fast, effective, and efficient expressway to student learning.

So, here is a collection of 50 stories about the *doing* of science. They are stories of the people, events, and processes that give us our rich scientific heritage. I have become fascinated and excited by the people and struggles I found while researching this book. I hope some of that fascination works its way down into you, and your students.

You will not learn formulas, theorems, and equations from these stories. Instead, you and your students will taste the exciting rollercoaster ride that goes pushing into the unknown—the thrill of discovery. You will gain an appreciation for the process of science, and for the great variety of personalities that have graced the world of science. I hope you will come to view the accomplishments and discoveries of science from a new and more sympathetic perspective, a perspective that lets you see beyond the facts of science to the exciting journey that led to each one of them.

In selecting events and scientists to include in this book, I didn't want to automatically grab the 50 top moments in science. I wanted 50 moments and 50 people that would make good stories, that would help me communicate the excitement and wonder possible in doing science. I also tried to select stories from all of the major fields of science study, and to include a mix of race and gender of the scientists.

There are two people and one organization whom it is an honor to single out and thank for their contributions to these stories. Dr. Nelson Kellogg is the first and only person I have ever met, or heard of, with a Ph.D. in the History of Science. What a delightful find, and an inexhaustible fountain of information and inspiration, he has been!

Like Nelson, the staff at the Woman's History Project, in Windsor, California, were an irreplaceable and seemingly endless treasure chest of information about the women scientists included in this book. I could not have written many of these stories without the help and the resources of the Woman's History Project.

My greatest thanks and appreciation go to Roni Berg, an intelligent, insightful, and articulate woman who holds science in a very low regard. Science is boring to her. She doesn't like science. She was my official litmus test for each story, and has done a great deal to make the stories consistently readable, interesting, and understandable. For that help I am eternally grateful.

Lastly, I want to encourage each of you to do more than just read these stories and say, "Really? I didn't know that." Bring science back to life—for yourselves, for your children, for your classrooms, for your communities. There are 50 stories in this book. There are a thousand out there waiting to be discovered and told. Find them. Tell them. We will all be better off.

I hope you find the science and scientists that inhabit these pages to be more interesting and exciting than you ever thought they could be.

How to Use This Book

In addition to the actual text, each story in this book contains focusing and exploratory questions, references, and topics that link back to curriculum themes. These additional elements are included to assist the integration of the stories into the science curriculum and into your teaching. These stories should not be viewed as separate entities, but rather as integral parts of teaching the nature and wonder of science to your students. A word on each story's structure, order, and intended use is in order here.

A Point to Ponder. Allow a few minutes for class discussion on these open-ended questions before diving into the story. They have been written to focus student interest and attention around the story's central science themes, and to ease their thinking more into line with thoughts and dilemmas of the central character.

Story Text. These stories, while containing fictionalized dialog, are based on historical accounts of the scientists, their struggles, and their discoveries. The personality and manner of the scientists, as well as the scientific aspects of the story, such as methods, procedures, and hypotheses, are accurate. Fictional characters have been created for several stories.

Library Links. These are follow-up questions to springboard your students into library research and class discussion. They are designed to extend the science aspects of the story, and to help students appreciate the perspective of the time and culture in which the scientist worked and lived. Answers to each of these Library Links are located in a separate section at the end of the book.

Topics to Explore. These are a list of the major science curriculum themes and threads that are addressed in each story. They are included to give you an additional tool for integrating the stories into all aspects of your science teaching.

References for Further Reading. These are good sources, commonly available in public libraries, for further reading about the story's central scientist. Both children and adult references are included. Your school and public librarians are still your best resources for finding available material.

Alphabetical List of Stories by Scientist

List of Stories by Date

20th Century

Physical Sciences

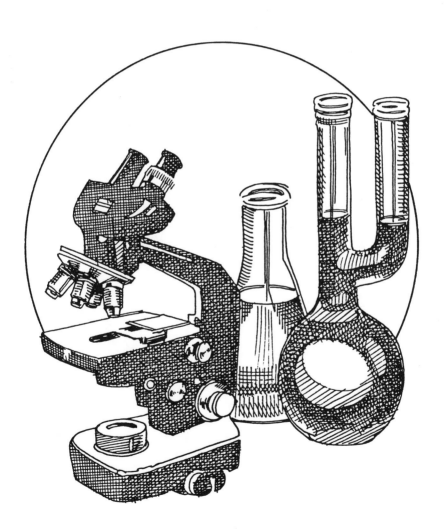

Physics—General

Teetering at the Beginning of Knowledge

A story of Archimedes's discovery of the lever principle in 259 B.C.

☑ **A Point to Ponder: What is a lever? Have you ever used one or played on one? Where?**

Steady, gentle waves rolled across the Mediterranean Sea and ran up onto a sandy Sicilian shore. A fierce, summer sun poured its heat down onto the proud island nation. Hiero II was king. Syracuse, the largest city in Sicily, was a bustling, growing center of commerce. By today's reckoning, it was 259 B.C.

Four men sat on a small knoll overlooking the south end of the Syracuse harbor. One of the men, Conon, was a famous teacher. The other three were his students. All four squatted under scrub olive trees for shade.

But 26-year-old Archimedes couldn't concentrate on his teacher's words about astronomy. The stars were all far away. Besides, it was a sparkling, bright-blue day, and there were no stars to look at. On a day like this day, astronomy bored Archimedes.

What fascinated Archimedes was a group of four young boys playing with a long piece of driftwood—probably a plank from some long-ago-wrecked ship. Laughing and dashing through the soft, white beach, kicking up sprays of sand on each sharp turn, the boys dragged the board over to a waist-high rock. They hoisted one end of the board on a rock, and then slid it along until it balanced exactly, teetering gently up and down in the breeze.

As seagulls circled overhead, one boy straddled one end of the board while his three friends counted, "One, two, three!" and jumped hard onto the other. Squealing with delight, the lone boy was tossed into the air, crashing to the sand with a soft thud and a cheer.

The boys slid the board off-center along the rock, so that only one-quarter of it remained on the short side. The longer, heavier side dropped to the sand with a dull "thud." Giggling, three of the boys climbed up the slick, inclined board to sit on the short, top end. Under the weight of the three boys, the short end slowly swung down toward the beach. At the last moment, the fourth boy bounded onto the rising end, crashing it back to the sand, and lifting his three friends back into the sky. All three boys squealed with glee. Two laughed so hard they fell off.

Archimedes was fascinated! One boy had easily lifted three, where before it had taken three to lift one! In the old, weather-beaten board, the boys saw a toy, but Archimedes thought he saw Euclid's mathematics at work. But exactly *how* did that old board make one boy strong enough to lift three friends? This was the question Archimedes had to solve.

"Archimedes!" snapped Conon. "Are my classes so boring that you can't pay attention? Maybe you'd rather play on the beach like a child!"

The other two students chuckled as Archimedes spun back to face Conon, his face flushed with embarrassment.

Conon stared sternly at his red-faced student. "Archimedes, you are a nephew of the king. Do not waste your time on the games of children. You are here to study the worthwhile sciences of astronomy and geometry."

"But Conon," interrupted Archimedes, "isn't it worthwhile science to ask how one small boy is able to lift a great weight by putting it on the end of a board that, itself, has great weight?"

"No!" snapped Conon, "lifting is for servants and has nothing to do with science. Now pay attention to your classes!"

But Archimedes couldn't concentrate on astronomy. "I want to understand how that board gave one boy such strength," he told himself as he walked to his family's home after class. "But how?" Archimedes was so deeply lost in thought, his head bowed, he missed two turns and was half an hour late getting home. Then he brightened. His head snapped up. "I'll experiment to see how it works. That's what Euclid would do."

Archimedes grabbed five of his niece's play blocks: two small cubes and one large one, a rectangular block, and a triangular prism to act as the balancing point. He found a thin strip of wood about fifteen inches long to act as his balancing board. He named it a *lever.* from the Latin word meaning "to lift."

He placed the prism on a table and carefully balanced his lever across it. His curly, brown beard touched the tabletop as he picked up the two small cubes, one in each hand, and leaned close to observe.

"Why are you playing with my blocks?" asked his six-year-old niece.

Surprised and a bit embarrassed, Archimedes snapped straight up, knocking his lever to the floor. "I'm not playing. This is a science experiment."

"Looks like you're playing. Can I play, too?"

"When you play very carefully to find something out, it's an experiment," answered Archimedes.

"Please?" she begged. "They're my blocks."

"All right, you can be my assistant," agreed Archimedes. "First, pick up that piece of wood."

Again, Archimedes placed the middle of his lever on the point of his niece's triangular prism. It balanced, wobbling slowly up and down. Archimedes lightly touched the balance point with his finger. "This, I think, we should call the 'fulcrum,' or point of balance."

On each end of this board he placed one of the small cubes. The whole thing balanced like two children on a seesaw, rocking slightly up and down.

"Now what does this teach me?" asked Archimedes, staring at the balanced cubes and thoughtfully stroking his beard. "That equal weights pushing down on equal lengths of board balance each other. Good. Now what did the boys do? Ah, yes. Three on one side; one on the other."

Archimedes picked up the large cube to represent the weight of the extra two boys. He held it over the balanced cubes.

"When are we going to play something fun?" asked his niece.

"Shhh!" whispered Archimedes. "This is an experiment, and it *is* fun."

"No, it's not," she grumbled.

Archimedes dropped the large cube onto one end of the lever. It crashed down, smashing to the table. The other end shot up. The small cube on it flew into the air. Archimedes's niece giggled.

"What does that teach me?" asked Archimedes. "That when unequal weights push down on equal-length boards, the heavier weight goes down, and the lighter one rises." Archimedes smiled and clapped his hands. "Learning is such a wonderful thing! Now, I wonder if I could balance the big cube with one of the small ones."

He held the large cube on one end of his lever and a small cube on the other. Slowly he slid the board across the fulcrum until the two exactly balanced. The end with the small cube was much longer than the end with the big cube.

"It's getting boring again," complained his niece. "Let's bounce something else up in the air."

"Shhhh. This is an important part of our experiment."

"Doesn't *look* important."

Archimedes carefully measured the length of board sticking out on each side of the balance point. "Ah ha!" he exclaimed. "The side with the small weight is exactly twice as long as the side with the big weight."

He compared the two cubes. The big cube was exactly twice as heavy as the small one. "What does this teach me?" Archimedes thought for a long moment. "To balance twice the weight, I need only half as much board. And half the weight needs twice as much board. I wonder . . ."

He stacked one small cube, the big cube, and the large rectangular block all on one side. The other side held only one of the small cubes. Archimedes guessed that the heavy weight was five times that of the single small cube. Now he tried to balance the board again.

Ha! It balanced. But the stacked heavy weight was almost on top of balance point. The end with one small cube seemed to hang way out in space, wobbling up and down. It reminded Archimedes of the three boys sitting on the short end of their board at the beach.

"I like this one," said his niece. "It looks funny."

Archimedes measured the length of each side of his board. The side with the one small cube was five times as long as the side with the stacked weights. To balance one-fifth the weight, he needed five times as much board.

Insight swept away Archimedes's confusion, like a brisk wind blowing away a fog.

Archimedes saw one of Euclid's proportions. So that's how the board made one boy so strong! Simple proportions. The force pushing up on one side was proportional to the length of board on the other side of the balance point. If one of the boys wanted to lift a stone 40 times his own weight, he could if he understood proportions. He need only get a long board, and have his side be 40 times as long as the side he wedged under the stone. Then when he sat on his own raised end, he would come down, and the heavy stone would rise!

"That's it," cried Archimedes. "I understand!"

His niece shook her head sadly. "Experiments aren't nearly as much fun as play."

Archimedes laughed and nodded. "You might be right. But think how much more we learn from experiments. Why, in one afternoon, I have learned how a lever lets people lift heavy weights, and that Euclid's mathematics really do describe how our world works in a practical and useful way."

"Maybe tomorrow you can learn something that's fun," said his niece.

Archimedes was the first to use mathematics as a way of understanding and describing natural occurrences. No one had ever made that connection before. But curious Archimedes did. He used that new understanding to create our very first scientific principles and concepts. That, however, is another story.

Library Link: How can someone very light lift someone very heavy on a seesaw? Why does this work?

Topics to Explore: physics, scientific method, Archimedes, lever principle.

References for Further Reading:

- *In the Children's Library:*

Bendick, Jeanne. *Archimedes and the Door of Science*. New York: Franklin Watts, 1962.

Lexau, Joan. *Archimedes Takes a Bath*. New York: Thomas Y. Crowell, 1969.

- *In the Adult Library:*

Clagett, Marshall. *Great Science in Antiquity*. New York: Abeland-Schuman, 1955.

Consult your librarian for additional titles.

The Fall of Galileo

A story of Galileo Galilei's discovery in 1598 that all objects fall at the same rate

☑ **A Point to Ponder: If you dropped a bowling ball and a marble side by side, which would fall faster?**

The cocky 25-year-old mathematics professor stood before his class at the University of Pisa, Italy, one cloudy afternoon in the spring of 1598. He held out two bricks for them to see—one in each hand as if he were weighing and comparing them. "Gentlemen, I have been watching pendulums swing back and forth. I have been watching them very carefully. And I have come to a conclusion. Aristotle is wrong."

The class gasped, "Aristotle? Wrong?!" Their eyes grew wide as if they had just been told the world were ending. The first fact every schoolboy learned in beginning science was that Aristotle was right. The writings of the ancient Greek philosopher, Aristotle, were the very foundation of the known science of the late 1500s.

"Class, I am prepared to prove my theory. Observe." Galileo smugly climbed up onto the edge of his desk and again held out the two ordinary bricks at eye level. "Observe carefully, gentlemen. Time their fall." He released the bricks. Thud! Both bricks crashed to the floor in the center of the fascinated knot of students.

Galileo crossed his arms and gazed down at his students. "Did you observe that?" They nodded, still dazed by the boldness of their teacher's words. Aristotle wrong? How could it be? But their teacher stood before them so confidently, as sure of himself as if he had just announced that the sky were blue.

"Now, class, what did Aristotle say about falling objects?" They all knew well each of Aristotle's theorems. Aristotle had said heavier objects fall faster because they weigh more. More weight meant greater attraction to the earth.

Galileo held out his hands to stop them. "And Aristotle is wrong. Observe this. Time this fall very carefully." Galileo picked up two bricks which he had cemented together. This new brick was twice the weight of a single brick. If Aristotle were right, the heavier brick would fall faster.

The ring of students actually held their breath in suspense as Galileo held out the heavier, double brick at eye level. All eyes were glued to the brick. The room was graveyard quiet. Galileo released the brick. Smash! The blow to the floor echoed around the room. Galileo looked down at his students. "Were you observing carefully? Good. Now, did the heavier brick fall faster than the single bricks?"

Still wide-eyed, the students nodded. Of course it had. Aristotle said it would. Galileo stomped his foot. "No! Think, gentlemen. Was the time faster?"

The students looked down at the floor sheepishly. "Well, maybe." "It might have been." "It all happened so fast." "Wasn't it supposed to be?"

Exasperated, Galileo demanded the bricks be handed back up to him. "Look. Really look this time!" Galileo held out a single brick in one hand and the double brick in the other. He let them fall together. Smash! The bricks dented the worn wooden floor. "Did the heavy brick fall faster?" he demanded.

The class shook their heads. No, it had not. They landed together.

"Again!" cried Galileo. His students were transfixed as Galileo again dropped the bricks. Crash! "Did the heavy brick fall faster?" No, again the bricks landed together. "Aristotle is wrong," declared their teacher with his smug, confident smile.

That evening a friend and fellow mathematician, Ostilio Ricci, found Galileo still testing, comparing the fall of his bricks from different heights. As Galileo described his experiment and his conclusions, Ostilio gasped, "Aristotle? Wrong?"

Galileo sighed. "Observe. The truth speaks for itself. If I show you the evidence, you will have to believe."

"But Galileo. You're only 25," stammered Ostilio. "How can you hope to prove Aristotle wrong?"

"Because he *is* wrong."

"But he's Aristotle."

"Who will you believe? Someone who has been dead for 2,000 years, or your own eyes?" Galileo leapt onto his desk and held out a single brick in one hand, the double brick in the other. "Watch their fall carefully," he instructed, and released the bricks. Crash! "Now, Ostilio, did the heavier brick fall faster as Aristotle said it would? Yes, or no?" It sounded more like a demand than a simple question.

Sheepishly Ostilio looked down at the floor. "Well . . . maybe. It *might* have. It all happened so fast. Isn't that how it's supposed to be? How can I not believe Aristotle?"

Galileo pounded his fist in frustration. "Use your eyes, man! Believe only what you can see." Again Galileo dropped the bricks. And again, and again, until the floor around his desk was ringed with gouges and dents.

"Enough!" cried Ostilio. But as a cautious scientist, he still had doubts. Questioning the work of Aristotle would shake the world of science to its very core. "In this demonstration, Galileo, I admit you are right. *This* double brick falls at the same rate as *this* single brick. Still, I cannot so easily believe Aristotle is wholly wrong. Search for another explanation. The world will not be eager to hear what you want to tell."

Galileo realized the world would need a more dramatic demonstration of this truth already so apparent to him. But what? His search led Galileo to the top of the famed Leaning Tower of Pisa with two cannonballs, one roughly ten pounds, the other about one pound. A crowd of eager students, skeptical professors and priests, and curiosity seekers formed a thick circle below. As he held the balls over the edge of the tower, Galileo explained that this demonstration would be the final test of whether Aristotle's or Galileo's "Theory of Falling Objects" were correct. From such a great height there could be no miscalculation, no mistake, no doubt.

Galileo dropped the balls. The crowd stood hushed and riveted as they fell. Down, down they whistled and thud—thud! The two balls smashed to the ground 191 feet below at almost the same instant. Aristotle was wrong. The results had spoken. The evidence was clear.

The world in 1598 was neither ready nor willing to hear the truth that Galileo's cannonballs spoke as they plummeted from the Leaning Tower of Pisa. Still, Galileo's work on falling objects became the foundation from which another well-known scientist, Sir Isaac Newton, was able to reach up to his own famous discovery. But that's another story.

Library Link: Before laser guns, digital watches, and even clocks, how would you time a falling brick?

Topics to Explore: physical science, physics, gravity, scientific method, evaluation, Galileo.

References for Further Reading:

- *In the Children's Library:*

Bixby, M. *The Universe of Galileo and Newton*. New York: American Heritage Books, 1964.

Marcus, Rebecca. *Galileo and Experimental Science*. New York: Franklin Watts, 1961.

- *In the Adult Library:*

Drake, Stillman. *Galileo*. New York: Hill and Wang, 1980.

Consult your librarian for additional titles.

A Weighty Matter

A story of Evangelista Torricelli's discovery of air pressure in 1640-1642

> ☑ **A Point to Ponder: Why is water pulled up into a straw when you suck? How high could you suck it up into a very long straw?**

On a clear, windy October day in the fall of 1640, three fashionably dressed men huddled around a public well just off the market plaza in Florence, Italy. One of the men, the famed astronomer and physicist Galileo Galilei, lowered a long tube into the well's murky water, a little more than eight meters below the stone rim of the well. From the well, Galileo's tube draped up over a wooden crossbeam two meters above the wall, and then down to a hand-powered vacuum pump held by the other two men, Evangelista Torricelli, a 32-year-old student of Galileo's, and Giovanni Baliani, another well-known Italian physicist.

Galileo lowered the tube inch by inch until a thin red line he had drawn across the tube rested right at the water's surface. Similar red lines were drawn across the tube at half-meter intervals up the rest of the tube.

Galileo turned, thoughtfully stroked his long white beard, and carefully studied the tube. The red ten-meter line rested just below the raised wooden crossbeam.

"As soon as you're ready on the pump, Evangelista, I believe we're ready here," he said. Officially, Galileo was under house-arrest. But the Church Inquisition Board, his jailors, occasionally let Galileo out under the promise that he would neither do, nor say, anything related to astronomy.

Torricelli and Baliani took their places, standing side-by-side, gripping the wooden handle of the pump. With a nod of Baliani's head, the two men began to pump the handle up and down, slowly sucking the air out of Galileo's tube.

A small crowd of curious onlookers gathered around the well and the three men. With grunts and grimaces, Torricelli and Baliani pumped harder and harder. Air was steadily pulled from the tube. Water was drawn up out of the well and higher and higher into the tube. Galileo called out the water levels to his two friends. "Five meters . . . six meters . . . seven meters. . . ."

Sweat poured down the pumpers' faces as the water level inched toward the eight, and then eight and one-half meter marks.

"Nine meters!" called Galileo. "Keep pumping!"

Torricelli groaned and clenched his teeth as he redoubled his efforts to keep the pump going. Evangelista and Giovanni pumped until the tube began to flatten in upon itself as a vacuum was created. But no matter how hard the two men worked, the water would not rise above 9.7 meters.

"The tube's collapsing. You can stop now," called Galileo.

Both men dropped, panting to the smooth stones of the plaza. Air hissed as it rushed back into Galileo's tube. The water level quickly sank back to its natural level in the well. The crowd wandered off.

Still stroking his beard, Galileo squatted beside his two friends. "The same as always, 9.7 meters. Always it rises to that point. But never higher. Why? Why?" With a thoughtful sigh, Galileo rose. "Come. We'll talk more at my house. I should be getting back."

Seated on Galileo's terrace, sipping tea to ward off the cool wind that swirled across them, Galileo said, "We know there is some force in a vacuum that pulls things in. But exactly what is that force? And why always to the same height?"

Torricelli shrugged. "How can we hope to understand why water is affected by a vacuum if we don't even know why this wind blows?"

Baliani shook his head and set down his teacup. "You'll never understand, Galileo. It is simply an act of nature. Just accept the way it is."

"No!" snapped Galileo. "Science cannot just accept anything. We must struggle to understand. It is our duty."

Baliani laughed. "But Galileo, how can you hope to understand the works of God?"

Evangelista turned and studied the leaves swirling in the wind. "A vacuum is a space with no air in it. The key is something about the air itself. But what?"

Other projects and tasks pulled the men's minds away from vacuums until after Galileo's death in 1642. Then, Torricelli took up the problem again. But this time, he had a new question. Would a vacuum treat other liquids the same way it treated water?

He repeated Galileo's experiment using heavier and heavier liquids. As his liquids grew heavier, the height to which a vacuum would raise them grew shorter. Finally he tried the heaviest liquid of all: liquid mercury. No matter how hard he pumped on his vacuum pump, the mercury would only rise 0.77 meters.

As the air hissed back into his short tube Torricelli realized the height was always proportional to the weight of the liquid. The weight. It seemed a vacuum always sucked up the same *weight* of liquid. Was that the long-missing key?

The next day, as a fierce storm rumbled into Florence, Torricelli invited Giovanni Baliani to his house to see if a second mind could help solve this old, troubling problem. Evangelista repeated his experiment with liquid mercury. However, no matter how hard they both pumped, the mercury rose only 0.75 meters into the tube.

Why only 0.75 meters? What was different about today that a vacuum couldn't raise the same weight of mercury it did yesterday? Search as they might, the two scientists could find only one answer, the storm. That was the only difference. But why would a storm and its howling winds affect a vacuum's ability to raise a weight of liquid?

Staring at the wind-whipped trees, Torricelli's mind suddenly latched onto a revolutionary new idea. What if the air, itself, had weight? Weights exert pressure. What if the pressure exerted by air were different at one spot than at another, and from one time to another? The higher pressure would push air toward the lower pressure. Pushed air was wind. Wind was caused by differences in air pressure and air weight.

Torricelli's mind raced back to his experiment. "Giovanni, what if Galileo's vacuum force is really just the weight of the air outside the vacuum *pushing* liquid up into the vacuum? What if a vacuum has no force of its own? A vacuum is just the absence of air. What if a vacuum only allows the weight of air outside a tube to push down on mercury in a bowl and force it up into the tube?"

"Then why only 0.75 meters today when before you measured 0.77 meters?" asked Giovanni thinking Torricelli's idea sounded too far-fetched to be taken seriously.

"The storm," answered Evangelista. "Somehow the storm lowered air pressure here. It lowered air weight. That must be why we have such strong winds today. That's also why the mercury only rose 0.75 meters. Less air pressure."

Air had weight. It was a real substance. No one had ever realized this before. But now it seemed so obvious and made such perfect sense. Torricelli felt giddy and weak in the knees from the magnitude of his discovery.

"How can this be?" asked a skeptical Giovanni, crossing his bulky arms. "A brick has weight. If I hold a brick, I feel its weight. Why can't I feel this weight of air?"

Torricelli thought for a moment before answering. "If you had always held that brick, Giovanni, you would no longer be aware of its weight. Because you have always borne the weight of air, you are no longer aware of the feel of its pressure."

Baliani opened his mouth to argue more, but could think of nothing to say. Could young Evangelista's wild idea be right?

Air had weight. It exerted a pressure on every surface on earth. It could change from day to day, and those changes caused the winds to blow. Such a magnificent set of discoveries to come tumbling into one person's head all at once! But how Torricelli's work led to the development of our modern barometer, and how it greatly improved our understanding of the earth's atmosphere and weather systems, is another story.

Library Link: Can you feel the weight of the air pushing down on you?
Do you know anyone who can feel changes in air pressure?

Topics to Explore: physics, scientific method, experimentation, Evangelista Torricelli, air pressure, air weight.

References for Further Reading:

- *In the Children's Library:*

Macus, Rebecca. *Galileo and Experimental Science.* New York: Franklin Watts, 1961.

- *In the Adult Library:*

McKenzie, A. E. *The Major Achievements of Science.* New York: Simon & Schuster, 1960.

Middleton, W. E. *The History of the Barometer.* Baltimore, Md.: Kaufman Publishers, 1964.

Consult your librarian for additional titles.

Apples, Moons, and Questions

A story about Sir Isaac Newton's discovery of the principles of gravity in 1666

☑ **A Point to Ponder: What would happen to you if there were no gravity?**

Unseen bees buzzed contentedly from tree to tree and bush to bush. Butterflies flitted back and forth above the rolling lawns of the garden. It was a lovely country estate garden where everything in the world seemed happily at peace. Everything, that is, except for the young man who sat glumly on top of the garden's one small hill, his back against a thick apple tree. It was as if his own private rain cloud hovered darkly over his head.

The 23-year-old teacher and scientist was Isaac Newton. With his fair complexion and long blond hair, many thought he looked much younger. His small, thin stature and shy, sober ways reinforced that impression.

Isaac's seven-year-old nephew, Joshua Marsh, an energetic bundle of thick, brown hair and questions, darted through a patchwork of wildflowers. "Why are you sitting way out here all alone when everyone else is talking and playing in the house?"

This was England in the year 1666. In London, the bubonic plague ravaged a terrified population. Universities were closed, and students and teachers, like Isaac Newton, had to bide their time in safe country estates waiting for the plague to loosen its death grip on the country.

Newton, who was staring up at an afternoon quarter moon, didn't even glance down. "I'm thinking; wondering."

"What are you thinking 'bout?"

Isaac sighed and lowered his gaze. "The moon."

Joshua was instantly excited. "I like the moon. Is there really a man living in it?"

Newton decided to use his young nephew as an excuse to think out loud. "The real question is, Josh, why doesn't it fall down to earth?"

"Maybe it doesn't want to," answered Joshua, hopefully.

Isaac laughed and reached out to ruffle young Joshua's hair. "That's as good as any of my answers. For that matter, if the earth rotates around the sun as Copernicus and Galileo have shown, why doesn't the earth fall down to the sun?"

Joshua scrunched up his face. "That's silly! The sun is up. We can't fall *down* to something that's really *up*!"

Newton sighed and shook his head. "Why, oh why, do I have to be stuck way out here when there are so many answers to learn?"

"You're living here because of the play. Remember?" answered Joshua, shaking his head as if his uncle had completely lost his mind.

"Not play, Josh. It's the *plague*, the bubonic plague."

Joshua nodded. "Oh, yeah."

"So here I sit, able to do little but *wonder* about the motion of the moon," continued Isaac. "What makes things move? Every motion needs some mover, some force, to create it . . ."

"Why?"

"Because without a force pushing on an object there is nothing to make it move. If an object is at rest, it will stay at rest until some force acts on it."

Proudly, Joshua crossed his arms over his chest. "I'm seven. Mother doesn't make me take afternoon rests anymore."

"This kind of rest is different, Josh."

Excitedly Joshua asked. "Is your kind of resting more fun, Uncle Isaac? Is that what you do?"

"No. I am a scientist. I discover questions. It often seems that's all I can do, discover more questions."

They both heard the familiar, soft "thunk" of an apple falling to the ground, and turned in time to see a second apple fall from an overhanging branch and bounce once before settling into the spring grass. It was certainly not the first apple Isaac Newton had ever seen fall to the ground, nor was there anything at all unusual about its short fall. All that was different were the specific questions in Isaac's mind that the falling apple interrupted.

While it offered no answers to the perplexed young scientist, the falling apple did offer Isaac an important new question, "The apple falls to earth while the moon doesn't. What's the difference between the apple and the moon?"

"That's easy," said Joshua. "The moon's big and yellow. The apple is small and red."

But like a nasty winter cold, the question wouldn't leave Isaac in peace. "What's the difference between the moon and the apple? The apple fell. So some force must have pushed it, or pulled it down to earth. Why doesn't that happen to the moon?"

Again he sighed. Questions, questions, questions.

Isaac's runaway mind wouldn't let him sleep that night. As thick clouds boiled in to block the stars, Isaac paced back and forth across his room. It began to rain, a steady, windless rain. Suddenly Isaac stopped and stared wide-eyed out the window. The rain was *falling*, falling to earth, just like the apple.

What force made the rain fall? The same force that made the apple fall? What force is it? Questions, questions, questions.

Then, in that dark, gloomy night the first glimmer of an answer crept into his mind. The rain, the apple, rocks, they all always fell *straight* down to the earth's surface. They fell that way here in England. They did in China. They also did in South America. Everywhere on earth objects fell straight down as if pulled by an invisible string straight toward the very center of the earth.

Again he paced and thought. "Maybe there is a force that attracts every object to the earth. But why only the earth? Maybe it is a more basic force that attracts every object to every other object, some universal attractive force, and things fall to earth instead of each other because the earth is so much larger! Then this force must be proportional to the size of each object. The bigger the object, the greater the pull."

Newton began to tremble with the excitement of discovery: a universal attractive force pulling every object toward every other object, its strength depending on the sizes of the two objects.

Then he collapsed sourly into a chair. His private raincloud reformed over his head. "But then why doesn't the moon fall down to earth? Why doesn't the earth fall down to the sun? Why doesn't this universal force make them fall?"

Questions, questions, questions.

The next morning, under a clearing sky, Joshua was out early, playing with a ball behind the house. His ball was tied to a string Joshua held tight in his fist. He swung the ball, slowly at first, and then faster and faster until it stretched straight out on its string, whistling over Joshua's head, as the two family dogs barked and leapt after it.

From his window, Isaac was thunderstruck at the simplicity of this obvious answer. "A string holds the ball in. But its motion makes it want to fly off, to escape. There are two forces pulling on the moon. And it doesn't fall because they balance each other!"

Isaac dashed downstairs. The moon circling the earth is just like a ball on a string!

Isaac burst out the back door. "Josh, I need your ball for an experiment." And he snatched the ball and string out of his nephew's hand.

"Hey! I'm playing with that!"

"I'll give it right back, Josh. I just need it a second."

Newton spun the string. The faster the ball spun, the harder it pulled on the string. Newton released the string. Joshua's ball soared across the lawn and landed in thick blackberry bushes.

"Hey! You lost it!"

"No, Josh. It escaped. And without a force holding it in, the moon would escape into space."

"That's not the moon. That's my ball, and I'm telling!"

Newton grabbed his nephew by the shoulders. "Oh, don't you see?" he laughed. "The spinning ball wanted to fly off. But the pull of the string wouldn't let it. The spinning moon also wants to fly off into space. But, just like a string, the pull of the universal attractive force won't let it!"

Joshua was suddenly very confused. "Is there really a string attached to the moon?"

"An invisible one," laughed Isaac. "The moon is just like an apple. They are both pulled down to earth, but the moon's motion keeps it from falling. There are two forces pulling on the moon, just like there were two forces pulling on the ball, and we just discovered what they are."

"We did?" asked Joshua, looking longingly at his ball buried deep in the thorny blackberry bush.

With the joy of this answer budding in his mind, Isaac turned for the house.

"You better get my ball back!"

"I will, Josh. But first come with me."

Newton ran to his study and began to scribble complex mathematical equations in his journal. "What's that?" asked Joshua, pointing a finger at the page Isaac was quickly filling.

"An answer this time instead of more questions, Josh."

"My ball gave you an answer?"

Isaac reached out and lovingly mussed his nephew's rich, brown hair. "Your ball, the apple, the rain, each of them held the answer. But I couldn't see it because I was asking the wrong question. I wondered why the moon doesn't fall. Wrong question. The moon *does* fall toward earth. But its motion and speed want to make it fly off into space, just like your ball. The two forces compromise, and instead of doing either, the moon falls *around* the earth, just like the ball fell around my hand until I let it go. In the same way, the earth is falling around the sun!"

Joshua looked more worried than confused. "The earth is falling?"

Isaac Newton paused, tapping his pen. "I think this force should be called *gravitation*. It's from the Latin. As I recall it means 'to come together,' more or less. Yes, gravitation, the universal force that pulls all objects together, the one force that will explain how and why the moon and planets act as they do."

Joshua pointed at his uncle's journal. "Is that gravitation?"

"No, Josh, this is mathematics. Mathematics will prove the existence and nature of gravitation. Your ball and the apple demonstrated it. My job was to discover the right questions."

Joshua pouted. "I hope your next job is to get my ball back."

But of course that was another story.

Library Link: Put two rocks on the ground. If gravity attracts all objects to all other objects, why don't the two rocks slide or roll toward each other?

Why do planets closer to the sun travel faster than planets at the outer edge of the solar system?

If the planets stopped traveling in their orbit around the sun, would they fall into the sun?

Topics to Explore: physical science, physics, astronomy, Isaac Newton, scientific method, Newton's Laws of Motion, evaluation.

References for Further Reading:

- *In the Children's Library:*

Land, Barbara, and Myrick Land. *The Quest of Isaac Newton*. Garden City, N.Y.: Garden City Books, 1960.

Rattansi, M. *Isaac Newton and Gravity*. London: Wayland Publishers, 1974.

- *In the Adult Library:*

Christeanson, Gale. *In the Presence of the Creator: Isaac Newton and His Times*. New York: Collier Macmillan, 1984.

Consult your librarian for additional titles.

Compressing the Truth

A story of Robert Boyle's discovery in 1668 of the "compressibility" of air

☑ **A Point to Ponder: Blow up a small balloon. Now try to squeeze the balloon and compress the air inside. Why is it so hard to do?**

As he did each week, short and stocky Robert Hooke stood grumpily at the front of the candlelit hall and rapped his gavel on the heavy oak table in front of him. "Will this meeting of the British Scientific Society please come to order?" Hooke pounded on the table and repeated his call several times before the twenty members present that day in early 1668 stopped their chatter and moved into the rows of high-backed chairs facing the head table.

"Gentlemen," repeated Hooke with his usual scowl. "During the past week we have received a report from the French Scientific Society which is of some interest."

"What's it about?" asked 41-year-old Robert Boyle from his chair in the middle of the front row. Boyle's long, tightly curled hair and proud, noble face were balanced by a warm smile and friendly, Irish manner.

Hooke brushed his scraggly hair back out of his eyes and glared at Boyle. Hooke was always ready for an argument. "If I wasn't being interrupted all the time, I could tell you."

With a light laugh, Boyle ignored the insult. "I just asked what the report was about, Robert."

"And I would tell you if you would be patient!"

Hooke cleared his throat to regain everyone's attention and tried to straighten his coat. No matter what Hooke did, his clothes hung like ill-fitting rags on a scarecrow. "This report by the French Society concerns the springiness of air."

"Ahh!" Everyone leaned forward to hear the news. The characteristics of air were of great interest in the seventeenth century.

Hooke told them that the French had conducted an experiment to see if air would expand back to its original volume after being squeezed, or compressed. They called this quality the "springiness" of air.

One of the French scientists had built a brass cylinder fitted tightly with a brass plunger, or piston. Several men pushed down hard on the piston, compressing the air trapped below. Then they let go. The piston sprang back up, but not all the way back up. No matter how often the experiment was tried, the piston never bounced all the way back to its original position.

The French claimed this proved that air was not perfectly springy. Once compressed, it stayed slightly compressed, just as a crumpled piece of paper can never be completely smoothed out. Did this also mean that, like crumpled paper, air was never as good again once it had been used? Did this mean that air could not be used over and over again in pumps and factory compressors? Squeeze or crush a piece of wood, and its strength was forever lost. Was air also only useful once?

An excited clamor erupted in the meeting hall of the British Society. Everyone wanted to talk at once about this French experiment. No one listened, and everyone yelled to be heard.

Only Robert Boyle remained seated, thinking quietly, re-creating the French experiment in his mind. Finally, he stood and raised his hands. "Gentlemen, the French experiment proves nothing. Their piston was too tight to bounce all the way back up."

Short, feisty Robert Hooke angrily jammed his fists onto his hips. "If they made the piston any looser, air would leak out around the edges and ruin the experiment."

Boyle shook his head. "But if the piston was too tight and rubbed against the sides, friction would affect the results. The experiment tells us nothing."

Hooke snapped back. "*Any* piston would either be a little too tight or a little too loose. I suppose *you* could design a better one?"

Boyle smiled and nodded. "I can, and I will. I will design a piston that is neither too tight nor too loose. It will be perfect. Then we can really find out if air is reusable and springy. I suspect we shall see that the French are wrong."

Hooke snapped at this bait. "I say yours will be no better than that of the French, and that air is *not* perfectly springy!"

Boyle eagerly rubbed his hands together. "Ah, gentlemen. It seems I have been challenged."

When the British Scientific Society met two weeks later, Robert Boyle stood before them at the head table, looking more like royalty than a scientist. His head was held high, his face radiating confidence. "Gentlemen, may I present the perfect piston for testing the springiness of air."

Boyle gestured to a large, glass tube which he had shaped into a lopsided U on the table before him. One side of the U rose over three feet off the table, but was very skinny. The other side was short and fat, like a soup mug. The short side was sealed at the top. The tall, skinny side was open.

Boyle poured liquid mercury into his tube so that it covered the bottom of the U and rose partway up each side of the U. A large pocket of air was trapped in the short fat side by the mercury.

Robert Hooke and the others stared in fascination at this strange-looking piston. Then Hooke scoffed. "That's no piston. It's a lopsided flower vase."

Many of the members laughed. Robert Boyle laughed harder than any. "Very funny, Robert. But what is a piston? A device for compressing air. And that is exactly what this tube will do. But I need a good weighing scale."

Several Society members rushed to a storage room to fetch one.

Robert Boyle lifted his glass piston onto the scale and carefully measured its weight. "Total starting weight of glass, mercury, and air is exactly seven pounds, four ounces. And now to begin."

Boyle carefully marked a line on each side of the glass U at the top edge of the mercury. As if lecturing a class of schoolboys, Boyle said, "I will now add more mercury into the tall side of my piston. The additional weight will force the mercury further up into the closed, fat side of my apparatus, compressing the air trapped inside. Note that air cannot leak out around the mercury, and that, since mercury is a liquid, it can never be too tight and rub against the sides of my piston. It is perfect."

Then Robert Boyle paused for a long, satisfied smile at Hooke before he lifted a beaker of liquid mercury and began to trickle silver liquid down the long neck of the open side of his piston.

The scientists crowded around the table to see this important measurement. Even Robert Hooke squeezed his way to the front row. The men could each feel that history was being made with this experiment.

Liquid mercury glistened in the candlelight as it flowed from the beaker in Boyle's steady hand. Slowly the mercury crept up the sides of the glass cylinder, compressing the air above. No one moved. Some actually held their breath, staring at the short chamber of Boyle's piston. As the column of mercury in the tall side rose higher and higher, its weight pushed the mercury up into the short, fat side.

By the time Boyle had filled the open neck of his piston, mercury rose over halfway up the short side. The trapped air had been squeezed to less than half of its original volume.

Again Boyle smiled as he drew a second line on the short chamber to mark the new level of mercury inside. "You can clearly see that the air in this chamber has been compressed."

Everyone nodded in agreement.

"And now to release the pressure and see if the air inside will spring all the way back to its original volume," announced Boyle as he opened a small valve at the base of the tall neck of his piston. Mercury flowed into a beaker below this drain.

All eyes stared at the mercury as its level slowly inched back toward the original lines marking the starting place for Boyle's experiment. As the mercury neared those lines, Boyle tightened the valve so that only a slight trickle remained. Again, he tightened the valve so only a slow drip, drip, drip of mercury plopped noisily into the beaker.

With a quick twist of his wrist, Boyle sealed the drain when his balance scale read exactly seven pounds and four ounces. In both sides of the piston, the mercury matched the original lines. "Behold!" cried Boyle with a sweeping and very theatrical gesture, "We have exactly the amount of mercury we had at the start, and our trapped air has sprung back to exactly where it started. Air *is* perfectly springy and can be used over and over and over. The French are wrong. *I* am right!"

Everyone leapt to their feet applauding and cheering, except for Robert Hooke who sulked in a corner chair.

Robert Boyle bowed over and over, like an actor during an ovation. A deliriously happy British Scientific Society proclaimed Robert Boyle a hero and rushed eagerly out into the Oxford, England, evening air to spread the exciting news.

Experimenting with his funny glass piston, Robert Boyle noticed something quite remarkable. When he doubled the pressure on a trapped body of air, he halved its volume. When he tripled the pressure, the air's volume was reduced to one-third. The change in volume of air when compressed was always proportional to the change in the pressure being applied to the air. Today we call it "Boyle's Law." No other concept has been more useful in understanding and using gases to serve the needs of people. But that is another story.

Library Link: Have you ever compressed air? When?

Topics to Explore: physics, scientific method, chemistry, Robert Boyle, gases.

References for Further Reading:

- *In the Children's Library:*

Irwin, Keith. *The Romance of Chemistry*. New York: Viking, 1986.

- *In the Adult Library:*

Conant, James. *Robert Boyle's Experiments in Pneumatics*. Cambridge, Mass.: Harvard University Press, 1950.

Consult your librarian for additional titles.

Boring in on the Flow of Heat

A story of Count Rumford's discovery of frictional heat in 1790

> ☑ **A Point to Ponder: What is heat? Is heat a thing? Can you catch it and hold it like a liquid?**

The King of Bavaria needed more cannons, and he needed them *now*. "More cannons!" cried ministers, dukes, earls, generals, and heralds. The person at whom they yelled was Count Rumford, the King's director of cannon manufacturing.

Dashing Count Rumford had floated into the King's court some months ago, with a charming smile and a grand bow, and had won the favor of the King of Bavaria. Actually, the Count was not really a count at all. He gave himself the title when he moved to Bavaria. But then, Rumford wasn't his real name either.

The Count was born Benjamin Thompson in the Massachusetts colony. During the Revolutionary War, he had been a well-paid spy for the British. As the colonists marched toward victory, Thompson fled to England. There, he was paid even more for spying on the British for the Prussians. By 1790, he had to hotfoot it to Bavaria. There, he changed his name to Count Rumford, and he planned to settle down quite comfortably with his large stash of spy money and the easy job of being in charge of the King's cannon manufacturing.

Then war broke out. The King wanted 1,000 cannons on the front line. "More cannons!" screamed everyone at Count Rumford.

The Count raced to the Bavarian cannon manufacturing plant, which, despite his title, he had never actually visited before. He planned to yell at the plant manager, just as the King had yelled at him.

The plant was a huge, deafeningly noisy warehouse. On one side, next to a long row of billowing open hearths, metal wheel rims and mounting brackets were hammered into shape around wooden wheels and cannon carriages. Hammer blows on red-hot metal strips echoed like high-pitched thunder across the plant. Steam rose from hissing water vats as glowing metal plates were cooled in their slimy waters.

On the other side of the warehouse the great cannon barrels were forged. Molten, liquid metal was poured into huge molds, like lava fresh from a spewing volcano. From these emerged solid cylinders for cannon barrels. Many were twelve feet long and over four feet across. The inside of the cannon barrel was hollowed out by a boring tool which scraped, drilled, and gouged its way down the interior.

Of course, the boring tools grew dangerously hot. Streams of water had to be constantly sprayed on them to keep them from melting. Hissing steam rolled out of the cannon barrels and billowed up to the ceiling where it slowly condensed and dripped down onto the workers below.

The din in that warehouse was incredible. The Count could scarcely hear his plant manager yelling right in his ear. But more than anything, the Count was fascinated by the boring out of each fearsome cannon barrel. He recognized that great amounts of heat flowed into the air and water from those cannon barrels. And the subject of heat had interested the Count for many years.

As Benjamin Thompson, he and several scientist friends had studied heat in England in the mid-1780s. At that time, all scientists believed that heat was an invisible, weightless liquid called "caloric." They believed that, as a substance grew hotter, more and more caloric squeezed into it. Eventually caloric overflowed and spilled out in all directions to heat whatever it touched. Caloric always flowed from hot to cold.

The question that instantly struck Count Rumford during his plant tour was: How could so much caloric pour out of the metal of one cannon barrel—especially from a cannon barrel that was cold to the touch when the boring started? Where had all that caloric been hiding in the metal before drilling began? If he could find out where all the caloric had been stored, and how much caloric each cannon barrel could hold, Rumford would unlock the secret of heat!

Rumford decided that this was an opportunity for some much-needed science, whether or not it slowed the delivery of the King's cannons. He stopped the tour, rode back to his estate, and returned with several large thermometers.

He directed half a dozen workers to stop work on the cannons and build a long trough to catch all water pouring out of a cannon barrel while it was being bored. This trough channeled the water past Rumford so he could both guess at the volume of the water flow and measure its increase in temperature. From those two measures he could calculate how much caloric flowed from the cannon barrel's metal.

The balding plant manager wrung his hands. "But Count, this will slow production. And the King demands more cannons."

The Count glared icily at his manager. "I am in charge of cannon production. The workers will do what I say."

The manager scurried off to his office, still wringing his hands.

Rumford directed his workers to bring a new cannon barrel and new drill bit for the boring tool. He also directed that extra hoses be sprayed on the drilling to prevent the formation of steam. Rumford didn't want any heat escaping in the steam that he could neither capture nor measure.

He carefully felt both the new metal barrel and the drill bit. Both were cool. How much caloric could be in them?

With a great screeching and grinding, the boring began. Hoses sprayed water onto the drill bits. Still the metal began to glow. "More water!" cried the Count. Each hose was opened full and water blasted into the cannon barrel.

Mercury quickly rose in the Count's thermometers, which he held in the middle of the trough. A torrent of heated water eight inches deep tumbled down the narrow section of the trough and past the Count.

Rumford was thrilled. More caloric flowed out of that cannon barrel than even his wildest dreams imagined could have been in it. And still the hot water flowed past him heated to 25°, even 30°F.

For 25 minutes, then 30 minutes, the boring continued, and the hot water flowed. Slowly the Count's face turned sour. "This can't be right," he said aloud. "How could one cannon barrel hold so much caloric and not melt?"

The Count lifted his thermometers and cried, "Cease work!" Now he had to get to the bottom of this. Just how much caloric was in this gun barrel? When would all the caloric flow out and leave only cold metal behind?

Then Rumford's face brightened. He pointed at a very dull, used drill bit leaning against the plant wall. "Use *that* drill bit!" he commanded.

"But sir, it's dull and won't cut well at all," complained the drilling operator. "It will take us forever to bore out a cannon barrel with that bit."

"Precisely," answered the Count. "Now we'll see if this barrel runs out of heat."

The plant manager wrung his hands. "Forever? But the King demands more cannons."

Again the grinding started. The dull drill bit inched its way deeper into the cannon barrel with agonizing slowness. Now even more heat poured into the water than before. The thermometer in Count Rumford's hand measured a 50° rise in the water temperature! The Count was fascinated. So much heat. So much caloric!

Thirty minutes flew by, and then a full hour. The dull drill bit glowed. And still the heat poured out.

Again the Count's face soured. "Cease work!"

Something was very wrong. More than 10,000 gallons of water had been sprayed onto the drill bits gouging out this one cannon barrel. The Count's thermometers said that every bit of that water had received enough heat to raise its temperature at least 30°. That was more than enough heat to turn the cannon barrel into a bubbling pool of liquid metal many thousands of degrees hot.

Something was very wrong, indeed.

"May we go back to the good drill bit now, sir?" asked the operator. Rumford's plant manager eagerly nodded his head.

"Do whatever you like," answered the Count with a casual, indifferent shrug. "My experiment is completed. Now I must decide what it means."

Count Rumford sat in a corner of the warehouse and watched the borers go back to work on his cannon barrel. Still heat flowed out. Heat could not be a liquid that was stored in substances. Too much heat had flowed out during this drilling. No, heat must be being created right in front of his eyes. But by what?

Rumford made a list of everything he saw before him. But there was only the metal and the motion of the borer. The Count's eyes widened. Motion. As the borer ground against the cannon's metal, its overall motion must be converted into quick, tiny movements by the individual particles making up the metal. It was that movement by these tiniest of particles, and their crashing into each other, that must create heat. Somehow *movement* was being converted into heat!

Of course, no one believed Count Rumford's new theory on where heat came from for over 50 years. "What particles?" they demanded. "I see no tiny particles!" But as atoms and molecules were discovered, Rumford's theory suddenly made perfect sense, and became the foundation for our understanding of heat created by friction, or the rubbing of two substances against each other.

Benjamin Thompson, or Count Rumford as he preferred to be remembered, was very pleased with his discovery, and couldn't wait to write long letters to his friends in England detailing his experiment. But how the King of Bavaria fared in that war is another story.

Library Link: Rub your hands against each other very fast. Did that motion create heat? What do we call this kind of heat?

Name as many sources of heat as you can.

Topics to Explore: physics, scientific method, heat, Count Rumford.

References for Further Reading:

- *In the Children's Library:*

Asimov, Isaac. *Great Ideas of Science*. Boston: Houghton Mifflin, 1969.

- *In the Adult Library:*

Tattner, Ernest. *Architects of Ideas: The Story of the Great Theories of Mankind*. New York: Carrich & Evans, 1938.

Thompson, James. *Count Rumford of Massachusetts*. New York: Farrar & Rinehard, 1935.

Consult your librarian for additional titles.

The Truth About Monsieur Le Blanc

A story about Sophie Germain's struggle to enter the world of math and science in 1794

☑ **A Point to Ponder: What would you do if you really wanted to go to school and no one would let you?**

Early December snows swirled down bitter-cold Paris walkways and alleys. The afternoon sky grew dark with smoke and coal soot from countless chimneys long before the sun set under lead-gray clouds. Five years after the fall of the Bastille, in December 1794, the still somber mood in Paris matched this dreary sky. The voices of the few Christmas carolers half heartedly wandering the streets were drowned out by the echoing thud of guillotine blades, still active in the larger Paris squares.

Every day during the aftermath of the French Revolution, it seemed, Paris lives were changed forever. Trials for members of the overthrown aristocracy continued. Heads were lost. Fortunes and property were seized. But no change that December of 1794 affected the world of science more than the changes to eighteen-year-old Sophie Germain.

For five years, Sophie had been cooped up in the family house on Rue St. Denis. Her parents feared for her safety in the violence outside. For five years, she had stayed indoors with her dark, solemn eyes, her plain, honest face, and her quiet, dignified manner, and she read.

Fortunately, Sophie loved to read, especially chemistry and math. Still, reading was not enough for Sophie Germain. She longed to hear the great scientists of her day, to ask them questions, to challenge their thinking. But Sophie was a girl, and there was no place for a girl in the world of science. Common knowledge said women were incapable of grasping scientific and mathematical concepts. Such intense thought would only make them dizzy and faint, if not actually ill.

But at 5:15 one frigid morning in December 1794, Sophie Germain's life began to change. That morning, Sophie's father again caught her studying at her desk. Actually, he caught her asleep at her desk wrapped in a blanket from her bed, pen still held loosely in her right hand, ink frozen in her ink horn, equations he could not begin to understand scrawled across her slate.

Sophie's father, Ambroise Germain, slammed his hand down on her desk. She squealed in fright, bolted upright, and sprawled backwards off her chair onto the floor.

Sophie's mother, Marie, wrung her hands and paced nervously near the door. The family's breath seemed to freeze in the icy air. Shadows danced across their faces from the lone candle Ambroise held. "Why, daughter," he bellowed, "do you insist on disobeying the best wishes of your parents?"

Even as Sophie groggily pulled herself from sleep, there was no hint of silly girlishness, or even fear or anger on her face; just a deep seriousness and an unstoppable, unyielding dedication to her beliefs.

Sophie's father began to pace before her as she sat next to her fallen chair on the floor.

"I'm not opposed to your studying, Sophie. But if you must study, study something *useful* like music, Latin, or art."

"What could be more useful than math and chemistry, father?"

"I mean for a woman!" he shouted and again slammed his fist on her desk so that her ink horn jumped and nearly tipped over.

Her mother added pleadingly, "You're a girl, Sophie; delicate and frail by nature. This much thinking will certainly ruin your health. We just want what's best for you, dear."

Ambroise returned to his pacing. "First I took away the heater in your room to keep you from this incessant night studying. Then I locked up all your clothes, and then the candles so you'd have neither warmth nor light. Finally, I hid all paper and pens. Goodness knows where you stole these from!"

He picked up Sophie's slate and shook it at her. Then he paused and frowned at the equations. "And what is this gibberish?"

"It's one of LaGrange's second order differential transformations, father."

Her mother's face looked as if she had just sucked on a lemon. "A different *what?*"

"Never mind what it is," growled Ambroise. "It's a silly waste of time. *That's* what it is. Why do you do this to us, Sophie?"

Sophie rose, slowly righted her chair, and sat, primly straightening her nightgown. "Have you heard of Archimedes, father? Did you know that when the Romans invaded his city, he was so engrossed in a geometry problem that he failed to respond to the Roman soldiers' questions, and they killed him. How fascinating math must be to command such attention!" Then she added quietly, "Besides, I have to study."

"Have to? Why *have* to?" asked her father with raised eyebrows.

Sophie lowered her eyes to her desk. She was sure her father wouldn't like this part. "To keep up with my class," she answered softly.

"Class? What class?" he demanded.

Now she proudly threw back her head and looked straight into her father's eyes. "Professor LaGrange's mathematics class at the university, Ecole Normale."

Ambroise shook his head and laughed. "Don't be silly, daughter. Girls are not allowed to even visit the university, much less attend classes."

"My friend, Gaston, loans me his class notes. I even submitted a paper this term."

"A famous professor at the university will never accept a paper from a girl," laughed her father.

Now Sophie smiled. "Yes he will, Father. I didn't use my own name."

Sophie's mother wrung her hands and moaned. "If word gets out our daughter's studying math we'll be the laughing stock of Paris. Besides, it can't possibly be good for your health."

That afternoon, Professor Joseph LaGrange leaned casually back in his leather and oak desk chair. On the table before him were spread nearly 80 term papers. Fellow professor Gaspard Monge puffed on his pipe in a second over-stuffed chair. The smoke curled up along book-lined walls to an ornate chandelier above. LaGrange picked up one of the papers and slid it across the table to Monge.

"I have selected the winning paper for the term. This one. It's brilliant, insightful, and concise. But I don't recognize the name of this student, Monseiur Le Blanc. Do you know him?"

Gaspard stopped his smoking and looked thoughtfully up to the ceiling. "Le Blanc . . . Le Blanc. No. It doesn't ring a bell. Let me see the paper."

Gaspard Monge pulled reading spectacles from his breast pocket and scanned through Le Blanc's paper. "I see why you chose it. Extraordinary. Obviously, a thoughtful and astute young man. Must have attended all your lectures to obtain such insight. It's surprising that I don't recall his name."

LaGrange shrugged and straightened himself in his chair. "Well, no matter. I'm sure we'll recognize him at the awards ceremony I've scheduled for tomorrow afternoon."

Gaspard nodded, rose, and stepped to the door. "Is your wife coming to the ceremony this time, Joseph? She's wanted to for years."

LaGrange looked shocked. "Certainly not! No woman has ever attended the award ceremony at the end of a term, and no woman ever will. It would be most inappropriate. Besides it would just confuse a female. They are not capable of understanding such things."

The next afternoon, just before the ceremony was to begin, Sophie Germain tiptoed nervously down the second-floor hall to Professor LaGrange's office. Gaston followed her, encouraging and prodding from behind at every step to keep Sophie from scurrying back home. The whole university was assembled in the auditorium one floor below to honor this term's winner, Monsieur Le Blanc.

Professor LaGrange opened the door immediately to Sophie's light knock, calling, "Le Blanc? Is that you? You're . . ." The final words of the sentence hung frozen in his mouth as he opened the door and saw who stood before him. "And who, might I ask, are you?" he asked in icy tones.

Sophie curtsied. "I'm Sophie Germain."

With a sneer, LaGrange gazed past her down the hallway, then at his pocket watch. "Yes, I'm sure. If you'll please leave now. I'm waiting for a remarkable, and rather late, young man."

Timidly, and with several encouraging prods from Gaston, Sophie said, "No, Professor LaGrange. You are waiting for me."

"You? Why would I wait for a girl?"

"Because I wrote that paper and signed it M. Le Blanc."

"*You?*" LaGrange's knees trembled a bit, his stomach dropped, and he grasped the doorframe for support. "You wrote it? But Le Blanc is a brilliant, thoughtful math student. You're a . . . a girl."

Sophie's cheeks flushed with embarrassment. "Still, I wrote that paper. I borrowed Gaston's notes each evening to study."

LaGrange began to feel faint. He collapsed into an overstuffed chair. "I selected the paper of a girl?" Then his eyes bored menacingly in on Sophie. His voice turned icy cold and hard. "Prove that you wrote it."

Thirty minutes later, as the faculty and students fidgeted in their seats, Professor Joseph LaGrange emerged from behind the stage curtain, pale and nervous. At his side marched an equally nervous, but very proud, Sophie Germain. The whole auditorium gasped. Professor Monge hissed, "Joseph, what is this? No woman has ever attended this ceremony, much less been its honored award recipient. You can't!"

Sheepishly LaGrange shrugged. "I have to. Both her paper and her mind are truly extraordinary. She deserves this award more than any student in years."

The shock waves Sophie Germain sent rumbling through the all-male scientific community of Europe did not stop with that one award in 1794. In 1816, Napoleon Bonapart himself awarded her the Grand Prize of the French Academy of Science. Her papers on the elasticity of solid objects became the foundation for the design of the Eiffel Tower. Her work on number theory was used in university classrooms for nearly two centuries. In 1823, she was the first woman ever awarded a Doctorate of Science from the University of Gottingen. But, of course, each of those is another story.

Library Link: Do you think the sort of discrimination Sophie Germain faced has disappeared from science?

Where do you think ideas like "women can't do science" ever got started?

Topics to Explore: mathematics, chemistry, women in science, scientific method.

References for Further Reading:

- *In the Children's Library:*

Perl, Teri. *Math Equals: Biographies of Women Mathematicians.* Menlo Park, Calif.: Addison-Wesley, 1978.

- *In the Adult Library:*

Grinstein, Louise, and Paul Campbell, eds. *Women of Mathematics: A Biobibliographic Sourcebook.* New York: Greenwood, 1981.

Osen, Lynn. *Women in Math.* Cambridge, Mass.: Massachusetts Institute of Technology, 1974.

Consult your librarian for additional titles.

Faster Than a Speeding Bullet

A story of Albert Michelson's measurement of the speed of light in 1928

☑ **A Point to Ponder: What problems do you think you would run into if you had to create an experiment to find out how fast light travels?**

Albert Michelson held the highly polished metal cylinder at arm's length, so he could focus his tired and blurry eyes on it. Slowly, he turned the cylinder over and over in his wrinkled, old hands. As he did so, he thought, "Odd that science has become so dependent on machines. We strive to measure things so big, so far, so small, and so fast that we can neither see nor detect them with our own senses." Then he tucked the small, octagonal metal cylinder into his pocket and buttoned his coat up tight around his throat.

Albert Michelson gulped one last breath of warm air and stepped into the bitterly cold February 1928 night on top of Mt. Baldy in California. He trudged along the short walkway to a small equipment building. Inside this shed, his great experiment sat idle, waiting for this new, mirrored cylinder.

Once inside the equipment building, Michelson blew on his frail, old hands to ease the sting of outside cold. "I'm 74 years old," he muttered. "Too old for fieldwork."

A longtime assistant, William Devers, grunted his sympathy as he re-checked the alignment of a field of mirrors. "All ready here as soon as I get that new cylinder aligned, Mr. Michelson."

Albert nodded and fished the new cylinder out of his pocket. For the past six months, his experiment had been waiting for this new, improved cylinder. He grunted and shook his head. "Science now depends on machines more than minds. Need more accuracy? Design a better machine. Need to see smaller? Design a better microscope. Need to see farther? Invent a better telescope. I hope this machine works for measuring *faster* as well."

Michelson turned to the shed's single window and squinted through the southern California haze at Mt. San Antonio, 22 miles away. He reached out his left hand and lifted the telephone receiver out of its cradle on the wall. He turned the hand crank and waited for his Mt. San Antonio team to answer. "Ready over there, Jensen?"

"Ready when you are, Mr. Michelson," came the raspy reply over the crude telephone.

Albert Michelson turned back to Devers, still busily checking the alignment of several mirrors and focusing lenses in the room. "As soon as the new cylinder is installed and balanced, we'll fire a test shot."

"Sure thing, Mr. Michelson."

If that worked, Albert would be ready to finally, accurately measure the speed of light. The ability to measure this fastest speed in the universe, the speed of light, had eluded humans for thousands of years.

Even in the sixteenth century, when Copernicus studied the planets, and the early seventeenth century, when Galileo invented the telescope, science knew that light did not travel instantaneously. But there was no way to measure its speed.

In 1676, the Dutch astronomer, Ole Christensen, detected a time shift in the eclipses of the moons of Jupiter depending on where the earth was in its own orbit. He realized that this time shift represented the extra distance light had to travel to reach earth when it was further away from Jupiter. From his observations of this time shift, he calculated that light traveled at 140,000 miles per second.

In 1877, a young Albert Michelson, with Edward Morley, improved that measurement to 185,000 miles per second through a carefully constructed set of experiments with revolving mirrors. However, limitations in the accuracy of their equipment kept them from being more precise.

In the late 1800s, measuring the speed of light had real importance only for astronomers. It was more of an interesting puzzle to the rest of science, but not of immediate importance. Then Albert Einstein discovered his famed energy-matter equation, $E=mc^2$. Instantly the speed of light, "c," became critical to a great many calculations. Now so much depended on accurately measuring how fast light traveled, that a 1% error, or even a 0.1% error, was too great.

Michelson was determined to measure the speed of light with no more than a 0.001% error. But how? Light traveled too fast for the human eye to see, or for any known clock to measure. Light traveled faster than anything Michelson could use to directly measure it.

In 1924, Michelson turned to the famed gyroscope manufacturer, Elmer Sperry, to improve upon the equipment available for his measurements. Four years later, the third, and most recent, round of equipment improvements was represented by the small, octagonal cylinder Devers was aligning now.

"The cylinder's in and balanced," called William Devers.

Michelson nodded, "Then, here goes." He clicked on a powerful electric motor that drove the air compressors that spun the cylinder in its vertical mount by blasting it with high precision jets of air. "Set the speed for thirty thousand revolutions per minute."

Devers nodded and adjusted the dials in front of him. "Thirty thousand rpm," he repeated.

Michelson clicked on the powerful spotlight. A beam of light blasted into the spinning cylinder. Seemingly instantaneously, light bounced off a series of mirrors and shot out into the night through a small hole Michelson had cut in the shed wall. "Good. Alignment is still okay."

The experiment Michelson had designed was really very simple. He shone a light onto this small mirrored cylinder as it rotated at a high speed. At some point, as the mirror turned, it would be perfectly aligned to reflect this light beam toward a larger, stationary, curved mirror at the back of the room. However, the rotating mirror would only reflect light back to the larger mirror for a very small fraction of a second before it rotated away.

The larger mirror at the back wall would thus get a short pulse of light from each of the eight faces of the rotating mirror. Each pulse was reflected off this mirror through a focusing lens and out through an opening in the wall, and on to the test site 22 miles away on Mt. San Antonio. There, it entered a second shed through a similar opening in its wall, hit a second stationary mirror, bounced back through a second focusing lens, and then back to Michelson's shed on Mt. Baldy. Here the light pulse reentered the hole in the wall, once again hit the back wall mirror, and finally reflected back to the rotating mirrored cylinder.

Even though the pulse of light would have completed this 44-mile journey in less than 1/4000th of a second, the rotating cylinder would have already turned a little by the time that light pulse got back from Mt. San Antonio. If the speed at which this small, mirrored cylinder rotated was set just right, Albert could force the reflected pulse of light to finally bounce off the spinning cylinder and hit a small target on the far side of his Mt. Baldy tool shed. By knowing exactly how fast the small cylinder rotated, he would know how long it took a pulse of light to make the 44-mile round-trip. That would tell him how fast the light had travelled.

While it sounded simple, it meant years of work to improve the equipment he used. First, Sperry had to create a better light. It had to be stronger, and more focused and intense, like the beam of a lighthouse, so that it would travel 44 miles. Next, Sperry had to create a more accurate motor drive so that Michelson would always know *exactly* how fast the cylinder was turning.

Next, he had to design better, smoother focusing lenses. And finally, he had to design a better mirrored cylinder, one that wouldn't vibrate or distort its mirrored sides under the tremendous forces of high-speed rotation.

Now, at last, all was in place. Michelson spoke into his telephone again. "The test flash was successful. This will be an operational run."

Again, he switched on the motor and light. Pulsing faster than the eye could see, the light stream shot out to Mt. San Antonio and came roaring back 1/4000th of a second later. It bounced off the rotating cylinder and onto the far wall about two feet to the right of the tiny target mark. "Increase speed to 31,000 rpm," commanded Michelson.

The spot of reflected light slowly crept toward the target. "Increase to 31,750 rpm."

Again the light inched closer to the target. Three inches to go. Two inches. Both men's eyes were glued to the tiny spot of light as it crept across the wall. Very slowly now, Devers increased the rotation speed of the metal cylinder to adjust the spot toward the target. 32,255 rpm. 32,258 rpm.

Michelson cried, "Stop! That's it!" The beam of reflected light struck exactly on target. Devers quickly recorded the rotational speed. From it, Michelson calculated the speed of light to be 186,284 miles per second. Over the course of twenty separate trials, the measured speed never varied more than 1.5 mph.

Using all the sophisticated equipment now available, researchers have determined that Michelson's calculations were less than 2 miles per second off, or, as he hoped, less than a 0.001% error. His work allowed other scientists to better understand the universe, design rockets, and create atomic bombs. But those, of course, are other stories.

Library Link: What travels at the speed of light?
Name some common tools you use to make your everyday measurements more accurate.

Topics to Explore: physics, experimental process, scientific method, Albert Michelson, speed of light.

References for Further Reading:

- *In the Children's Library:*

Jaffee, Bernard. *Michelson and the Speed of Light.* Garden City, N.Y.: Science Study Series, 1960.

- *In the Adult Library:*

Hughes, Thomas. *Science and the Instrument Maker: Michelson, Sperry, and the Speed of Light.* Washington, D.C.: Smithsonian Institution Press, 1976.

Consult your librarian for additional titles.

A Beeline to Physics

A story of Shirley Jackson's early attempts to study matter, energy, and motion in 1955

☑ **A Point to Ponder: What is physics? Do you have to be in a special lab to study physics?**

Ten-year-old, pigtailed Shirley Jackson squatted on the bottom back step of her family's inner-city row house hunched over a two-quart mayonnaise jar. Inside, a dozen honeybees buzzed back and forth, some darting across the jar and crashing into the clear glass sides and lid, several hovering in the middle of the jar. Three walked across the bottom of the jar, groping for an escape.

This was not the first jar of bees Shirley had collected at the neighborhood park. By now she knew to poke six small air holes in the lid after she screwed it on good and tight to keep the angry bees from getting out. To Shirley, staring at that jar, the only sound in the world was the ferocious buzzing of bee wings, that and the occasional "bonk" of a startled bee smashing headlong into the sides of the glass jar.

Actually, Shirley Jackson also heard all the normal sounds of a sweltering Washington, D.C, August Saturday in 1955. It was so hot that the trees and grass seemed to suffer along with the people. Heat waves shimmered up off of virtually everything, and the blacktop on Georgia Street where the Jacksons lived grew sticky and began to melt. Cars droned by, and kids yelled and squealed down at the corner where someone had managed to turn on a fire hydrant, blasting jets of cool water out across at least this one intersection of the city.

But Shirley had learned to ignore the sounds of the outside world when she was conducting an experiment.

"Whatcha up to, Shirley?" It was Shirley's father just swinging through the alley gate and into their small backyard after hauling a load of trash to the dumpster. His T-shirt was soaked with sweat.

"I'm studying, Dad," she answered without looking up from her bees.

He wiped the sweat out of his eyes and leaned over her shoulder on his way up the back stairs. "Studyin' what? Looks like a bunch of no-sense congressmen buzzin' around in there."

"Daaad! They're bees!" she whined in mock disgust. "And I think I'm studying physics."

Mr. Jackson shook his head and wandered on up the stairs. " 'Physics!' Pretty fancy word for a fourth-grader."

"I'm going to be a *fifth*-grader!" she shot back without looking up. Then added, "And physics is what our teacher said scientists study."

He continued, pretending not to have heard. "Why don't you study the physics of how to get Congress to pass a decent bill for the working man?"

Just as he reached and opened their back door, Shirley turned and looked up. "Dad, is it okay for me to be a scientist?"

He smiled and placed his hands on his hips. "And why wouldn't it be all right for my little brain child to be anything she wants?"

She barely whispered, " 'Cause I'm a girl. And I'm black. Our teacher said she didn't think there were any black women scientists."

Mr. Jackson sat next to Shirley on the bottom step. "When I got my job at the Post Office there weren't many blacks there either. Now we got lots. If there aren't any black women scientists now, it just means my girl gets to be the first. Did I ever tell you about Benjamin Banneker? No? Well, he was born a slave. But still he got so good at math and astronomy, that he got to help plan the layout for our nation's whole capitol, just fifteen blocks from here. Don't you ever let anyone say you can't."

As late afternoon shadows crept across the Jacksons' tiny backyard, Mr. Jackson again found his daughter squatting on the bottom back step, hunched over jars of bees.

"Now, whatcha doin' out here with my good packin' tape?"

Again Shirley answered without looking up. "I'm doing a physics experiment."

Mr. Jackson chuckled. "What kind of experiment you doin' on a scorcher of a day like this?"

Shirley began to carefully unscrew one of the jar lids. "I want to see what happens when I mix honeybees and yellow jackets."

Mr. Jackson peered closer. "I thought yellow jackets were the same thing as bees."

"No, Dad. Yellow jackets are wasps. I read that at the library."

Mr. Jackson shook his head and scrunched up his face. "Oooweee! Mixin' bees and wasps is worse than mixin' taxpayers and senators!"

After unscrewing the first lid and leaving it sitting loose on top of its jar, Shirley began to unscrew the second lid. "I caught fifteen bees for this jar, but only nine yellow jackets in the other. That's all I could catch. I've tried to memorize how they each move, so I can see if it's different once they're mixed together."

As the yellow jacket lid was unscrewed, Mr. Jackson became concerned. "Now you be careful, Shirley, or some of your experiment's liable to get out and sting you."

"No, Dad. That's what the tape is for." Shirley attached the wasp lid with two small pieces of tape. Then she carefully inverted that wide-mouth jar and set it down on top of the jar with bees. She removed the tape and slid out both lids.

Wasps and bees met at the border of the two mason jars. Instantly, the buzzing increased to a frantic pitch. Wasps dove for honeybees. Bees fled, crashing into the glass. Several bees grouped together and drove at one of the wasps, stingers bared. Stung and beaten warriors from both sides slowly dropped to the glass bottom of the jar.

"Oooweee! You got a regular war in there, Shirley!"

Shirley watched, fascinated, unable to pull her eyes away from the wild, helter-skelter motion.

"What'd you say you were studyin'?" asked her father.

"Physics," answered Shirley, still staring at her experiment.

"Don't you mean 'biology,' or 'sociology,' or 'warfare'? Something like that?"

"No, Dad. Physics. That's the study of what makes up the world. It's where you study matter, and motion, and energy. My teacher taught me that. Those bees are made of the same molecules and atoms that we are. They're just put together a little differently. And look at how much energy and motion they get with just their little bits of matter!"

"Well you just watch out that some of that 'matter and motion' don't sneak out and sting you."

Inside her jars, only two yellow jackets and one honeybee still buzzed wearily back and forth, desperately searching for an escape. All the rest lay dead or dying on the bottom.

"That was something to watch," said Shirley's father, slowly shaking his head and thinking of the wonder of nature, survival of the fittest, and the miracle of life.

"It sure was," whispered Shirley, thinking only of atoms and molecules and how they made up everything in the whole world, and how, if you could describe them, and know what made them stick together in different patterns, you could describe everything.

Three days later, Mrs. Jackson maneuvered through the back gate, struggling with two bulging bags of groceries. There sat Shirley on her step, intently studying a row of jars before her.

"Shirley Ann! What are you doing with all my mason jars?"

"Not *all*, Mom. I'm only using five. It's for another physics experiment."

Mrs. Jackson peered through her glasses and around her grocery bags. "Are those bees? You get those right out of here, young lady! I don't want bees nesting around my house."

With one of the long, disgusted sighs children save especially for the times parents don't show the intelligence God gave a grasshopper, Shirley said, "Nooo, Mom. They're trapped in these jars. They can't get out. And it's an experiment."

A dozen bees flitted back and forth in each jar. But on the floor of each jar lay a different pile of food: flecks of orange clover pollen in one, a mound of sugar in a second, a thin layer of honey in a third, grass in a forth, and a tall pyramid of salt in the last. "I'm studying how the bees act differently with different food."

Her mother glared at her. "Why don't you make it part of your experiment to see what happens when you move every last one of those bees on out of here?"

Finally Shirley pulled her bright, black eyes away from her jars. "It's just physics, Mom. Matter turns into energy; energy turns into matter. But the atoms stay the same all the time no matter what you do. I read all that in a library book. I want to see how bees convert these different kinds of matter into energy, and then into more bee matter."

Mrs. Jackson held firm. "Shirley Ann Jackson. I want those bees out of here *now*!"

Shirley tried once more. "If you could look inside a bee, Mom, all you'd see is atoms and electrons that look exactly like yours. Really, you and bees are exactly the same. If only I knew how to describe it better."

Her mother set down one bag and pointed toward the back gate. "Out!"

Later that afternoon, Shirley skipped home from the library with a thick, new book. After dinner she bounced up into her father's lap and shoved the volume into his hands.

"Dad, can you read this to me tonight?"

He held the heavy, hard-bound book at arms length to focus on the title, and then reached into his breast pocket for well-worn reading glasses. Adjusting them onto the bridge of his nose he said, "Let's see. What do you bring me tonight? *Fundamentals of Differential and Integral Calculus*? Is this some kind of joke, Shirley? I can't read this!"

Shirley brought her hands together in mock prayer. "Pleeease, Dad. Remember I told you that physics is where you study the motion and energy of molecules and atoms? And that if I could describe them, I could describe anything? Well, Mrs. Kramer at the library told me that math is the language that describes physics."

Mr. Jackson's eyes grew big. He stared at his daughter slightly bewildered. "Math is what?"

"It's true, Dad! The librarian told me. Math is the language of physics. You have to teach me this math so I can describe bees, and mountains, and wind, and people."

Mr. Jackson smiled lamely, patted his daughter on the knee, and dropped the weighty calculus book on the floor. "Maybe another night, Shirley. Tonight why don't I read you one of the Oz books?"

Eighteen years later, Shirley Jackson became the first African-American awarded a doctoral degree from the famed Massachusetts Institute of Technology (MIT). Since then she has become a renowned theoretical physicist working for the Bell Laboratories in New Jersey, where she develops computerized mathematical models of subatomic particle motion. But that is another story.

Library Link: What do physicists study now?

Have we always known that matter and energy were so closely related—that matter and energy are really different forms of the same thing?

Topics to Explore: physics, matter and energy, scientific method, Shirley Jackson.

References for Further Reading:

- *In the Children's Library:*

Hayden, Robert C. *Seven African American Scientists*. Frederick, Md.: Twenty-First Century Books, 1970.

- *In the Adult Library:*

Turner, Joseph, ed. *Black Women Achievements Against Odds*. Washington, D.C.: Smithsonian Institute Press, 1989.

Consult your librarian for additional titles.

Physics—Electricity

A Spark of Genius

A story of Benjamin Franklin's discovery in 1750 that lightning and static electricity are the same

☑ **A Point to Ponder: Is there any naturally occurring electricity in the world, or is it all manufactured at power stations?**

It started with an invitation to a turkey dinner two days before Christmas at the home of Mr. Benjamin Franklin for his friends and neighbors. I, myself, was both. Franklin, the 44-year-old statesman, publisher, and inventor, greeted us with the sly giggles and the mischievous twinkle in his eye that said some gimmick, some new invention, was afoot.

"Come in! Come in," he chortled, whacking us merrily on the back and whisking us into the kitchen where we stomped our feet and rubbed our arms to shed the outside winter cold. On Franklin's kitchen table, we saw not a winter feast, but only two large Leyden Jars.

Of course we were familiar with Leyden Jars. They were a must for any fashionable party. Static electricity was a very popular plaything in the American colonies in 1750. People would shuffle across a rug and reach out for a metal door knob to get a spark, a sharp "pop!" and the thrill of a quick jolt running through a finger while observers laughed and applauded.

Leyden Jars gave the same effect, only stronger. Invented just four years earlier, they quickly became all the rage in Europe and spread to the colonies as a favorite toy. A Leyden Jar was a large glass jar, partially filled with water and wrapped with tinfoil around the outside. A rod extended through an insulating cork out the top of the jar to a knob. Once a Leyden Jar was charged with a hand crank, anyone who grabbed the knob while touching the tinfoil got a resounding shock.

Franklin's Leyden Jars looked different. They were coated both inside and out with tinfoil; they were larger than most; and they were linked together in series by a wire. Franklin seemed very self-satisfied as we gawked at the differences in his jars.

"No, no! Don't touch," he cautioned. "I have made a few improvements, and found a way to pack more electricity in the jars. Oh, it's all quite basic experiment and physics really. But these now carry a sizable punch, as you shall see."

He brought out a large and very live turkey, which was to be our dinner. To our amazement Franklin said his calculations showed that these jars packed enough electrical punch to kill the bird and spark the fire that would cook it. With the turkey held tightly under one arm, he began to enthusiastically describe his modifications to standard Leyden Jar design, and how he had learned to make electricity flow down a wire from one jar to another.

He talked more and more excitedly about his experiments on ways to harness this amazing electrical force and put it to use.

"Like preparing our turkey dinner?" asked one of the group jokingly.

We all laughed. But Franklin was serious. "Exactly!" he answered, and, getting carried away by his own enthusiasm, reached out one hand and laid it on the nearest Leyden Jar.

There was a sharp crack, and a sizzling blue arc leapt from the jar to Franklin's fingers. He shot back half a dozen feet and crashed to the floor, the turkey squawking wildly and flapping about the room. Dazed, Franklin sat up slowly, rubbed his eyes to clear them, and adjusted his spectacles. Then his face lit with the glow of discovery.

"That was exactly like a lightning bolt," he repeated over and over again. "Exactly like lightning." In 1750, everyone believed there were two kinds of electricity: playful static electricity, and the fiery electricity that leapt from clouds as lightning. Franklin was the first to think that they might be the same.

Our turkey dinner was prepared in the usual fashion that night. But all through its preparation and consumption, Franklin was lost to us, deep in thought about this new discovery, and about the design of an experiment to prove it. He decided that the best way to show that all electricity was the same, whether explosive lightning or playful static, was to design a big Leyden Jar-like electric circuit to let electricity flow from the clouds just as it did from a jar.

Franklin's circuit would be made of a sharp metal wire fixed to a kite and tied to a twine kite string. This arrangement would gather electricity from the clouds. Electricity would flow down the twine to a large iron key tied to the bottom, which would act as an electrical storage jar. The other end of the key would be tied to a nonconducting ribbon which Franklin would hold. Thus, electricity would be trapped in the key, just as it was in a Leyden Jar. All Ben needed now was a good thunderstorm.

"I am not entirely sure what electricity is," he told me. "But I am beginning to understand how it works. Rather than being a kind of fire, I see it more as a fluid, able to flow down wire or cord from place to place, and able to build up in a jar like water in a lake."

When an afternoon storm brewed up dark and threatening a few weeks later, Franklin rushed to launch his kite. The winds howled, and the clouds boiled above us. A cold rain pounded down about our upturned collars. Twice, I had to help brace Franklin as a savage gust of wind grabbed hold of the kite and tried to rip it from his hand. The kite twisted and tore at the air like a rampaging bull.

Then it happened. No, a lightning bolt did not strike the kite as has often been reported. And a good thing, too. A French scientist was killed a few months later by a lightning strike when he tried to repeat Franklin's experiment. No, what happened that stormy afternoon was that the wire began to glow a faint blue. The fibers on the twine rose and bristled straight out. We could almost see electricity trickling down the twine.

Franklin reached out a cautious hand closer and closer to the key. And pop! A spark leapt to his knuckle and shocked him—just like a Leyden Jar.

Franklin's son was along with us. He reached out a hand and a blue arc sizzled from key to finger. It made him cry out with fright, and he leapt back behind his father.

Lightning and static *were* all the same, fluid electricity!

Satisfied, Franklin reeled in the now tattered kite, and we hurried inside for congratulations, hot cider, and a careful review and discussion of the experiment. Although it would take men like Michael Faraday of England, and Samuel Morse of the United States another 50 years to fully understand the nature and flow of electricity, Benjamin Franklin, on that stormy afternoon, led the world of science in a great step forward. But the struggles of Faraday and Morse are another story.

Library Link: Electricity is a powerful and dangerous form of energy. If you were beginning to experiment with electricity, how would you protect yourself from harm?

Why was a Leyden Jar filled with water?

Topics to Explore: physical science, energy, electricity, Benjamin Franklin.

References for Further Reading:

- *In the Children's Library:*

Cass, Sandak. *Benjamin Franklin*. New York: Franklin Watts, 1986.

Wilson, M. *American Science and Invention*. New York: Bonanza, 1960.

- *In the Adult Library:*

Wright, Esmond. *Franklin of Philadelphia*. Cambridge, Mass: Harvard University Press, 1986.

Consult your librarian for additional titles.

The Thread of Invention

A story of Thomas Edison's invention of the light bulb in 1879

> ☑ **A Point to Ponder: Why does the filament of a light bulb emit light when electric current flows through it, but a regular electric wire doesn't glow in the same circumstances?**

October 19, 1879, dawned bleak and drizzling in Menlo Park, New Jersey, with a deep cold that made you shiver even with a coat pulled up tight around your neck. Inside the long, beam-ceilinged warehouse-turned-laboratory, 32-year-old Thomas Alva Edison slumped into a chair glumly scowling at the cluttered work table before him. Dim shadows waved back and forth around the room from flickering gas lamps mounted along the bare laboratory walls.

As he stared at the slowly spinning, tinfoil-covered cylinder mounted on a horizontal metal shaft before him, Edison pounded his fist on the table and muttered, "The sound should be better—clearer! Tinfoil must not be the right recording surface. But what is?" While an amazed nation called this device "Edison's Talking Machine," the label on its base said simply "phonograph."

Edison rubbed his bloodshot eyes and reached into a vest pocket for his watch. These last several weeks had been an intense work period. As was his custom, Edison rarely left the lab during such periods, grabbing only occasional catnaps for rest. Today he had been struggling at this work table since 2:45 in the morning.

In the wavering light, Edison squinted to read his watch. 5:20. No. 6:21. Then he glared up at the gas lamps around him. "Bah! And I should be able to make my electric light work, too! But I can't find the right material for the filament!"

At 7:15, one of Edison's assistants, James Stiller, entered the long lab, stamping his feet and shaking his arms to shrug off the outside cold and damp. Harvey Lampert, science reporter for the *New York Times*, stepped in with him. Stiller spoke in hurried, whispered tones. "There it is, on the table in front of Mr. Edison. Remember to speak clearly and strongly. He's almost deaf now, and it's just getting worse."

Startled, Edison turned as they neared his workbench. Short, burly James Stiller stepped forward nervously and brushed back his rich, brown hair. "Mr. Edison? This is Harvey Lampert from the *New York Times*. He's come for a demonstration of the phonograph."

Edison cupped a hand to his ear. "The what?"

"The phonograph!"

Edison brushed them off with a wave of his hand. "Why bother? The sound's not accurate yet."

Tall, lanky Harvey Lampert was dumbfounded. "Why bother? Why, Mr. Edison, I'd say a machine that talks is a stroke of true genius!"

"It's what?"

"I said, 'it's genius!' "

"Genius, young man, is one percent inspiration and 99 percent perspiration. The phonograph still needs much more of the latter."

James Stiller scurried to connect a bank of batteries to the phonograph and placed Harvey Lampert in front of the mouthpiece. "Now say something, anything."

While Harvey Lampert giddily recited "Mary Had a Little Lamb," Edison scowled and disgustedly rolled between his fingers some of the lampblack and tar he used as a sealant.

Stiller set the phonograph for playback. Harvey Lampert watched the rough needle vibrate along the grooves which had been etched in the tinfoil as he talked. He gazed at the electromagnetic circuits that amplified the needle's motion onto a vibrating diaphragm. And out came his voice, clipped, tinny, and a little scratchy, but definitely Harvey Lampert's voice.

Edison winced and rolled the lampblack and tar harder and faster into a fine thread. Harvey Lampert squealed with glee. "Incredible! Stupendous! Front-page stuff!"

And then, as if he were alone in the room, as if he were jolted by an electric current, Edison leapt to his feet. "Carbon! Lampblack is almost pure carbon! Why didn't I think of it sooner?"

He rushed across the lab to a series of benches along the far wall strewn with electrical equipment, barking orders over his shoulder as he went. "Stiller, prepare one of the light bulbs. I've got a new filament to test." Stiller shrugged and followed his boss. Lampert, bewildered, stumbled along behind.

Harvey Lampert rubbed the eraser end of his pencil behind one ear. "Mr. Edison, is this some new wrinkle with the talking machine?"

"What?"

"The talking machine, sir. My readers want to know."

Edison glared at the reporter. "The electric light bulb, man. You're about to witness the death of that awful gas lamp."

Lampert scoffed. "Surely you jest, sir. The Science Committee of England just voted that an electric light is impossible."

With a fierce glare Edison brushed past the reporter and rolled the lampblack and tar into a fine, even thread. Then he held it over a Bunsen burner to harden it into a carbonized black wire. He carefully clamped the wire to electrical prongs and bolted this wiring into a large glass bulb James Stiller had prepared.

As Edison attached a vacuum pump to pull air out of the glass chamber, the confused reporter leaned close to James Stiller. "What, in Heaven's name, is he doing?"

"Don't you see? It's the light bulb filament, the part that glows. Mr. Edison has tried over 100 different materials for that filament. None work. Some don't glow bright enough. Some give off too much heat. Some glow the wrong color. Some burn up. He's tried 40 metals alone. He's tried things like coconut fiber. Why, he's even sent one assistant to South America for a certain vine fiber, and another to Japan for bamboo. Nothing he's tried will withstand the electric current and deliver even, steady light."

Smugly, Lampert shrugged. "That is precisely what the English Science Committee said."

Stiller now bristled with confidence. "You just wait until he's created a vacuum inside the bulb so the filament will resist burning. Then you'll see."

"See what? Did you say something?" Edison asked as he spun around.

"No, nothing, Mr. Edison."

"We're ready then. Connect the battery, Stiller."

All three men stared breathlessly at the light bulb as James Stiller connected the battery cables and threw the switch. Two of the men watched with a hope of success after years of long struggle and failure; one watched with a reporter's sense of seeing history in the making. The filament began to glow.

Edison peered closely at the glass bulb and held his hand above it. "Good brightness. Not too much heat." Twenty seconds, then 30 seconds, ticked by. Hot spots flared along the filament's length. It sparked and broke. The light faded to a dull glow.

Harvey Lampert tapped his pencil on his notepad and smiled. "I believe I told you it wouldn't work. Didn't I?"

James Stiller's downcast face gave him his answer. "It was close . . ."

Edison ignored the other men and stared at the crinkled filament. "That was close. But somewhere it got enough oxygen to burn itself up."

Edison rubbed his temples, deep in thought. "Of course. Oxygen is locked into the lampblack." Then he brightened. "What I need is something with a simpler structure to carbonize, like thread. Stiller, bring me a spool of thread. Quickly."

Stiller asked, "Thread, Mr. Edison? Some special thread?"

"What? Thread, man. Normal sewing thread. It will work better, so find it!"

Stiller scurried out the door and soon returned reverently holding a spool of blue cotton thread he had begged from a neighbor woman.

Edison baked that spool of ordinary blue cotton thread until it had blackened to pure black carbon, a delicate carbon thread with no oxygen to allow it to ignite. Carefully Edison removed the spool. As if he were handling the most sensitive, deadly explosive, he peeled the carbonized thread off its spool. Out of an entire spool, he was able to retrieve only one short length.

This fine black line, no thicker than a hair, was attached to the electrical terminals and bolted into the glass bulb. All air was slowly pumped out. James Stiller threw the switch.

The carbon thread glowed a bright yellow-white. And it glowed, and it glowed. Five minutes . . . ten minutes . . . one hour . . . two hours. "My God, man. You've done the impossible!" cried Lampert.

On October 20, 1879, the *New York Times* announced that the electric light bulb had, at long last, been invented by the "Wizard of Menlo Park," Thomas Alva Edison. That first cotton thread filament burned for over 40 hours. It still took another seven years of testing before Edison's light bulbs would last for many hundreds of hours each. And it took another decade for anyone to create a system for delivering electricity to homes, factories, and offices across the nation. But that is another story.

Library Link: Why do we have to have a glass bulb around the filament in a light bulb?

Topics to Explore: physical science, physics, energy, electricity, scientific method, evaluation, Thomas Edison.

References for Further Reading:

- *In the Children's Library:*

Green, Carol. *Thomas Alva Edison: Bringer of Light*. Chicago: Childrens Press, 1985.

Lampton, Christopher. *Thomas Alva Edison*. New York: Franklin Watts, 1988.

- *In the Adult Library:*

Adler, David. *Thomas Alva Edison: Great Inventor*. New York: Holiday House, 1990.

Buranelli, Vincent. *Thomas Alva Edison*. Englewood Cliffs, N.J.: Silver Burdett Press, 1989.

Consult your librarian for additional titles.

A Ray of Insight

A story of Wilhelm Roentgen's discovery of X-rays in 1895

☑ **A Point to Ponder: Why do your bones appear dark gray and your skin very light gray, almost white, on an X-ray?**

"Bertha! Please come down here, Bertha. I have something to show you!" 50-year-old physics professor Wilhelm Roentgen stood at the bottom of the basement stairs and yelled up to his wife late on this evening of November 8, 1895. "Bertha! Hurry, please!"

"I'm coming, Wilhelm. What's so important it can't wait 'till I'm up in the morning?" Wearing slippers, nightgown and heavy coat, Bertha Roentgen clopped down the old wooden steps of their Wurzburg, Germany, home into her husband's cramped and cluttered basement laboratory. Her breath became visible as small, steamy clouds when she reached the bottom stair. She shivered and wrapped her arms tight around her waist. "So, what's so important? It's freezing down here!"

Wilhelm remained bent over his desk, intently studying a photographic plate. So she added with a touch of irritation, "This better be good. I was snug and warm in bed!"

Wilhelm looked up and excitedly rubbed his hands through the fiery head of hair that stuck up in the front. "Bertha. Look at this picture."

Wilhelm proudly stroked his full beard with one hand, and slid the other into a pocket on his frayed and stained cardigan. Smugly, he nodded toward the picture on his desk. Bertha bent over the desk and studied the black and white photographic plate.

"It looks like a picture of a key, Wilhelm."

"Of course it looks like a key, Bertha. It *is* a picture of a key!"

She slowly raised her head and jammed her hands onto her hips. "You brought me down here out of a warm bed to look at a picture of a key? Who cares about a picture of a key?"

"Bertha! Wait until I tell you how the picture was taken," Wilhelm blurted out, trying to calm his wife and also to pique her curiosity. "This film was never in my camera. It was exposed sitting in the dark in its case in my bottom desk drawer."

Bertha cocked her head and raised her eyebrows. "The cold in this basement must have frozen your brain. You're a university professor, Wilhelm. You know you need light to expose a photograph."

"It never saw normal light, Bertha. It was exposed by rays."

"Rays? What rays?" she demanded.

"Cathode rays from that Crookes tube," he announced, pointing at the large glass vacuum tube mounted high on the far wall. Inside the thick, egg-shaped cylinder Bertha saw two thin platinum plates, mounted parallel to each other along the length of the cylinder.

As Bertha squinted at the Crookes tube she asked, "What kind of ray is a cathode ray?"

"I don't exactly know. Crookes thinks they might come from another world."

"You don't know? What do they do? What do you use cathode rays for?"

Wilhelm shrugged and his eyes sparkled. "No one knows. That's the great wonder of it. They're new. They're mysterious. And no one knows what they can do. But I'll find out!"

"You don't know?"

Wilhelm's brow furrowed as he struggled for the right words. "Cathode rays are created when an electrical current flows through a vacuum. The rays seem to be able to pass through black paper, cardboard, and even wood! *They* exposed the picture of the key. But you can't see them, so I still have no idea what they really are."

That disgusted look crept back across Bertha's face. "You brought me down here in the middle of a freezing night, and you don't even know what kind of rays?"

Wilhelm shrugged. "Isn't it exciting?"

Sir Edward Crookes of England discovered that electric current could be increased (amplified) in a vacuum. He invented a vacuum tube with two wires in it: one the transmitter wire, or cathode, and the other a receiver wire, or anode. Whatever electric current flowed into the cathode wire would be amplified in the wire leading from the anode. This tube was called a Crookes tube.

"But the point, Bertha," said Wilhelm, recovering his composure, "is that the only key in this room is an old gate key in that small box at the front of my desk."

Bertha opened the box to which her husband pointed, and took out the long brass key. "Wilhelm," she gasped. "It's a perfect match to the key in the photograph!"

Triumphant, Wilhelm nodded. "And look. That box is along a straight line from my bottom drawer back to the Crookes tube. The rays from that tube passed through the blackened cardboard I had around the tube, across the room, through the box, through my desk, and exposed the photographic plate, making it look foggy. *But*, they couldn't pass through the metal key."

Now Bertha looked alarmed. "What kind of rays could do that?"

Wilhelm smiled mischievously. "It's late and cold, Bertha. I'll tell you in the morning."

"What?!" she shrieked. "You've got me wide-awake with wonder. I want to know now!"

Wilhelm led his wife back upstairs for coffee and told her of his initial experiments with his Crookes tube and the mysterious rays that flooded out of it. He told her how the Crookes tube glowed an eerie green when he turned on the power, and how, even when he covered the tube with blackened cardboard, some kind of ray escaped through the cardboard and struck the fluorescent salts he had painted on a screen across the room, making it also glow faint green.

"And now this. These rays seem to pass through everything except metal."

Two nights later, Wilhelm Roentgen again stood at the bottom of the basement stairs, hands trembling with excitement. "Bertha! Bertha, come down right away!"

She clambered down the steep steps. "Is this about those . . . those rays, again, Wilhelm?"

"X-rays," he answered, blocking her way at the bottom of the stairs.

"What kind of rays?"

"I named them X-rays, Bertha. X in mathematics stands for the unknown. And these are still so unknown. I named them X-rays." Wilhelm took a deep, excited, breath to regain his composure. "Before you go in, I must tell you about my most recent experiment. I wanted to find out what the rays would and would not pass through. They pass easily through paper, wood, cement, cloth with hardly any disruption at all. They partially pass through most metals. That is why the key was dark gray instead of black. What these rays will not pass through at all is lead.

"As a final test to confirm this, I held this lead disk," he showed her a palm-sized lead disk. "between the Crookes tube and my fluorescent screen." Again he took a deep, excited breath. "Now look at what happens."

Wilhelm ushered his wife into his lab and handed her the lead disk. "Hold it up. Higher. There, good. I'll turn out the light so you'll see better."

He switched on electric power to his Crookes tube. The tube glowed an eerie green. "Oh, my!" exclaimed his wife.

"Now, look back at the screen, Bertha," he commanded.

Bertha turned her head and shrieked. The fluorescent screen behind her was also faintly glowing green except for a pure black circle where the shadow of the lead disk fell on the screen, and for the dark gray outline of every bone in her hand and arm. Even her wedding ring was clearly outlined on the screen. When she moved a finger, several of the gray bones on the screen moved with it.

Bertha was fascinated and terrified at the same time. "Wilhelm, are those my bones?" she gasped.

"Every one of them," he said proudly. "Just imagine what my X-rays can be used for!"

Bertha threw down the lead disk and backed away, rubbing the arm she had seen on the screen. "This is a bad thing, Wilhelm. It makes me feel that I am about to die, like I have been touched by evil magic!"

"No, Bertha, not evil," Wilhelm reassured her. "X-rays are a natural wonder. They can do great good!"

Bertha hurried up the stairs, still rubbing her arm. "The greatest good those things can do is to stay away from me!"

Within a month, Wilhelm Roentgen's X-rays were the talk of the world. Skeptics called them death rays that would destroy the human race. Eager dreamers called them miracle rays that could make the blind see again, and could beam complex charts and diagrams straight into a student's brain.

Doctors called X-rays the answer to a prayer. Of course, it would take another 60 years and the work of many scientists to make X-rays safe for patient and doctor. But that is another story.

Library Link: A Crookes tube is an early example of a well-known type of electronic vacuum tube. Can you think of any modern uses for this type of tube?

Why do you have to wear a heavy, lead-filled vest when you get a tooth X-rayed at the dentist's office?

Topics to Explore: physics, medicine, technology, Wilhelm Roentgen, scientific method, observation.

References for Further Reading:

- *In the Children's Library:*

Aaseng, Nathan. *The Inventors*. Minneapolis, Minn.: Lerner Publications, 1988.

- *In the Adult Library:*

Nitski, Robert. *The Life of Wilhelm Roentgen, Discoverer of the X-Ray*. Tucson, Ariz.: University of Arizona Press, 1977.

Consult your librarian for additional titles.

Physics—Electrical Communications

The Code for Success

A story of Samuel Morse's invention of the telegraph in 1852

☑ **A Point to Ponder: Which would be easier to create, a telephone system or a telegraph system? What's the difference between a telephone and a telegraph?**

Science is often a cut-throat race for invention and discovery. While many scientists individually struggle toward a common goal, usually only one is proclaimed the winner—the discoverer, the inventor. The rest get little for their efforts beyond the bitter taste of anonymity. Yet rarely is a discovery or invention due entirely to one person's efforts. Never has that been more true than in the frantic race to invent a workable electric telegraph system.

The gates of Locust Grove opened onto a hundred-acre estate just south of Poughkeepsie, New York, whose rolling hills bent right down to the lapping shores of the Hudson River. Bouncing along in a rented carriage from the Poughkeepsie train station, the short, pudgy lawyer Richard Stanlin had little time to notice the beauty of his surroundings as he struggled to stay on his bucking seatboard and to shield his eyes from the driving summer rain. Stanlin bounced through the Locust Grove gate and up to the sprawling, Italian-style villa of Samuel P. Morse.

Dismounting and rubbing his numbed bottom, Richard took a moment to soak in the grandeur of Morse's estate. He whistled softly to himself. "My, my. Samuel has certainly done well with his telegraph company."

The year was 1852. A bustling country was moving westward and Morse's telegraph was sprouting up as fast as settlers could stake their claims. His system had also invaded Europe. But each expansion seemed to uncover a dozen new challenges to Morse's telegraph patent, and to his claim as "Inventor of the Telegraph."

Stanlin climbed the stairs to Morse's massive front door carrying a bulging briefcase in one hand and mopping rainwater from his balding head with the other. He was shown into the study, where he faced a tall, proud man of 61, Samuel Morse. Morse's eyes were black as coal, but his passion made them glow like embers. His bushy, white beard hung down across his chest.

There was no pleasant chit-chat with Morse. A quick shake of the hand, a nod toward a straight-backed chair, and he dove right to the heart of the business that had forced Stanlin to endure the long journey up from New York. "Can you do it? Can you protect my patents?"

Richard removed and wiped his thick wire-rimmed spectacles. "This is a complicated matter, Mr. Morse. I need to better understand all the claims and counterclaims."

"It's very simple," bellowed Morse, bearing down on the seated figure before him. "I am the one who invented the telegraph."

Stanlin opened his leather briefcase and removed a thick packet of documents. "I only need to ask a few questions about the science aspects of your invention."

Morse groaned, as if deeply pained by needless questions, and threw himself into a high-backed, leather chair facing Stanlin. "I'll say it again. It's very simple. The telegraph is mine. I invented it."

Richard squirmed in his chair as if to escape Morse's fierce gaze. "Perhaps it would be better to say you invented *a* telegraph. There does seem to be more than one."

Morse's bushy, white eyebrows drew together like thick puffs of cotton atop his eyes, and he pounded his fist on his desk. "No! I invented *the* telegraph. Period."

Richard adjusted his spectacles again and thumbed through a stack of notes and documents in his lap. "Maybe. Maybe not," he muttered in a low tone. He paused while searching for the correct paper. "Ah, here we are. Isn't it true that Baron Paul Shilling created a working electromagnetic telegraph in 1823 in Russia? That's over twenty years before the successful Washington-to-Baltimore demonstration of your system."

Morse dismissed the thought of the Russian scientist with a wave of his hand. "Shilling's system couldn't transmit over great distances. It lost signal strength. Besides, it was too complicated, with five wires and five separate magnetic needles. You had to transmit and then decode all five needles to send one simple letter. Lousy system."

Stanlin nodded. "I see. What about von Steinheil's system in Munich, Germany? His electric telegraph was already in wide use by the Bavarian government in 1839, five years before your 1844 test."

Morse's mouth twitched back and forth as he seemed to struggle for the correct words. "Don't you see, man? My system is better. I transmit dots and dashes. They can be recorded and easily read. The German system had a needle that swung from side to side by electromagnetic force. It was awkward and slow.

It had to be watched constantly. If an operator blinked, he could miss a letter. Look at whose system is in place in Europe now. Mine."

Stanlin scribbled rapid notes before he replied. "I see. But what about Sir Charles Wheatstone in England? His system has been in practical use running along railroad lines in England since 1838. Why can't he claim to be the inventor of the electromagnetic telegraph?"

Morse rubbed his bushy eyebrows and nodded. "Sure his system works—after a fashion. But it's an awkward, outdated system. Five wires and five needles. You have to set all five needles at the transmitting end in a certain position depending on the letter you want to send. Then five separate electric circuits force the magnets at the receiving end to flip the five needles there to the same positions—all to transmit one letter! Mine has one wire and one clicker on each end. You see the difference? Mine is better!"

"But was it first?"

Morse growled fiercely, so Stanlin flipped to his next sheet of paper and a new question. "I see. Mr. Morse I would like to review the individual components of your system. As I understand it, first the sending operator pushes down a knob, or clicker, on the sending end to complete an electric circuit. Did you design that clicker assembly?"

Morse cleared his throat. "Actually, my assistant Alfred Vail designed the metal spring and clicker assembly."

Stanlin scribbled more notes. "I see. And that circuit is powered by a battery which you designed?"

Morse cleared his throat again and shifted in his chair. "No, Alessandra Volta of Italy invented and designed the batteries."

"I see. And as long as the clicker is held down, an electric current is sent out along a single wire. Using a single wire was your idea?"

"Actually, Joseph Henry," muttered Morse.

"I see. And that single wire is mounted on poles, instead of being buried in the ground as the European systems are. Was that your idea?"

Morse crossed his arms angrily. "Ezra Cornell, a New York engineer, designed that."

"I see. And the wire is insulated. Did you design that unique insulation?"

Morse scowled. "Joseph Henry, again."

Stanlin adjusted his spectacles and turned to a new page in his notebook. "I see. I believe another unique aspect of your system is the glass insulators between each pole and the transmitting wire. Was *that* your idea?"

Morse mumbled something. Richard cupped his hand to his ear. "What was that, Mr. Morse?"

"I said that using broken glass bottle bottoms was the idea of Leonard Gale and Joseph Henry!" shouted Morse.

"I see. And I believe every few miles along your system there is a battery-powered relay to boost and maintain signal strength. Did you invent and design the relay?"

For over a minute, Morse stared angrily at his lawyer. Then he sighed, "Joseph Henry did."

"Henry again. I see. And at the receiving station this wire is wrapped tightly around a horseshoe-shaped magnet, so that when current flows through the circuit, the magnet is activated and pulls down the clicker on the receiving set. Is that correct?"

"Of course," answered Morse.

"I see. And did you design the system for wrapping the wire around the magnet?"

"No. That would be Joseph Henry."

Stanlin scribbled more notes. "I see. Henry again. And did Alfred Vail design the receiving clicker and handset, as he did at the transmitting end?"

Morse began to pace back and forth across the expansive study. "Of course he did. He designed all our mechanical pieces."

At last Stanlin smiled. "Ah, but I know you designed the notched board which records the incoming sequence of dots and dashes."

Morse paced all the faster, staring down at his carpet and mumbling disgustedly to himself. Then he glared up at Stanlin. "I *did*. But we stopped using mine. Leonard Gale designed a better pen and paper recorder."

Stanlin shook his head and looked imploringly up at Morse. "I see. But Mr. Morse, isn't there anything in your telegraph system that *you* invented or designed?"

Morse stopped and pounded one fist into the palm of his other hand. "By thunder, man, don't you understand? I got the *idea*. I pulled all the pieces together. I made it work. Besides that, I created Morse code, the fastest, easiest system in the world for transmitting written information. The telegraph is mine!"

Richard Stanlin regrouped his papers, snapped shut his briefcase, and rose from his chair. "I see. This has been most informative. I must tell you this does not appear to be the strongest case I have ever represented. But, we shall see. Good day, Mr. Morse."

Two years later, in 1854, the Supreme Court of the United States confirmed that Samuel Morse was the true inventor of the telegraph and upheld all of his patent claims. One man, Samuel Morse, emerged as a worldwide hero, and was proclaimed a scientific genius. Unfortunately, the names of Wheatstone, Steinheil, Shilling, Vail, Gale, and Henry quickly faded from history. But that is another story.

Library Link: Do we still use an electromagnetic telegraph system in the United States?

What is a patent, and how can it protect an inventor's work?

Topics to Explore: physics, electricity, communication, scientific method, Samuel Morse, telegraph.

References for Further Reading:

- *In the Children's Library:*

Hays, Wilma. *Samuel Morse and the Telegraph.* New York: Franklin Watts, 1960.

Lathan, Jean. *Samuel B. Morse: Artist-Inventor.* Champagne, Ill.: Garrard Press, 1967.

- *In the Adult Library:*

Kirby, Mona. *Samuel Morse.* New York: Franklin Watts, 1991.

Consult your librarian for additional titles.

The Call of Greatness

A story of Alexander Graham Bell's invention of the telephone in 1875

☑ **A Point to Ponder: How were messages and news sent across country or overseas before we had satellites? Before we had radios? Before we had telephones? Before we had telegraphs?**

Thomas Watson stretched his cramped back and wiped the sweat from his eyes. The muggy heat of this early June day in Boston was stifling, making even breathing seem an unbearable effort. He had shrugged off the discomfort of the small, poorly ventilated, third-floor flat and worked all morning. But now, Thomas Watson wanted to stop.

Throwing down the wire cutters he held, Thomas said, "Alexander, we're not getting anywhere. Let's take an afternoon off."

Alexander Graham Bell raised a heavy eyebrow. "Sorry, Thomas, a day off is a luxury we can't afford. We've got to find some way to convert human voice into electric signals."

"But Alexander, it's hot, too hot."

Alexander shook his bushy, black beard. His eyes seemed to burn with excitement, even in the heat. "Don't you see, Thomas, we're in the midst of a race, a grand race into the unknown. A day off might mean the difference between winning and losing."

Watson sighed, "After two months in this rented oven, we still can't send anything but 'clicks' down an electrical line, and Morse did that 30 years ago with his telegraph."

But Alexander Bell wouldn't give in. "Someone will make a telephone work, and I want to be the first. He who wins the race is a hero. He who comes in second is forgotten. That's the way of science, Thomas. Now back to work!"

It was 1875, and Alexander Graham Bell had devoted his life to the study of speech. He had studied how speech was formed, how complex sound waves travelled through the air from mouth to ear, and especially how to teach the deaf to speak. He dreamed of electronically converting audible sound waves into wave patterns on paper, so that deaf students could speak a word and actually see if they were producing the word correctly by comparing their wave patterns to those of people with normal hearing. Bell knew all about sound and speech, but he didn't know electronics.

Thomas Watson was a Boston-area mechanical engineer, drawn in by Bell's energy and enthusiasm. He loved the thrill of the hunt for the solution to a problem.

But as the two men struggled to create this aid for the deaf, they recognized the vast potential of their talking device as a communications system for the whole world. Eagerly, they shifted their focus and joined the race to invent the telephone.

Bell and Watson's early optimism faded as they encountered nothing but technical problem after technical problem. By now, even problem-solver Thomas Watson was tired of the seemingly endless hunt for solutions.

In theory, it was simple. Bell had talked the problem through a hundred times, each time hoping he'd uncover some missing clue. As Watson puffed and fanned his face, Alexander clasped his hands behind his back and tried yet again. "As we talk we send pressure waves out through the air. I can measure these waves and watch the pressure vary. So why can't I convert these air pressure waves into electrical waves? That is, into a changing electrical current?"

Watson mopped his face with a handkerchief. "Because it's too hot?"

"No, James!" Alexander scowled and then continued. "Physical waves in the air don't seem to have any effect on electrical current. So how can I make changes in air pressure create changes in electrical current?"

It seemed they had tried everything that sweltering morning of June 2, 1875, when they stopped for a noon break.

After a brief meal, Bell rose. "Back to work, Thomas. I want to check some of the connections in the hearing room. You stay here and keep working on the talking unit."

Bell and Watson had set up the living room of their tiny apartment as the *talking*, or *sending room*. Here were large batteries, spools of wire, and the equipment they hoped would change speech into electrical currents. From the talking room a wire led down the hall and into a bedroom that had become the *hearing*, or *receiving room*. Here sat more bulky, rectangular batteries and equipment Bell hoped would one day convert the electrical current back into air pressure waves that would match normal speech.

Left alone in the talking room, Watson halfheartedly slumped into a chair and drummed his fingers on the table before him. Drums. Watson's sleepy, overheated mind wandered off to think about drums. "If my finger taps on a drum, the drum skin vibrates. I wonder. If I made the skin covering the drum very, very thin, would the air waves of speech make it vibrate?"

Then Watson bolted upright, catching himself about to doze off, and briskly rubbed his face to wash away the sleep. "I've got to get busy or Alexander will be furious."

But wait. What was he just daydreaming about? Drums? Something nagged at his mind, whispering that there was a valuable thought here. "Oh, it's too hot to think," he grumbled. But, like a nagging fly, the thought buzzed around his awareness. What if that very thin drum skin, or membrane, were stretched over the opening of a small, sealed canister? Then, whenever something pushed the membrane inward, whatever was in the canister would be compressed. When the membrane was pulled out, whatever was inside would expand. The bigger the push or pull, the greater the compression or expansion.

Watson sighed and shook his head. "So what? That still doesn't have anything to do with electricity." He felt along the table, searching for his fan. But that nagging thought buzzed past his ear again. "What if the stuff in the canister would carry an electrical current whenever it was compressed? And what if the membrane were thin enough so that the air pressure of sound waves would be strong enough to push the membrane in, and to pull it back out?"

Watson struggled to remember. Hadn't they tested a canister like that? No. They had *made* one, but never tested it. Where had they left it?

Watson fumbled through two storage boxes. Ah! Here was the canister, just a bit smaller than his fist, with long wires trailing out of both sides. But how should he hook it up? What would it do? Lazily, he unplugged the two sending boxes they had tried that morning and attached the wires from the new canister.

The sweat dripped off Thomas's face. He sank wearily into his chair. "I'll let Alexander decide what to do." Idly, he began to pluck the reeds of the telegraph they used as a test unit and fan himself in the shimmering afternoon heat.

Alexander burst into the room, his face flushed red. "Watson, what did you do?" he demanded.

Embarrassed at being caught idle, Watson started to confess. "I'm sorry, Alexander. But it's so hot . . ."

"Whatever you did, do it again!" continued the excited Bell.

"You mean fan myself?"

"No, man! The talking unit, the reeds. I heard you. I heard notes, not clicks. I heard the notes through the receiver!"

The heat was forgotten instantly. Both men eagerly examined the sending unit Watson had halfheartedly thrown together.

"What's this?" demanded Bell with a scowl, pointing to the canister Watson had hooked up.

Watson shrugged. "It was in one of the boxes. We never tested it."

Alexander brightened. "This is the canister we filled with activated charcoal." Then he exploded in understanding. "Powdered charcoal! Charcoal is carbon, Thomas. When sound waves push the membrane inward, the carbon in the canister is squeezed, compressed. The tighter the carbon is packed, the better it conducts electricity! When the membrane is pulled outward, the carbon inside expands, loosens. The grains are farther apart, and electric flow decreases. This is it! This is how we can convert air waves of speech into electrical waves. How simple it is once you see it. Great idea, Thomas!"

Thomas blushed. "Well, I always do my best thinking when it's on the hot side."

Three days later, they were able to transmit a voice from room to room. They still couldn't understand the words, but they could tell whose voice it was.

Nine months later, on March 7, 1876, Alexander Graham Bell spoke the first clear words ever transmitted over an electrical device, "Mr. Watson, come here. I need you!" as he spilled battery acid over his clothes.

By the turn of the century, over 2 million Bell telephones were in busy use in America, and the name Alexander Graham Bell was a household word. Elisha Gray, the man who came in second by several months in the race to invent the telephone, was almost completely lost to history. But that's another story.

Library Link: Why was it easier to send Morse's telegraph dots and dashes through an electric line than voice?
What happens when you talk that allows others to hear you?

Topics to Explore: physical science, energy, electricity, communication, Alexander Graham Bell.

References for Further Reading:

- *In the Children's Library:*

Quiri, Patricia. *Alexander Graham Bell.* New York: Franklin Watts, 1982.

Shipper, Katherine. *Mr. Bell Invents the Telephone.* New York: Random House, 1952.

- *In the Adult Library:*

Bruce, Robert. *Bell: Alexander Graham Bell and the Conquest of Solitude.* Boston: Little, Brown, 1973.

Costain, Thomas. *The Chord of Steel.* New York: Doubleday, 1960.

Consult your librarian for additional titles.

A Signal to His Father

A story of Guglielmo Marconi's invention of the radio in 1894

☑ **A Point to Ponder: What makes a radio signal fly out of a wire and into the air?**

1894. What a wonderful year for a clever, eager young man to be alive—particularly if he was fascinated by electronics! Morse's telegraph, still new and exciting, was speeding messages all over the world. Electric motors hummed in the world's factories. Alexander Graham Bell's telephone system spread across America and Europe, letting ordinary people, hundreds of miles apart, talk to each other. The world of electronic communications, like a budding rose, seemed to promise glory and beauty yet unimagined.

This buzzing electronic excitement found no better receiver than twenty-year-old Guglielmo Marconi in Bologna, Italy. "Father! Alonso! Luigi! Come up quickly. It works!"

Mr. Marconi slowly set down his newspaper and followed his two scampering sons up to the small third-floor guestroom Guglielmo had converted into a laboratory. As Alonso and Luigi eagerly poked and prodded the assembled wires, tubes, and switches, Guglielmo's father leaned against the door. "Well, I certainly hope you made something work after what this equipment has cost me!"

Guglielmo stood proudly next to a large porcelain electrical throw switch. "Just watch, Papa. Your son is going to send the world's first electric message through the air!"

Luigi and Alonso gasped in awe and wonder. Their father grunted and crossed his arms. "I just hope it's worth all the effort."

Despite his Italian name, fair-skinned, slender Guglielmo closely resembled his Irish mother, especially in the bright, thoughtful, blue eyes that danced with the energy of electric communications.

All through Guglielmo's studies with his two younger brothers at their father's estate, nothing drew his interest as much as the recent work by the American Michael Faraday. Faraday discovered that an electric current flowing through one wire could force an electric current to flow through a nearby wire, even if the two wires never touched! It was as if the electric current flew from wire to wire by magic!

One afternoon in March of 1894, a question began to gnaw its way into Guglielmo's thoughts. If a simple electric current could fly through the air from one wire to another, why couldn't he also make a *useful* signal, a message, leap through thin air from wire to wire?

For the next eight weeks, this idea had been Guglielmo's all-consuming passion. He was determined to make a message jump across open space from one wire to another. And now his batteries, wires, and circuits stood ready for their first demonstration. Guglielmo coughed politely for attention, and gestured to a battery and a large glass tube before him. A small sign in front of this tube read "transmitter."

"As soon as I connect the switch, battery power will flow into this tube causing a small crystal to vibrate over 10,000 times a second. I call this tube my *oscillator*. That oscillating, or vibrating, signal runs down this wire, and . . ."

Here Guglielmo paused for effect as he slowly pointed across the room to more wires and tubes with a sign reading "receiver." ". . . leaps across the room to that wire, which receives my signal and sends it running through that second oscillator. Finally, my signal will cause that compass needle to move. Watch that needle!"

Guglielmo threw the switch, connecting his transmitting oscillator to its battery power supply. Instantly, the compass needle shifted away from north to align with the electric current flowing through the receiving wire.

Alonso and Luigi exploded in wild cheers. "Hooray! That was wonderful! What happened? What did you do to the compass? Is it broken?"

Mr. Marconi shrugged. "It would be easier to just walk across the room and spin the compass needle by hand. For all this equipment cost me, you should carry the signal across on a golden pillow!"

Guglielmo winced. "I'll make it work better, Papa. This was only the first step. I have a problem. The electric current in the receiving wire is too weak to do any more. I don't know how to make it stronger yet."

Mr. Marconi shrugged and turned to leave. "For all the equipment I've gotten you, and all the time you put into it, I had hoped for more."

For a month, Guglielmo Marconi studied every scientific paper he could find that even mentioned electric current. It seemed there were only three possible ways to boost current strength in the receiving wire: put more battery power into the transmitter, increase the efficiency of the transmitter, or somehow increase the efficiency of the receiver. Unfortunately, as of 1894, very little work had been done toward any of these solutions. Marconi would have to rely on his own intuition and experiments.

One day, he found that a large glass jar filled with packed iron filings could receive a signal better than a plain electrical wire, and create a much stronger electric current flowing to his receiving oscillator. With this iron-filled tube wired into his receiver circuit, Guglielmo could move the receiver farther away from the transmitter and still have his electric signal jump from transmitting wire to receiving wire.

Guglielmo thought of a new demonstration, and chuckled with mischievous glee. This demonstration should *really* impress his father!

Two days later, Guglielmo was ready and called down to his father and brothers.

"Should we come up?" shouted Alonso.

"No. Go into the living room. You'll see. Ready? Here goes!"

Guglielmo threw the switch up in his third-floor lab. The front doorbell began to buzz. Mr. Marconi called up, "Just a minute, Guglielmo. Someone's at the door."

But when he opened the door, there was no one there. Mr. Marconi shrugged and closed the door. "Buzz!" Mr. Marconi threw open the door. No one was anywhere in sight. "What's going on here?"

"Papa, did you like that?" cried Guglielmo bounding down the stairs. "*I* made it ring. I transmitted a signal from upstairs and hooked my receiver to the doorbell."

Alonso and Luigi squealed with surprise and delight. Slowly Mr. Marconi shook his head. "Why did you do that? Who cares if you can make a bell ring in the living room? These are just silly party games you're doing, Guglielmo. After all I spent buying every contraption and electric whatnot you ever wanted, I had hoped for more than this."

Guglielmo's wide smile evaporated. His shoulders sagged. His jaw tightened. "I'll do better, Father. It just takes time."

Another month of testing produced two new ideas to make the receiver work better. First, Guglielmo replaced the iron filings in his glass receiver jar with nickle and silver filings. He called it a "signal condenser." Second, he held a metal plate horizontally just beneath the signal condenser to reflect extra airborne signals up into the condenser, and to block the signal from leaking out of the condenser and down to the ground.

On his next demonstration, Guglielmo was able to send a signal to the house next door. His brothers cheered. His father shrugged. "So now you bother the neighbors. Believe me, I talk to them enough already. If you're going to play with all that expensive equipment, Guglielmo, find a way to make it useful."

Though disappointed by his father's continued indifference, the fire for success still burned bright in Guglielmo's eye. "I will, Papa. I just know I will. It's only a matter of more time."

Guglielmo found that larger metal plates meant better signal reception. With his new giant metal plate he sent a signal 200 meters to the top of a hill behind the Marconi estate. Luigi waved a flag to let his brother know that the signal had been received. Of course, it did take four strong men to lift the receiver's metal plate and a horsedrawn cart to carry it. But it worked!

Guglielmo's father scoffed. "So now you have to hire four men and a horse just to send a message 200 meters? Why not ride up on the horse and hand someone the message? Be practical, Guglielmo. You won't get anywhere this way."

Even now, his father's reaction did not discourage Guglielmo. It only made him more determined. "I will, Papa. You'll see."

With another two months of testing, Guglielmo made two more important advances. First, he found a way to greatly increase the power flowing through the transmitting wire. Second, he discovered that thin, light, copper tubes placed eight to ten centimeters apart worked just as well as a heavy metal plate. He also found that this receiver design worked best if raised up off the ground.

Guglielmo welded eight of these eight- or nine-meter-long copper tubes onto thin metal spacer bars and raised the whole assembly on a wooden pole. As he did, Guglielmo Marconi raised the world's first antenna, now a common sight rising from rooftops all over the world. The receiver wire ran from these copper tubes into Guglielmo's signal condenser jar and oscillator.

Alonso put the antenna and receiver on a cart to see how far he could travel and still hear Guglielmo's signal transmitted from his third-floor lab. First, Alonso stopped half a kilometer away. He got the signal fine. He moved on to a full kilometer from the house. Again it worked, and Alonso wheeled his cart farther down the dirt road.

By midafternoon, Mr. Marconi asked, "Where's Alonso?"

Guglielmo beamed. "Just a second, Papa. I'll see." Guglielmo threw the switch sending a signal to his brother. Alonso had to fire a gun into the air to signal back that the message had come through loud and clear. He was over two kilometers away in the next village!

At home, all eyes turned to Mr. Marconi to see his reaction. He nodded his head and rubbed his chin. Slowly, thoughtfully, he said, "Now you've got something, Guglielmo. *This* could be useful." He broke into a wide grin. "*This* could be worth all the trouble."

Guglielmo sighed with relief and smiled. Once he won his father's approval, Guglielmo knew everything else would be easy.

Still, it took Guglielmo Marconi another two years of hard work to refine his transmitting and receiving systems (his radio) to the point where he could send messages to ships at sea. He needed another two years to send a signal across the Atlantic Ocean. It took other researchers another decade to learn how to send voice signals over a radio. But that's another story.

Library Link: How does an antenna pick up a signal from the air?
What were the first uses of radio signals?

Topics to Explore: physical science, electricity, communication, scientific method, Guglielmo Marconi, radio.

References for Further Reading:

- *In the Children's Library:*

Gunston, David. *Marconi, Father of Radio.* New York: Crowell-Collier, 1967.

- *In the Adult Library:*

Marconi, Degna. *My Father, Marconi.* New York: McGraw-Hill, 1962.

Consult your librarian for additional titles.

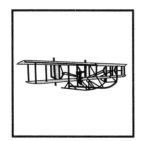

Physics—Transportation

All Steamed Up

A story of James Watt's invention of the steam engine in 1778

☑ **A Point to Ponder: What were steam engines used for around the turn of the century? Do we still use them for anything?**

Heavy-set, 46-year-old Mathew Boulton shook his fists up at the grimy ceiling and scowled down into the work pit. "Oh, no! You're not giving up again?!" Even though there was an edge of irritation in his voice, like the rumble of distant thunder, his face, as always, remained bright as a spring day.

Down in the pit, frail James Watt angrily threw down the rag he was using to wipe his hands. "I mean it this time. This whole project is one big disaster." He seemed on the verge of tears. Then he scooped the rag back up and nervously attacked the grime covering his fingers. His thin, pale face was drawn. His skin was even more sickly-white and pasty than usual. His voice was high-pitched and shrill.

Somewhat concerned that his prized scientist and inventor had stumbled up against yet another problem, and somewhat irritated that he had to sit through another of James Watt's whining fits, Mathew Boulton sighed, pulled back the jacket of his business suit, and rested his hands on his broad hips. "What went wrong this time?"

"First, I do not feel at all well." James Watt ran his hands through his thinning and receding hair. He was only 41. But on the many days when work did not go well, he looked more like 61.

"You never feel well, James. I mean what went wrong with the fire engine?" It was already 1778. Designing and creating this fire engine, an early name for what we call a "steam engine," was taking James Watt years longer than Mathew had originally thought. Another major setback might mean that someone else would create a practical, working fire engine first. Then all Mathew Boulton's investment in James Watt and in the shop would be lost.

James crossed his arms and sulked. "I simply cannot make a two-stroke steam engine. I don't know why I let you bully me into trying."

"But James, your own calculations show that a two-stroke engine will be 70% more efficient than even your best one-stroke design," said Mathew, now sounding serious and stern. "And increased efficiency is the key to a sellable engine. Just try a little longer."

James angrily stomped up the stairs out of the work pit. "Well certainly not today! I need rest and my head aches. Besides I think I'm coming down with something."

Mathew Boulton shook his head and muttered after James, "You're always coming down with something."

Inside a steam engine, burning wood, coal, or gas superheated water, turning it into high-pressure steam. This steam expanded and drove a piston up into a metal cylinder. Then the steam flow was shut off and gravity pulled the piston back down where a burst of steam could force it back up again.

That was how a one-stroke engine worked. In a two-stroke engine, steam not only pushed the piston up, but also forced it back down. This would create power from both the up and the down stroke of the piston. James Watt was trying to create the first two-stroke steam engine.

He was still sullen and brooding when he reached the Birmingham, England, house he shared with his wife, Ann, and their four children. Ann met James at their front door. "Oh my! You look gloomier than a thundercloud today!"

James rubbed his hands together and picked at the grime under his nails. "I couldn't get my hands clean at the shop," he whined.

"Then scrub them with a stiff brush."

"No. Then they'll hurt and be chafed. Do I look sick to you?"

Ann nodded in understanding. "So you had a bad day on the engine, did you? Well, change out of those filthy clothes. Dinner's almost ready."

"Ann," he announced in his thin little voice. "I'm quitting. This engine is impossible. Everything is wrong. Two-stroke engines cannot be created."

Ann, of course, had heard all this many times before and was in no mood for an evening of whining. Fiercely, she turned back to face her husband. "Is your one-stroke engine the finest and most efficient in the world?"

"Well, yes . . ." he stammered. "It's three times more efficient, Ann. You know that. Once I blow steam into a cylinder to force the piston up, I don't cool the cylinder with water to condense the steam. My engine keeps the cylinders hot by condensing the steam in a separate chamber."

"Right," said his wife with a nod. "And for every inch of those improvements, you whined about quitting a hundred times. Why should it be different now?"

"But the one-stroke was simple physics," whined James. "I merely analyzed the heat content of the steam and the energy transfer from heat to mechanical motion. That was easy. But this two-stroke business, this is too hard. Besides, I don't have any of the right tools, and I don't feel well."

Ann shrugged and shook her head. "I'll help you up to bed. You can eat up there and whine to yourself tonight. Maybe you'll figure it out tomorrow."

The next afternoon, Mathew Boulton warily approached the wide work pit in the fire engine shop. "James?" he called with a soft voice and a big smile. "How's it going today?"

James Watt looked up from the drafting paper on which he was furiously drawing. "How do you *think* it would be going with *me* working on it?"

Mathew sighed. "Still having problems?"

James Watt laughed. "Heavens no! What problems could someone as brilliant as I am have designing something as simple as a two-stroke steam engine? I've already finished the physics assessment and designed the steam flow. Look."

Mathew blew out a long sigh of relief and smiled. It was always like that with James Watt, one day disaster, the next, no problems at all. He climbed down into the pit next to the partially assembled fire engine and looked at the drawings.

"It's brilliant, James," said Mathew with a great booming laugh. The two-stroke engine had been created.

James smiled thinly and shook his head. "Don't overreact, Mathew. For someone of my caliber, this was easy."

Mathew decided to use James's good mood to push toward the next step. "There's only one more tiny change we need to make. Right now your piston just moves up and down. We need to make that motion go round and round on a wheel to drive the conveyor belts, pulleys, and machines in an industrial plant."

James Watt's face paled. His skin grew clammy. His mouth tightened and drooped. He wrung his hands. "Oh, that's impossible! It's too hard," he whined. "I'm going home. I don't feel at all well."

And so it was that step by step, over the eight-year period from 1774 to 1782, prodded on by his wife and his manager, James Watt designed, tested, and implemented an efficient, working steam engine and ushered in the great industrial age. How his family and coworkers put up with his whining along the way is another story.

Library Link: How does a steam engine work?
Name the most common uses of steam engines in this country.

Topics to Explore: physical science, energy, transportation, steam engine, James Watt.

References for Further Reading:

- *In the Children's Library:*

Crane, William. *The Man Who Transformed the World: James Watt.* New York: Messner, Inc., 1963.

Nahan, Andrew. *James Watt and the Power of Steam.* Sussex, England: Wayland, Hove, 1981.

- *In the Adult Library:*

Rolt, L. T. *James Watt.* New York: Arco Publishing, 1963.

Consult your librarian for additional titles.

The Drive for Perfection

The story of Berta and Karl Benz's invention of the motor car in 1886

☑ **A Point to Ponder: Of the many advances, discoveries, and inventions necessary to make modern automobiles possible, which do you think was most important?**

At 5:00 in the afternoon, Karl Benz slid out from under the engine he had struggled with all day in his Manheim, Germany, workshop. He leaned wearily against a wheel as he wiped his grimy hands. His drooping, walrus-like mustache was matted with oil and sweat. Every inch of his body radiated weariness, except for his eyes. Black as coal, they still radiated inexhaustible energy, even as the deep lines in his face spoke of going straight to bed.

Benz's slender wife, Berta, breezed into the drab and grimy workshop like a breath of fresh air.

"How are the modifications going, Karl?" she asked with a rich, warm smile.

He sighed noisily past his thick mustache and dismissed her question with a wave of his hand. "Problems. Nothing but problems."

Berta laughed and tossed a clean rag to her husband, noting that the one he was using was only making his hands greasier. "You always say that, Karl."

"And it's always true!" he angrily protested.

Berta found a reasonably clean stool, spread a towel over it, and sat next to her husband. "Back in 1876, your machine shop was going broke. Problems, right?"

Karl Benz nodded. "Ya. We had so many problems!"

Berta continued. "And you solved them all by building stationary gasoline combustion engines for factories. Then in the depression of 1880 when no one could afford new factory equipment, you were broke again."

Karl threw up his hands. "Now that was a big problem!"

Berta persisted. "But you solved it by dreaming up a gasoline engine for a moving vehicle. You always have problems, Karl, and you always manage to solve them. That's the way of science and invention. Now come home to supper."

Karl looked up at his wife, his black eyes twinkling. "You win, Berta. I guess I'm pretty lucky to have you to tell me when I'm being a fool."

But at supper this October evening of 1886, Karl continued to brood. Over soup he explained, "When the engine was on a three-wheeled vehicle, the lone front wheel steered like a bicycle, and the engine was connected to the rear wheels by a drive chain, like a bicycle. Simple and reliable. But a three-wheel vehicle can barely carry two people and no cargo. So we went to four wheels."

"I already know all this," said Berta, pouring more soup.

"*But,*" continued Karl, raising his bushy eyebrows to signal his annoyance at being interrupted. "The extra weight creates too much pressure, pops the drive chain. So I improved and reinforced the drive chain. But I started thinking that I should shift to a solid drive *shaft*. But my test design tends to lock up when the vehicle turns a corner. And making two front wheels steer smoothly together is a nightmare! The steering is far from smooth enough."

Again Berta laughed. "Oh Karl. Don't you remember you said the same thing in 1882, when you couldn't see how to ignite the fuel and air in the combustion cylinders? Then you invented spark plugs. You also said it in 1884, when you couldn't get enough of an electric charge in the starter. For four months, I had to hook my sewing machine to your engine and pedal the sewing machine to build up a good charge."

Karl chuckled at the comical memory of his wife pedalling furiously on her sewing machine to get his engine to start.

Berta went on. "Then you invented a battery-driven . . . oh, what do you call it?"

"Accumulator," whispered Karl, as if he were sneaking the answer to his wife.

"Oh, yes! An accumulator to store a large enough electric charge. *And* you invented a gear box and put three forward gears on the engine to increase its speed from seven miles per hour to well over twenty. I think the new drive chain works perfectly well. But if you really want a drive shaft, you'll solve that problem, too, Karl. But not tonight. It's late."

Berta rose, kissed her husband on the cheek, and began to clear the table. Karl remained at the table with his chin in his hands. "I'm just not at all sure the drive chain and front-wheel steering are at all reliable."

While Karl slept late that night, Berta tossed and turned, trying to think of a way to show her skeptical husband how good his vehicle really was. Then it hit her. She and their two teenaged sons were due to visit her mother in the town of Pforzheim, well over 50 miles away. They had planned to go by train. But why not take the automobile and prove to Karl that it was roadworthy?

Fifty miles! No one had ever driven a self-propelled vehicle of any kind more than a mile or two around town. This would be a world's record—if the car made it all the way to Pforzheim.

Four days later, Berta and the boys were up and off before daybreak. To avoid waking Karl, they pushed the Benz a short distance down the road before starting the noisy engine.

By noon, they had thundered 30 miles across the countryside to Heidleberg without a hitch, other than being sore and stiff from the jostling of the bumpy road. Berta was exhilarated by the ease and speed of their drive. Both boys were thrilled by the envious stares they got from children they passed along the road.

At two in the afternoon, they sputtered into the village of Wieslock, out of gas and needing water for the radiator. They found a pharmacy that sold petroleum distillate as a solvent. Berta figured this kerosene-like distillate was as close to gasoline as she was going to get in a small town and filled the gas tank.

Heading out of Wieslock, the dirt road got rougher and narrower. Twice, they got stuck in ruts. Both boys had to push and strain to get the vehicle out. Once, they were forced to detour into a field to avoid a large muddy spot that seemed eager to trap the narrow Benz. Before they could get back to the road, trees closed in and blocked the way. They had to back up. But the Benz had no reverse gear. Berta and Eugene slowly rolled the vehicle back across the field while Richard steered.

Climbing up to the town of Bretten presented them with their first big hill. It was too steep. The Benz couldn't climb it. Again, Berta and Eugene pushed as Richard steered and stomped on the gas pedal to make the Benz climb as best it could. Mud splattered up into Berta's face and caked her clothes.

On another hill just past Bretten, the car overheated and Richard had to walk back to town for water. An hour later, the automobile died in a dark forest. Berta realized no fuel was reaching the cylinders and used a hat pin to clean a large grain of grit out of the fuel line.

Then the insulation around one of the ignition wires short-circuited and the Benz again sputtered to a halt with a shower of sparks. Berta fashioned a replacement insulator out of one of her garters.

Night was falling as they neared Pforzheim, and the Benz had no lights. Happily, the last few miles were downhill. Just at twilight, Berta was at the Pforzheim telegraph office wiring Karl that they and the Benz had set a world record and driven over 50 miles in just one day!

Karl Benz wired back, "Fifty miles? And my vehicle made it? Incredible news. Glad you're safe."

Berta and the boys returned three days later in triumph, having completed the world's first 100-mile round-trip by automobile. One hundred miles! It seemed as miraculous as flying to the moon. A huge crowd lined the street in Manheim to watch Berta drive proudly back to the Benz Automobile Shop.

Inside, Karl eagerly asked how the car behaved on the return drive, as he carefully wiped the dirt and dust off his once-shiny automobile.

"Fine," answered Berta. "Except I wish it had a horn. I would have liked to properly announce our arrival back into Manheim."

"Ach!" sighed Karl, shaking his head. "Another problem!"

Within four years, the first four-wheeled Benz automobiles, complete with front-wheel steering and solid drive shaft, rolled out of the factory. By the turn of the century, the Mercedes-Benz automobile had become the standard of automotive excellence. But that's another story.

Library Link: Virtually all components and systems in an automobile have been redesigned and improved many times since the time of Karl Benz. But have any completely new systems been invented for cars since his day?

Topics to Explore: physical science, internal-combustion engine, transportation, automobile, Karl Benz.

References for Further Reading:

- *In the Children's Library:*

Bingham, Mindy. *Berta Benz and the Motorwagon: The Story of the First Automobile Journey.* Santa Barbara, Calif.: Advocacy Press, 1989.

Lomask, Milton. *Great Lives: Invention and Technology.* New York: Charles Scribner's Sons, 1988.

- *In the Adult Library:*

Williams, Brian. *Karl Benz.* New York: Bookwright, 1991.

Consult your librarian for additional titles.

Launching a Scientist

A story about Robert Goddard's first attempts at rocketry in 1887

☑ **A Point to Ponder: What force really makes a rocket rise into the air?**

On a brisk Saturday afternoon in September 1887 Boston, when the leaves were just beginning to turn, two six-year-old boys played in front of a modest two-story house.

"It won't work," repeated freckle-faced Percy Long.

"It will too!" insisted the smaller, dark-haired boy.

"You can't fly, Bobby. Only birds fly!" yelled Percy.

But young Bobby Goddard was not going to back down. "This is called science. You just count once I jump from the front porch railing."

Bobby fished a ten-inch-long, shiny zinc rod out of his pocket. It was as thick as his wrist.

"What's that?" asked Percy suspiciously.

"It'll help me fly. Now you just remember to count. Get ready!" Bobby slammed open the front door and dashed into the living room. There, he slid his shoes along the thick wool carpet, shuffling furiously back and forth across the room.

"Hurry up!" called Percy from outside. "I can't wait around all day."

"Just a second!" Bobby shuffled two more laps across the carpet. "Here I come!" He sprinted back out the open front door, stepped once on the low bench he had positioned next to the railing, once on the railing itself, and, with a mighty leap launched himself into space, holding the zinc rod high over his head with both hands. "Count!"

"One . . . two . . ." THUD! Bobby slammed into the soft dirt of his mother's flowerbed just below the railing.

Percy Long laughed so hard he almost fell over. Bobby had crumpled two flower bushes, flattened half a dozen blooming primroses, and left a deep hole where his elbow and knees hit. "I told you you couldn't fly!"

Bobby sat up thoughtfully and rubbed his sore knee. "Maybe I didn't get enough of an electric charge . . ." He climbed out of the flowers and back onto the porch.

"Where are you going?" demanded Percy. "Giving up?"

"No. I'm going to try it again. This time I'll get a better static electricity charge. So you be ready to count!"

Bobby stepped back into the house and began to shuffle across the living room carpet. Back and forth, scraping his shoes across the carpet, time and time again. "Here I come!" Being careful not to touch anything and lose his electrical charge in a harmless spark, Bobby raced back onto the front porch. One foot on the bench. One foot on the railing. And six-year-old Bobby Goddard launched into the clear blue sky again. Again, he lifted the zinc rod high overhead.

Percy counted. "One . . . two . . . three . . . four . . ." SMASH! Bobby wiped out two hydrangea bushes as he crashed down and rolled out onto the grass.

Again Percy laughed. But Bobby leapt to his feet. "Don't laugh. I flew longer that time! It worked better."

Percy squeaked to a stop in the middle of a laugh. It was true. Bobby had stayed up almost twice as long that time.

"Bobby Goddard!" called his mother from the porch. "I have told you a thousand times not to leave this door open." She reached the porch railing, looked over, and gasped, "My land! What have you done to my flowers?"

"He was crashing, Mrs. Goddard," said Percy with a shrug.

"I was flying, Mom," corrected Bobby, and he glared over at Percy.

"Flying?" exclaimed Mrs. Goddard. "Where on earth do you think you're going to fly to?"

"Not on earth, Mom. I'm going to fly to the moon."

"Well, so far it looks like you've only managed to get as far as my flowerbeds. And right now, young man, you will fix the damage you've done."

Bobby lowered his eyes, and softly sighed. "Yes, ma'am."

Bobby's father marched out onto the porch still carrying the newspaper he had been reading. "What's all the commotion out here?" he asked.

"Bobby's been wrecking my flowerbeds. That's what!" snapped Mrs. Goddard.

"I was flying, Dad," explained Bobby.

"Mostly, he was crashing," corrected Percy.

Mr. Goddard squatted down on the porch and looked at his son standing before him. "How were you trying to fly, Bobby?"

"Electricity, Dad. If I could only get a big enough electric charge."

Mr. Goddard nodded. "So that's what all that shuffling across the living room was about. You were building up a static electricity charge. And here I thought you were just wearing out the rug!" He thought for a moment. "But what I don't understand, son, is the zinc rod. What was it supposed to do?"

Bobby shrugged and answered, "You told me yesterday that when I shuffle my feet on a rug, electricity rises up from the carpet to my feet. I knew zinc was a good conductor, so I figured if I held a zinc rod up real high when I jumped, maybe the electricity would rise up through me to the zinc, and maybe it would carry me up with it as it went."

Mr. Goddard quickly covered his mouth with both hands to cover up the laugh that threatened to jumped out of his throat. Bobby looked glum and dejected. "Well, it sort of worked. I flew longer the second time." Then he sighed. "Maybe I just jumped harder."

Mr. Goddard rose and turned to his wife. "Now what do you think of this boy, Fannie? I tell him one thing about electricity, and he puts it together with two or three other ideas and comes up with an experiment!"

"What he came up with was the destruction of my flowerbed!"

"What he came up with was a crash," Percy reminded everyone.

Mr. Goddard nodded and looked back at his son. "So your experiment was a failure?"

Sadly Bobby nodded. "I guess so."

"Good!" exclaimed Mr. Goddard.

"What?" Bobby was startled.

"Failure is how a scientist learns," explained his father. "You try something. It flops. That leads you to a better idea for the next try. The important thing is to never stop trying. Now before your next try, you might spend some time thinking about what kind of force could be strong enough to overcome gravity and thrust something up into the air. I think it's time I told you about Sir Isaac Newton's laws of motion."

Percy fidgeted back and forth from foot to foot. "I, uh, think I have to go home now." He leaned close to Bobby and whispered, "Yuck! That sounds boring!"

On a cloudy afternoon three days later, Mrs. Goddard climbed the basement stairs with a load of wash and glanced out the kitchen window. She dropped the laundry basket and screamed. Her son balanced on top of the high wooden backyard fence. In his hands Bobby held two enormous balloons. "He must be six feet off the ground!" she gasped. Then she sucked in a great breath and yelled, "Bobby Goddard, you get down from there this instant! But be careful!"

She raced out the door just as Percy Long's countdown reached, "Three . . . two . . . one . . . . Go!"

Mrs. Goddard screamed as Bobby leapt from his precarious perch high into the air. "Now count!" As he jumped, Bobby relaxed his tight grip on the necks of the two bulging 24-inch balloons. With a piercing screech, air rushed out the bottom of each balloon.

Percy counted. "One . . . two . . . three . . . four . . . fi-" Thud! Bobby crashed to the soft grass. The whine of his two balloons slowly died away to a faint hiss as they deflated. Bobby sat up and shook his head to clear the stars in front of his eyes as his mother rushed over. "What on earth do you think you were doing?" she demanded.

"I was flying, Mom," he answered.

"You mean crashing," corrected Percy.

At dinner that night, Mr. Goddard asked, "What's this I hear about you trying to fly again?"

"He just about broke his neck, is what he did," said his mother.

"I was using balloons for thrust, Dad, like what you told me Mr. Newton said. When the air rushes out the bottom of the balloons, it pushes the balloons up. I figured they'd take me up with them."

Mr. Goddard smiled. "Did you hear that, Fannie? What do you think of our boy now?"

Softly Bobby asked, "Is this another failure, Dad?"

"You just need more lift, Son, more power. A lot more power. Oh, and maybe it's time to stop sending yourself up with your rockets. Safer for you to watch from the ground. Yup. A few more experiments and a little more power. I think you'll get it."

Forty years later, on March 16, 1926, Robert Goddard launched the world's first liquid-fueled rocket. It rose 50 feet from the ground. By 1937, one of his rockets thundered over 9,000 feet into the air, and the space age was launched. In another 25 years rockets blasted free of earth's gravity regularly to place satellites and manned capsules into orbit. But that's another story.

Library Link: What forces pull a rocket back to earth?

Why does a space shuttle get so hot as it rises through the atmosphere or as it reenters the atmosphere to return to earth?

Topics to Explore: physics, chemistry, scientific method, Robert Goddard, liquid-fueled rocket.

References for Further Reading:

- *In the Children's Library:*

Farley, Karin. *Robert H. Goddard.* Englewood Cliffs, N.J.: Silver Burdette Press, 1991.

Lomask, Milton. *Robert H. Goddard.* Champaign, Ill.: Garrard Publishing Co., 1972.

- *In the Adult Library:*

Lehman, Milton. *This High Man: The Life of Robert Goddard.* New York: Farrar, Straus, 1963.

Consult your librarian for additional titles.

A Warped Idea

A story of Orville and Wilbur Wright's invention of a motorized airplane in 1903-1905

☑ **A Point to Ponder: Will a balsa-wood glider get more lift if you throw it into the wind, or with the wind?**

William Tate rocked slowly back and forth on the weather-worn boards of the front porch at his general store and post office in the tiny coastal village of Kitty Hawk, North Carolina, creaking rhythmically. Tate's face, like the wooden buildings around him, seemed etched and worn by the constantly blowing salty winds.

A ring of five reporters, one of them from as far away as Washington D.C., huddled around him. It was 1905. The Wright Brothers were flying again, in their hometown of Dayton, Ohio. Their latest world-record flight covered 25 miles with loops, spins, and plenty of turns to demonstrate complete mastery of the skies. At last man could truly fly! The imagination of the world soared with each take-off of *The Flyer III*, the Wright Brothers' current model. The reporters had come to Kitty Hawk to get the full story of how those flying wonders had started.

William leaned forward in his rocker, as if sharing an important secret. "Back in July of 1901, when Wilbur and Orville first showed up, I thought they were crazy dreamers. Oh, they were both very polite and all. But I figured you'd have to be crazy to think man could really fly."

One of the reporters moved up onto the porch to escape the fierce summer sun and pounding wind. "Mr. Tate, we just want to see where it all started. Did the Wright Brothers start here?"

"Oh, it didn't start here," answered William. "Turns out they had over two years' research under their belts before they ever came out here. Oh, aerodynamics, wing design, and such. Started in a bike shop they owned in Dayton. That's where they made the first of their two great discoveries."

It was the spring of 1899. And that discovery put Orville and Wilbur ahead of a dozen others trying to be the first to fly. On a warm spring afternoon 26-year-old Wilbur, four years older and much taller than Orville, yelled in the back door of their bike shop, "Orville. Drop everything and come out here!"

Dropping his tools and leaving a befuddled customer inside, Orville dashed out the back door to find his brother lying on his back on the small hill behind the Wright Cycling Company, hands tucked behind his head, looking up into the sky.

"Wilbur! What are you doing? I got customers in there."

Urgently Wilbur motioned his brother to come nearer. "Forget them. Watch these buzzards."

"Watch birds? Are you crazy?"

"Watch!" commanded Wilbur without taking his eyes off the lazily circling birds. "Watch what they do with their wings."

Orville knew that if his brother was anything, he was steady and dependable, not impulsive as he, himself, tended to be. Rather than ask any more questions, Orville plopped down into the soft, spring grass next to his brother and watched. Within a minute, Orville saw what had captivated Wilbur. "That's incredible! They control their flight by changing the shape and position of their wings as they glide—not by flapping."

Three things were needed to fly: lift, power, and control. Two of these were well understood. Lift was the upward pressure needed to get a plane off the ground, and the correct wing design for lift was well-known. Power, through motors with propellers, was readily available. But control, making the plane go where you wanted instead of where the wind took it, was a different story. Control was what nobody had figured out. But Wilbur's buzzards had.

"There. See that?" asked Wilbur. When a left wing tipped up, the right wing tipped down. When one wing curled forward, the other curled back. Every time the bird slipped out of balance or wanted to turn, it changed the angle at which each wing met the oncoming air, moving them always in opposition to each other.

"That's it," cried Orville. "If we change the slope and curve of a plane's wings, we control its flight. But how can we move rigid glider wings?"

Wilbur sat up with the flush of a wonderfully simple idea. "Do you still have the long shipping box for that order of inner tubes we received last week?"

Orville ran back into the shop, his customer both gone and forgotten. Rummaging through a dark corner of the storeroom, he found the three-foot-long cardboard box.

Wilbur took the box from his breathless brother and held it with one hand over each end. "Their wings always move in opposition. Watch this." Wilbur rotated one hand counter-clockwise, and the other clockwise. The box warped into a spiral. "See? One wing curls up. One wing curls down. We'll do the same to our aeroplane's wings—warp the wings to give us control of the flight."

William Tate rocked back in his chair. "That was the beginning of the Wright Brothers' successful design. But it took two years of testing before they arrived here with their first full-sized glider. Yes, I said glider. They didn't attempt powered flight until they tested gliders for two more years."

Scribbling notes, one reporter asked, "Why'd they come way out to . . . to *this* place?"

William held out his hand to gesture at the blowing sand and dust. "Wind. Yer standing on one of the windiest spots in America. Wind to get the glider up in the air. Well, that and the sand dunes for a soft landing area. I showed 'em down to Kill Devil Hills dunes myself, you know."

The reporters all chuckled. "Why'd they need a soft landing pad? They crash a lot?"

"It's not funny," snapped Kitty Hawk Postmaster Tate. "Every crash of that glider meant two, three weeks' lost time for repairs, and lost money for replacement parts. The Wright Brothers were short on both."

The reporter from the *Washington Post* thumbed back through his notes. "You said wing warp was the *first* of Wilbur and Orville's great discoveries. How many did they have?"

"Two," answered William with a confident nod of his head. "Had the second one right here. Well, I mean down at the dunes. I helped. Late September 1902, it was.

"They set up a tent camp down there. I'd go down in the evenings. Orville always cooked. Wilbur always washed dishes and kept the camp neat. Then Orville'd pull out his harmonica, and Wilbur'd drag out his mandolin and they'd play till it got chilly. Down at that camp I realized they were real scientists. Had to test, to prove, to understand each little step, takin' notes and data here all fall. Then they'd high-tail it back to Dayton to test new designs in their wind tunnel all winter, before they rebuilt *The Flyer*, and came back out here next year."

One of the reporters tapped his pencil impatiently. "You were saying about their second discovery?"

William nodded and began his slow rocking again. "Orville was up flying the glider that day. Wilbur and I launched him. We'd each hold one of the wing tips and run down a steep sand dune until there was enough speed to lift the glider into the air.

"There was a steady, warm wind that afternoon and Orville shot up like a bird, using the wing warp to keep himself just so into the wind, or using it to start his long graceful turns. I tell you, the gulls were envious of Orville that day!

"Then he nosed up too steep and almost stalled. His right wing dipped. He threw the wing warp hard left to compensate, level her out. But the glider just shuddered. Then the tail kicked around. I stood right there on the sand watching it. The glider nosed into a spiraling dive. Orville couldn't pull it out. And crash! The glider splintered out on the beach.

"Except for some bruises, cuts, and some blood on his shirt, Orville was all right. The glider was wrecked. It was a mighty sad evening in camp that night, I tell you. That is, until Orville sat straight up on his cot, nursing a stiff neck, and called out 'Wilbur, I know what happened. The tail got lift.'

"And that was their second great discovery. Under some conditions, the vertical tail section could act just like a wing and produce lift, only it was lift to the side instead of up and down. That's what kicked the glider out of control and into a dive. All they had to do to correct for this was make the tail rotate into a turn. So they hooked the tail to the wing warp controls. When the wing warp eased the glider into a turn, the tail rotated to stabilize and help the turn.

"Those two discoveries gave Orville and Wilbur control of flying. And that's why they were the first to fly."

William Tate eased back into his rocker and crossed his arms, obviously satisfied with his telling of the story.

"But what of the world's first motorized aeroplane flight, the one on December 17, 1903?" demanded one of the reporters. "That's when history was made."

"Oh, that," answered Tate with just a hint of a sneer. "I suppose *that's* what'll become famous. Probably even go down in the history books." He shook his head in disgust. "Oh, I mean, it was a pretty thing, and all. Man flying by motor, without relying on the wind. But that was bound to happen because Wilbur and Orville did their homework, their science. But the real miracles happened, ya see, in their bike shop lab, and in the glider out here on the dunes. Now what *I'm* waitin' for is when flyin' turns practical. You know, carryin' people and cargo where they need to go. But I suppose that's another story."

Library Link: Birds have always been our model for the design of flying machines. What about birds would be hardest to copy in a pair of manmade wings? What holds an airplane up in the air?

Topics to Explore: physics, aerodynamics, mechanical engineering, the Wright Brothers, scientific method.

References for Further Reading:

- *In the Children's Library:*

Freedman, Russell. *The Wright Brothers: How They Invented the Airplane.* New York: Holiday House, 1991.

- *In the Adult Library:*

Renstrom, Arthur. *Wilbur and Orville Wright.* Washington, D.C.: Library of Congress, 1983.

Wescott, Lynanne. *Wind and Sand: The Study of the Wright Brothers.* New York: H. N. Abram, 1975.

Consult your librarian for additional titles.

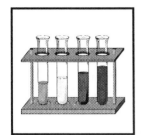

Chemistry

An Explosive Idea

A story of Roger Bacon's discovery of gunpowder in 1261

☑ **A Point to Ponder: What really creates an explosion?**

Finally, the massive bell mounted in the tower high atop the chapel tolled, marking the end of evening prayers. Many of the Franciscan friars at the Oxford, England, monastery rose and shuffled quietly down the long central aisle of the echoing stone chapel to retire to their rooms for the evening. Others remained kneeling to complete personal reflections.

A few, however, rose quickly, and eagerly made their way past the bright rows of glowing candles into the common room. There they gathered in small clusters to discuss news and the church. A select few always gathered in one corner to discuss the subjects of astrology, nature, and alchemy, which was an early form of chemistry. In the world of 1261, these three subjects comprised the full range of what we would call *science*.

But in 1261, or the Middle Ages, science was not a safe topic for a Franciscan friar to discuss. In the common mind, science and magic were almost the same thing. Science dabbled with vast forces no one really understood, and the Mother Church did not look favorably on her friars exploring forces she thought better left to faith and Church policy.

The 47-year-old, balding friar, Roger Bacon, was consumed with a passion for the study of science. Always in the center of the evening science discussions, he was well-known as one of the most outspoken and insatiable science experimenters of his time.

"Brother Roger," said friend and fellow friar Timothy Chitters, with a slow shake of his head, "don't forget that curiosity killed the cat. I'm afraid your curiosity will get you into trouble."

"Nonsense!" snorted Roger with a wave of his hand. The hair on his head formed a scraggly ring around his large bald spot, looking like an unkempt, brown halo. "Without direct experience, how can anything really be known?"

"The Church has said we should accept the existing science policies on faith," cautioned Timothy.

Flickering candlelight and shadows danced across the small ring of friars who nudged forward to listen to the debate. "I disagree," said Bacon, "I believe it is our duty to investigate the mysteries of nature outside known bounds. Scientific knowledge is always a good and powerful force. The knowledge we discover and give to the Church actually strengthens it."

"Talk like that and you might get to 'investigate the mysteries' of excommunication!" broke in another friar from the shadows behind Bacon.

"Brother Roger," continued Timothy, "General Master Bonaventure has decreed that common metals can't be turned into gold, and that the study of alchemy should be stopped. How can you disagree with the head of our Franciscan Order?"

Most of the friars nodded and mumbled their agreement.

Only Roger Bacon shook his head, the shadows on his face flickering back and forth with the candlelight. "But I know that when we combine the right elements of nature in the right way, they become more than the mere sum of those ingredients. Something wondrous happens. Who knows what they can turn into? No one, until we investigate. Come up to my room tomorrow and I will show you."

Of the entire group, only one man, Friar Timothy Chitters, climbed the stairs to Roger Bacon's room the next morning. Along one wall was a long row of jars, vials, and sacks filled with Roger's collection of natural ingredients.

"Ah, come in, Brother Timothy. You're just in time. I have been experimenting these past weeks on combining common saltpeter with other things."

"I know," replied Timothy. "I have smelled some of those experiments even out in the gardens."

"Combinations which are not made properly can be offensive," agreed Roger. "But until we mix them and see what happens, how will we know?"

Roger lifted a large jar of saltpeter onto his table. Saltpeter was the term used in 1261 for the chemical potassium nitrate, which is a major ingredient of many fertilizers, and doesn't always smell very nice. He also picked up a bag of common charcoal. "Yesterday I combined these two ingredients in several different ways and proportions, but nothing happened. Today I think I will add a third ingredient to try to create some reaction."

As Timothy watched, Roger Bacon measured out a small pile of granular saltpeter and added an equal amount of granulated charcoal. Then he turned and studied the row of bags and jars. "Aha! Sulphur might be a good activating ingredient."

Roger carefully added a small amount of the bright yellow powder to the gray-black pile in the middle of his table. He slowly stirred the mixture together.

Nothing happened.

"Maybe we need a catalyst to make the ingredients react," suggested Roger. "Help me move the table, Brother Timothy."

"What's going to happen?" asked Timothy, wary of becoming too deeply involved.

"I don't know," answered Roger. "If I knew, I wouldn't have to do the experiment."

They moved the table next to Roger's window so that sunlight touched the mixture.

Nothing happened.

"Maybe nothing will ever happen," suggested Timothy hopefully.

"When light alone won't start a reaction, it may mean the ingredients are too cold. We should let the mixture warm up," said Roger. "The right temperature is important."

They stood and watched for some minutes. Nothing happened.

"When light and warmth fail, maybe fire is the correct catalyst," said Roger.

He brought in one of the candles from the hallway and touched its flame to the pile on his table.

In a scorching flash of white-hot light, the table exploded. A reverberating blast rattled teeth and rumbled across the monastery like thunder. Roger was thrown against a wall. Timothy was flattened, trembling, to the floor. The small table had disintegrated into thin splinters of wood flung all over the room. The wall around Roger's window was blackened. Outside, friars and townspeople looked fearfully into the clear morning sky. Thunder with no clouds?

Hearts pounding, legs still weak and rubbery, Roger and Timothy slowly rose to their feet. Both men's eyebrows had been singed off by the blast, their ears rang, and their eyes stung from the acid smoke swirling around the room.

"Something certainly happened that time!" said Roger. "*That* is what I call a reaction!"

Timothy was awestruck. "I think you've discovered thunder, Brother Roger," he whispered in a small, reverent voice. "What will the Church think if one of its friars can control the very thunder of Heaven?"

"But the question is, *how* did we do it?" said Roger. "We must repeat the experiment but vary the mixture and procedures to see what makes the reaction work."

Ten minutes later a second blast belched sparks and smoke out of Roger's window. A second mighty clap of thunder rattled windows half a mile away.

A rumor raced through the fearful town that the end of the world was at hand.

Roger and Timothy stumbled back to their feet, faces blackened, holes torn and burned in their cassocks. "You see, Timothy," said Roger, "this is the way of alchemy. Combine ordinary ingredients in the right way, and they can become far more than the mere sum of their collective parts."

But Roger Bacon was a curious scientist, not a practical inventor. It took the vision of another friar, Berthold Schwartz of Germany, almost a century later, to see that Bacon's thunder explosion might be controlled by placing it at the bottom of a metal tube. It was Schwartz who first placed a metal ball on top of a pile of Roger Bacon's "gunpowder" in the bottom of a tube, and fired that ball through his wall and straight through a neighbor's house.

But how Berthold Schwartz turned Roger Bacon's discovery into the world's first gun is another story.

Library Link: Why does an explosion create a sound?
What is *alchemy*?

Topics to Explore: chemical research, scientific method, combustion, explosives, Roger Bacon.

References for Further Reading:

- *In the Children's Library:*

Blish, James. *Doctor Mirabilis*. New York: Dodd, Mead, 1971. (Fiction)

- *In the Adult Library:*

Easton, Stewart. *Roger Bacon and His Search for a Universal Science*. New York: Columbia University Press, 1952.

Consult your librarian for additional titles.

The Measure of His Success

A story of Antoine Lavoisier's discovery of the conservation of matter in 1771

> ☑ **A Point to Ponder: If you mix one pound of dirt with one pint of water to make mud, how much dirt is in the mud? How do you know?**

Matter is neither created nor destroyed during a chemical reaction. It can change from one form to another, but it can always be found, or accounted for, both before and after that chemical reaction takes place. We use this principle every day and call it "Conservation of Matter."

But only 200 years ago, this principle was unknown. The study of chemistry ground to a standstill as scientists struggled to find a way to study and understand what happened during chemical reactions. The key they needed was Conservation of Matter, and the story of its discovery begins with a woman.

Marie Lavoisier sat at her writing desk along the sunny, east wall of the upstairs laboratory in her home. Bright morning rays of sunlight splashed across her desk, bathing the room a warm yellow. Marie's forehead furrowed into thin creases of concentration as her bright blue eyes carefully read and reread a report written by Robert Boyle, the famous English scientist of almost a century before. Marie was translating the report from English into French for her husband, Antoine, to read.

Antoine strolled in with a broad and somewhat sleepy smile, fashionably dressed in the ruffled white shirt, long velvet coat, and knee socks that were the aristocratic fashion of Paris in the 1770s. "Good morning, my love. What's got you up and working so early this morning?"

Without looking up from her translation, Marie said, "Read this report by Robert Boyle, Antoine. I think you will find it interesting."

"Boyle?" questioned Antoine with an upturned lip. "His work is so . . . old. It's not modern. What could he possibly have done that would interest me?"

Again Marie spoke without stopping her translation of the final paragraphs. "It describes an experiment with tin, during which he noted an unexplained weight change."

Antoine's eyebrows rose. He quickly crossed the room. "Really? A weight change? Let me see."

The scientific world of chemistry in 1771 was itching to tear apart the substances of the world into their basic building blocks, or elements. But it needed a way, a method to break through from compound and substance to element.

Lavoisier was convinced chemists and alchemists would never find such a system because their basic experimental approach was all wrong. During experiments, chemists carefully observed and described the changes in a substance that their eyes could see. But they did not bother to actually *measure* anything. Lavoisier claimed it was far more important to record what could be specifically measured before and after an experiment. Weight was one of those properties he could always measure.

"Hmm, the weight of his tin sample increased when he heated it," muttered Antoine as he scanned through his wife's handwritten translation.

"Look here, Marie. He describes the presence of calx, which is a light gray tarnish that often forms on metals, after the heating."

"I know. I've already read it," answered Marie, now copying the sketches accompanying Boyle's report.

"Hmm. And he had no idea where the extra weight came from? Oh, look here! He proposes that it might have been *created* during heating. Nonsense!"

"I know," repeated Marie. "I already read it."

Antoine rolled the pages of Boyle's report into a tight tube which he tapped against his other palm. "Marie, I think it's time for me to repeat Mr. Boyle's experiment. I shall see if *measurement* can detect the source of this extra weight!"

Marie smiled, her bright blue eyes sparkling in the morning light. "I knew you would. I've already got a sample of tin for you to work with."

Antoine carried a small sheet of this tin to his delicate balancing scales to measure and record its weight. "The tin alone weighs 120 . . . 121 grams."

Marie nodded and recorded the weight in a large notebook.

Next Antoine placed the tin in a heat-resistant glass flask and sealed its lid to completely enclose the tin.

"Why seal the flask?" asked Marie.

"To trap the entire reaction inside, my love. Now, we shall see about a weight gain." Antoine carried the sealed flask back to his balance scale. "Flask and tin together weigh 815 . . . 16 . . . . No, 817 grams."

Again Marie recorded the weight of flask and tin in her logbook.

Antoine slowly heated the flask on a gas burner until the tin was covered by a thick layer of gray calx. He turned off the burner, let the flask cool, and carried it back to the scale for a second weighing. "Now we'll see if tin and flask have gained weight. 817 grams. Odd. It's exactly the same weight as before heating. There was no weight gain."

Antoine pried off the flask's lid. Air rushed in, as if into a partial vacuum. He removed and weighed the calx-covered tin sample alone. "122 . . . 123 grams. What is this? The tin *did* gain weight! It gained 2 grams."

Antoine began to pace back and forth in front of his scales. "But where did the weight come from? When I weighed the flask there was no weight gain."

"Then it must have come from inside the flask," offered Marie.

"Of course!" shouted Antoine, remembering the rush of air into the flask as he pried off its lid. Quickly he replaced the tin in the flask, reattached the lid, and reweighed the whole thing on his scale. "See? 819 grams. Now there *is* a weight gain. The tin gained 2 grams, and that two grams had to come from the air inside the flask. Some of the air must have been absorbed into the tin calx. Two grams of new air rushed in to replace it when I opened the lid."

Marie suggested, "Perhaps, if you used a bigger piece of tin, you could absorb all the air in the flask."

"Exactly right!" exclaimed Antoine. "I'm surprised I didn't think of it first myself." Antoine repeated the experiment with a larger piece of tin to see if more air would be absorbed into calx. No. Only two grams of air combined with tin to form calx.

After the weighing, Antoine was bitterly disappointed. But Marie said, "Strange. The rest of the air in the flask must be incapable of combining with tin."

"Yes," agreed Antoine, suddenly brightening. "I just came to the same conclusion myself. Air must really be a mixture of two separate gases, active air and inactive air."

"But how much of each is there in air?" asked Marie.

"We shall have to repeat the experiment to see, my love!" exclaimed Antoine.

They repeated the experiment a third time. But now, after heating and calx formation, they opened the flask lid underwater with their flask held upside down. Water rushed up into the flask to fill the vacuum left when active air combined with tin. They marked, and then measured the portion of the flask that filled with water.

"Almost exactly 20%," said Antoine as he finished his calculations. "Active air is 20% of the air we breathe, and inactive air makes up the other 80%."

But Marie had turned, thoughtfully gazing out a window. Then she spun back, her face flushed. "Antoine, with your measurements you have just proved something very important."

"I always do," smiled Antoine, his face dripping self-satisfaction. "I shall call active air *oxygen*. It's from the Greek words for 'acid former.' And I shall call inactive air *azote*, from the Greek for 'lifeless.' Azote makes up 80% of our air. What an incredible discovery I've made. And it's still only morning."

Marie stamped her foot. "Antoine, listen to me! You just proved something far more important than that. Boyle thought weight, or matter, might have been created during his experiment. Most chemists also believe matter can be created or lost during a reaction. But you have just proved that matter is neither created nor lost during a chemical reaction. It always comes from somewhere, and goes somewhere. You can always find it if you measure carefully."

"I proved that?" repeated Antoine, thoughtfully pacing in front of his scales. "Yes, I think I did! Yes. Matter is never lost or created. It can change forms. But its mass, or weight, can always be found both before and after an experiment."

Suddenly Antoine was ecstatic. "Yes, Marie. I have just discovered a great guiding principle with which I can tear apart and analyze all sorts of chemical reactions! I knew Boyle's article would have value. I'm glad I had you read it."

Marie smiled, realizing her husband was once again going to take all the credit for a joint effort. That was the way it always went in the Lavoisiers' upstairs laboratory in the early 1770s, when oxygen and nitrogen were first separated and named, and when the all-important principle of conservation of matter was discovered. But how long patient Marie was willing to let her husband grab all the fame for their joint efforts is yet another story.

Library Link: In what way is a burning candle the same as a rusting hunk of iron?

What is the air around us made of?

Topics to Explore: chemistry, scientific method, combustion, oxygenation, Antoine Lavoisier, Theory of Conservation of Matter, Theory of Burning.

References for Further Reading:

- *In the Children's Library:*

Grey, Vivian. *The Chemist Who Lost His Head.* New York: Coward, McCann & Geoghegan, 1982.

Irwin, Keith. *The Romance of Chemistry.* New York: Viking, 1959.

- *In the Adult Library:*

Asimov, Isaac. *The Search for the Elements.* New York: Basic Books, 1962.

Consult your librarian for additional titles.

A Breath of Fresh Air

A story of Joseph Priestley's discovery of oxygen in 1774

☑ **A Point to Ponder: On earth, what uses, or needs, oxygen? What produces it?**

Preachers in the Protestant Church of England of the early 1770s were supposed to take time to reflect, study, and counsel. But Reverend Joseph Priestley had no such time. His every spare moment was spent in the kitchen of his family's small country house.

No, he was not practicing to become a chef. He was creating and studying gases. This would be Reverend Priestley's third venture into the world of science. As a not-very-successful priest and part-time schoolteacher, he found himself drawn more and more to the amazing possibilities of the sciences.

Priestley's first scientific endeavor, inspired by a meeting with the famous colonist Benjamin Franklin, had been an exploration of electricity. His second project had been a study of light and color. This third undertaking would be a study of the mysterious and wondrous world of gases.

Priestley's fascination with gases had grown from two reports he read in 1771. First, Jan van Helmont, of Brussels, wrote that he put some soda and vinegar in a bottle to see what would happen. Bubbles appeared. He corked the bottle, and watched to see what the bubbles would do when trapped. Fewer and fewer bubbles formed. Then the bottle exploded in his face, and he was badly cut by flying glass.

"An invisible spirit was loose in the bottle," van Helmont wrote. "I named this spirit *gas*, as something which cannot be contained in a vessel or reduced to a visible body."

Priestley's imagination soared on reading those words. He felt compelled to seek out and study this wild, untamed gas.

The second report that drove Priestley to gases described an experiment by several German scientists who heated *mercurius calcinatus,* a mercury-based, orange-red powder used in skin ointments. The report described "new air" that seemed to rise up from the heated powder, and which made a nearby candle burn at more than twice its normal brightness.

What caused something to burn was, in the 1770s, still one of the world's greatest mysteries. The most popular scientific theory said that all materials able to burn contained a mysterious, invisible substance called "phlogiston," or "fire stuff." When something burned, its phlogiston escaped into the flame. How truly incredible, thought Priestley, that an invisible gas might force substances to give up their phlogiston more quickly!

Two great mysteries, wild gases and the wonders of burning, seemed to merge into one great experiment in Priestley's mind. Trap, tame, and study this new air, or gas, and he might uncover the secrets of burning!

Priestley could easily see the problem that had tripped up other researchers. They had not been able to successfully trap the gases they produced and keep them from mixing with regular air. Since these wild gases seemed to be just as invisible as air, how would he ever know if he were looking at a wild gas, or ordinary air, or even a mixture of gas and air?

Clearly, Priestley's gas experiments would require a new and cleverly designed apparatus. But it would also have to be simple. On a minister's salary, Priestley had precious little money to spend on his experiments.

In early 1773, it struck Joseph that the way to keep his gases from mixing with air was to trap them underwater in an inverted, water-filled glass jar where there was no air. All he'd need were his wife's large washtub, a wire mesh stand to place in the tub, and glass bottles he already possessed.

Now, how to create the gases he would study? In all Priestley's readings he had seen only two ways: mix something with a liquid so that the gas would rise as bubbles, or slowly heat a solid so that it gave off gaseous vapors. Priestley decided to begin his burning experiment as the Germans had—by burning solid *mercurius calcinatus* powder.

But how best to heat it?

Priestley sealed one end of a metal gun barrel with putty and linseed oil. He placed a small amount of his orange-red powder in this gun barrel and shoved it down deep into the coals of the kitchen fire. He wedged a glass tube and cork into the barrel's open end, with the tube snaking its way into his washtub and an inverted, water-filled glass jar.

The gun barrel began to glow red-hot. The powder heated too quickly. Priestley's putty seal evaporated. Precious little gas was trapped, and that was contaminated by putty fumes and smoke. His first try was a failure.

Priestley needed a way to control the heating of his metal sample. That meant being able to always watch his reaction. On a hot July day in 1774, with a merciless sun blazing through the windows and turning his house into an oven, Priestley realized that sunlight and more glass jars might just do the trick.

On Sunday, August 1, 1774, after a frustrating four-day delay because of constant rain, Joseph Priestley opened his windows to a gloriously clear, warm day. The sunlight he needed flooded in through his kitchen window. He placed a twelve-inch focusing lens just where it would catch the most direct sunlight.

He poured *mercurius calcinatus* powder into a small bottle and sealed it tightly with a glass tube and cork stopper. The glass tube snaked across the floor and up into the Priestley washtub, where two water-filled glass jars stood inverted on a wire mesh stand. The water level in the tub was well above the mouths of these bottles. Priestley's glass tube ended just under the open mouth of one of these bottles so that whatever wild gas he produced would bubble into, and be trapped by, that glass jar.

Joseph placed his bottle of orange-red powder just where the magnifying lens focused its burning beam of sunlight. Slowly the powder heated. Clear bubbles began to drift up from the end of the glass tube into jar #1. The water level in the jar began to go down.

Priestley stared, fascinated. Here it was. The magic burning gas, bubbling up into his bottle. Jar #1 was already half full of this wondrous gas. Priestley's eyes were glued to it. He could see straight through the gas. The gas was completely colorless and didn't distort light at all. The only evidence that anything was in the jar at all was the steady stream of bubbles flowing up from the glass tube to burst above the water's surface.

Suddenly Priestley realized jar #1 was almost full. He quickly shifted the tube beneath jar #2. A second jar began to fill with gas.

As jar #2 filled with gas, Priestley moved his focusing lens away from the window to stop the heating process. The stream of bubbles rising through his tub of water slowed and finally stopped. Joseph Priestley was now the first human to have successfully trapped this mysterious gas. But what was it?

First, he examined the small sample bottle. His red-orange powder had turned into a thick silver liquid—pure mercury. But this mercury sample was almost the same size as the original powder had been. It looked like the escaping gas hadn't reduced the amount of the sample at all. Priestley was awed.

Now he turned to this new gas itself. Keeping the first jar of new gas inverted, Priestley carefully raised it out of the water. He held a lit candle beneath its mouth. The dim glow around the candle's wick erupted into a brilliant ball of fire. Joseph gasped and almost dropped both candle and jar.

Yes! This strange gas did quickly suck phlogiston out of a burnable substance. But was the gas poisonous? Priestley placed a new jar, filled with ordinary air, upside-down on the wire stand next to his second jar of gas. The gas in both jars was now isolated from room air. He placed a mouse in each jar and waited. Neither mouse died. But the mouse in ordinary air began to struggle for breath in 20 minutes. The mouse in the jar of this strange gas breathed comfortably for over 40 minutes!

What sort of amazing gas could make wood burn and turn to ash more than twice as fast as air, but would also sustain life twice as long as air? There seemed only one name for this amazing gas: "pure air." There was one more test he had to try. Could a human breathe pure air?

Priestley made a new batch of pure air from his remaining *mercurius calcinatus*. He carefully raised the jar up out of his water-filled tub. He jammed his nose up into its wide mouth. His heart began to beat faster. What would happen when he breathed this gas into his own lungs? He closed his eyes, gathered his courage, and breathed in as deeply as he could.

Joseph felt nothing different or odd from this breath. He tried a second breath and felt happy and filled with energy. Priestley set the jar aside and waited. Nothing happened, except that his breath felt particularly light and easy for some time after. He fancied that the fashionably rich would soon be clamoring to get a whiff of pure air at parties.

The not-so-good priest, Joseph Priestley, in a makeshift kitchen lab was the first human to isolate and study a pure gas and a gaseous element. But it took another scientist, Antoine Lavoisier in Paris, to give Priestley's pure air the name by which we know it today, "oxygen." It also took the work of a dozen other scientists to fully explore the properties of this wondrous, life-giving gas. That, however, is another story.

Library Link: Why do people feel good when they breathe pure oxygen?

Priestley started with a solid metal and wound up with liquid mercury and oxygen gas. What kind of a metal compound must the original metal have been?

Topics to Explore: chemistry, scientific method, oxygen, Joseph Priestley.

References for Further Reading:

- *In the Children's Library:*

Irwin, Keith. *The Romance of Chemistry*. New York: Viking, 1986.

Marcys, Rebeca. *Joseph Priestley, Pioneer Chemist*. New York: Franklin Watts, 1961.

- *In the Adult Library:*

Bainbridge, Beryl. *The Road to Milton Keynes*. New York: G. Brazallin, 1984.

Consult your librarian for additional titles.

A Liter of Mystery

A story of Amedeo Avogadro's discovery of molecules in 1811

☑ **A Point to Ponder: Hold your hands tightly together, forming a small bowl. How many molecules of air do you think you are holding in your hands? Can you see any of them? How do you know they are there?**

The college professor sat on the worn, wooden table that served as both lectern and desk in his classroom, legs slowly swinging back and forth. "Well, what do you think of *that*, students?" An impish twinkle danced across his eyes. "These are two important papers in the study of chemistry, but I think I see a mystery for us to solve." The two scientific papers he had just read to the class were still curled in his hand.

Thirty-five-year-old professor Amedeo Avogadro pushed off of the table and landed squarely on both feet with a sharp "thump!"

"I said, 'What do you think?' "

This time it sounded more like a demand than a question. Avogadro slowly paced up one row and down the other, his steady footfalls echoing across the quiet room like crashing boulders. "Can you see the mystery about atoms that's hidden in these reports?"

The students sat absolutely still, staring down at their desktops, afraid to glance up for fear they'd catch the eye and attention of their teacher. They weren't at all sure what to think. Was this another of Professor Avogadro's pranks, or was there really a scientific mystery here?

Amedeo Avogadro taught a natural science class at Vercelli College in the Italian mountain town of Turin. March snow still clung to the peaks and steep slopes above Turin, but the city itself, in this year of 1811, had finally shrugged off winter's blanket. As the world slowly warmed, 25 students sat each day and listened to Professor Avogadro lecture, discuss, and quiz them on whatever aspects of science caught his fancy.

In the two papers Avogadro had just read, the English chemist Dalton and the French chemist Gay-Lussac each described an experiment in which they combined hydrogen and oxygen atoms to create water. Each reported that it took exactly two liters of gaseous hydrogen atoms combined with exactly one liter of oxygen atoms to produce exactly two liters of gaseous water vapor. Dalton claimed that this experiment proved that water is the combination of two atoms of hydrogen and one atom of oxygen. Gay-Lussac also claimed it proved that a liter of any gas had to contain exactly the same number of atoms as a liter of any other gas, no matter what gas it was.

The world rushed to embrace the work of these two giants of science. Their studies were heralded as a major breakthrough in chemical study. But from his first reading of these papers, Professor Avogadro was bothered by a nagging doubt. Something wasn't quite right. Some deep part of him said that the study of chemistry would take a wrong turn if he couldn't identify and solve this mystery.

"So what do you think? Do you agree with these scientists? Do you see the mystery? Extra credit for the one who finds it."

The students struggled to see some hint of a mystery in the reports. Most of them desperately needed the extra credit, but no one could guess the professor's mystery. Eighteen-year-old Lorenzo timidly asked, "But, Professor, how can Dalton know how many atoms of oxygen are in a liter, or even that they were all used to make water? Atoms are far too small to see or count."

Professor Avogadro tossed down the two papers and ran his hands through his thick, bushy hair. A full beard almost hid the smile that started small, grew into a wide grin, and finally became the full, roaring laugh for which Avogadro was known. "Who agrees with Lorenzo? Lorenzo says that Dalton may be a famous English chemist, but how can he possibly know that there are the same number of atoms in a liter of oxygen as in a liter of hydrogen? Tiny, invisible atoms don't wear name tags so they can be spotted and counted, you know!"

And Avogadro laughed and laughed. The students all joined in. It must be one of Professor Avogadro's jokes after all.

Feeling very confident, Lorenzo added, "Dalton and Gay-Lussac are just guessing that a liter of hydrogen gas has the same number of atoms as a liter of oxygen gas. Do they think nature has time to count out exactly how many atoms she puts in a liter jar of gas?"

"Is *that* what you all think?" asked Avogadro with a raised eyebrow.

Again the students laughed and nodded. But they were dismayed to see a fierce scowl spread across their professor's face. He held up the report by Gay-Lussac. "But Gay-Lussac *tested* for remaining uncombined oxygen atoms and hydrogen atoms after he formed water vapor. There were none left. All atoms were used."

Avogadro thoughtfully tapped the rolled-up report against his table. "Maybe nature is a more careful counter than you thought, Lorenzo. It would seem that there really are the same number of atoms in a liter of oxygen as in a liter of hydrogen. But who sees the mystery?"

The class shifted nervously in their chairs. What sort of a mystery could he see in combining hydrogen and oxygen to make water that would be worth extra credit?

Romano, sitting in a chair on Lorenzo's right, slowly raised his hand just barely above his shoulder, not at all sure he had really found the mystery. "Professor, Gay-Lussac combined *two* liters of hydrogen with only *one* liter of oxygen. Wouldn't that mean that each oxygen atom had to split in two to combine with a hydrogen atom?"

Avogadro's eyebrows arched expectantly, but then sank. "Not quite it, Romano. Each oxygen atom actually attaches itself to two hydrogen atoms when you make water. So, with twice as many hydrogen atoms as oxygen atoms, no oxygen atoms have to be split."

Romano's face dropped in disappointment, and he sank back into his seat.

"But," continued Avogadro. "Romano's getting warm. He's on the right track. Where's the mystery?"

Suddenly Lorenzo's face brightened. His hand shot bravely into the air. "I know! I know!"

Avogadro nodded. "Ahhh. Let's listen to Lorenzo."

Lorenzo stood, and then paused, making sure he had all of his thoughts in order, afraid he'd forget the great mystery that had flashed into his mind a moment before. Then he nodded to himself and began. "Both Dalton and Gay-Lussac started with exactly *two* liters of hydrogen and *one* liter of oxygen. That's a total of *three* liters of gas. But they both ended with only *two* liters of water vapor gas. If every liter of every gas has to have exactly the same number of atoms, then how can all the atoms from three liters of oxygen and hydrogen fit into just two liters of water vapor gas? Wouldn't there have to be lots of leftover atoms?"

Professor Avogadro bounded up onto his table and wildly clapped his hands. "Yes! That's it exactly! Lorenzo has found our mystery. Something is wrong here. Either there *are* the same number of atoms in every liter of gas, and three liters worth of atoms can't possibly fit into two liters, or some liters of gas can have more atoms than others. Both statements can't possibly be true!"

The Turin cathedral bell chimed 3:00.

Avogadro sighed. "That's all for today, class. Tomorrow we must solve Lorenzo's mystery."

The students gathered their books and left, with Lorenzo marching at their lead as proudly as a national hero.

The next day, Avogadro's students filed into class to find their professor at the front of the classroom, smiling broadly as he sat on his table and swung his legs.

"Students, yesterday Lorenzo found a problem with Dalton's and Gay-Lussac's theory. The number of atoms didn't add up. Did anybody find a solution?"

Each student tried to sink inconspicuously lower in his seat, fearing Avogadro would call on him.

The professor raised his eyebrows. "No? Then I guess we're stuck with mine. First, a question. If one atom floating free is called an 'atom,' what do you call two atoms of hydrogen and one atom of oxygen hooked solidly together?"

The class looked confused. Was this another of Avogadro's jokes? Romano cautiously raised his hand. "Isn't that a trick question. It's called 'water.' "

Avogadro laughed. "True enough, Romano. But what do you call any group of attached atoms?"

Some students thumbed madly through notebooks. Some scratched their heads in thought. None knew.

"Of course you don't know," laughed Avogadro. "That's because until I invented one last night, there has never been a word for a group of attached atoms.

The word I invented is *molecule*. It's Greek and means 'to move about freely in a gas.' And that's the answer to Lorenzo's mystery!"

Avogadro sank back onto his table with a satisfied smile. Lorenzo paused, pen frozen in mid-air. "Professor Avogadro? Could you say the part about the answer to my mystery again?"

"Let's suppose that atoms of free oxygen do not float around all by themselves, but, rather, are attached to other oxygen atoms as molecules of oxygen. Suppose the same is true for hydrogen. If that is so, then Gay-Lussac and Dalton simply used the wrong word. Liters of gas don't have the same number of atoms. They have the same number of molecules. Instead of 'atom,' in Dalton's theorem, substitute the word 'molecule.' Two *molecules* of hydrogen plus one *molecule* of oxygen make two *molecules* of water; and a liter of any gas holds the same number of *molecules*."

Young Romano slowly shook his head. "But Professor Avogadro, if a molecule of water has two hydrogen atoms and one oxygen atom, what's in a molecule of hydrogen or oxygen?"

"Ahh!" cried Avogadro with a broad smile. "Good question, Romano. I asked myself the very same one."

Romano beamed and turned to enjoy the envious glances of his fellow students.

Avogadro continued. "If this new theorem is going to work, I asked myself, how many atoms must be in a molecule of either oxygen or hydrogen gas? I could find but one simple answer that works. It seems to me that a molecule of hydrogen must contain exactly two atoms of hydrogen, and a molecule of oxygen must contain exactly two atoms of oxygen. Now think, students! Would that work?"

The students thought—but mostly about how they were afraid to volunteer to guess at their professor's question.

Avogadro slammed his open hand down onto the table. "Ah, students! The answer is right in front of you! Two *molecules* of hydrogen (that would be four atoms) plus one *molecule* of oxygen (two atoms) produce two *molecules* of water (two atoms of hydrogen and one atom of oxygen each). It works! It balances. And we always have the same number of *molecules* in every liter of gas, even though we don't always have the same number of atoms! The mystery is solved."

The students wrote notes furiously. Avogadro smiled in a self-satisfied way and concluded, "Now we can say that equal volumes of a gas will always have the same number of molecules at the same temperature and pressure. Dalton and Gay-Lussac were almost right. They just needed a new word: molecule."

And so it was that, without ever touching a test tube or conducting a chemical experiment of any kind, without even a background in chemistry, Amedeo Avogadro solved a classroom mystery and discovered the existence of molecules.

But whether Lorenzo or Romano got the better grade on their final exam is another story.

Library Link: What's the difference between an atom and a molecule?

Topics to Explore: chemistry, scientific method, Amedeo Avogadro, molecules, gas laws.

References for Further Reading:

- *In the Children's Library:*

Irwin, Keith. *The Romance of Chemistry.* New York: Viking, 1959.

- *In the Adult Library:*

Nash, L. K. "The Atomic Molecular Theory," Case 4 in *Harvard Case Histories in Experimental Science*, edited by J. B. Conant, vol. 1. Cambridge, Mass.: Harvard University Press, 1957.

Consult your librarian for additional titles.

The Smell of Success

A story of Charles Goodyear's invention of vulcanized rubber in 1837-1839

☑ **A Point to Ponder: How many things have you used in the past week that were made at least partly of rubber?**

"*Mother*! He's doing it again!" whined seven-year-old Charles Jr. from the hallway of their small, rented house.

"Mommy! I hate it when Daddy makes the house stink!" cried four-year-old Carol, running across the bare living room floor to throw herself onto her mother's lap.

"I'm hungry!" complained five-year-old William, not wanting to be left out.

Susan Goodyear sighed deeply, shook her head, and put down her knitting. Turning her head toward the kitchen, she called to her 37-year-old husband, "Charles? I thought we had an agreement. No more experiments until you found a job and had enough money to feed and clothe this family."

Charles Goodyear poked his head around the corner of the kitchen doorway. "Trust me, Susan. This time it will work. I know it will!"

Susan Goodyear set her daughter back down on the wooden floor and rose from her chair, one of only two in this otherwise bare room. "Charles, you were supposed to buy groceries. Did you buy more rubber gum instead?"

Charles broke into his quick, winning smile, thoughtfully scratched at the muttonchop sideburns that were so fashionable in this year of 1837, and tugged at the hem of his threadbare and patched coat. "Oh, I got some groceries, Susan. I bought the gum with the money that was left over."

"How could there be any left over, Charles?" she snapped. "There hasn't been any leftover money in this house for five years!"

Susan Goodyear was a patient and forgiving woman. But five years of smelly rubber experiments and no income to support the family had pushed her to the limits of even her angelic endurance.

"Don't worry. I figured it out this time," announced Charles, fanning the summer heat away from his face. "A nice man at a leather shop showed me how they tan hides into leather by boiling them in lime. So I thought, if it works for leather, why not for rubber? Success at last! Oh I can just smell sweet success, can't you, Susan?"

"We sure can smell it!" whined all three of the children.

Susan raised her eyebrows and tightened her lips. Hands on hips she said, "You've said that about each of your last 100 experiments!"

"But, Sweetheart, every one leads me closer. Last time I tried adding magnesium to create strength, because it works with iron and steel. But now I realize magnesium can't do its job until the rubber is cured, or tanned. That's what's new and exciting about this experiment."

Charles Jr. slouched sullenly in the hallway. "Mom, why do we have to live in a house that always stinks? Burnt rubber is the worst smell in the whole world. The other kids laugh at me."

"Mommy," whined little Carol. "Why don't we have any furniture? All the other kids have furniture in their houses."

Again feeling left out, William added, "I'm hungry! There's never any food around here."

"There. You see?" demanded Charles's wife with tears rising into her soft, brown eyes. "Once again, you have put your experiments ahead of your family!"

"Oh, no, Sweetheart. Inventing reliable rubber clothes is how I'm going to take care of my family. This batch is bound to work. Boiling with lime is the key. You'll see. Rubber is just harder to work with than I had anticipated."

Rubber was well-known by the nineteenth century. Columbus had found children playing with rubber balls on his second voyage to the New World. Spanish explorers smeared the milky-white sap of rubber trees on their clothes for waterproofing. The Englishman Joseph Priestley discovered in 1770 that the gum of the tree rubbed out his writing mistakes. He was the one who named the stuff "rubber."

Some thought rubber could have and should have many more important uses. Charles Goodyear was one of these. But his dream of creating practical rubber pants, coats, hats, and boots to protect his family had turned into a family nightmare.

In 1832, Charles lost his Philadelphia hardware store because he spent far more time experimenting with rubber than he did minding the store. By 1835, the Goodyear family was broke and survived by selling Susan Goodyear's fine handmade linens and the children's books. By 1836, Charles began to sell their furniture and any decent clothes they had left. Now, in 1837, after five years of the reeking stench of boiling rubber wafting out from the kitchen, there was very little left of the Goodyears' possessions.

The problem was that rubber didn't adapt well to changes in temperature. Summer heat turned it into a sticky goo. Winter's subfreezing cold turned rubber brittle so that it cracked, chipped, and broke. To make rubber useful, Goodyear had to find a way to make it pliable, but sturdy, at all common temperatures.

Charles excitedly ducked back into the kitchen to finish this latest batch: a mixture of rubber, turpentine, magnesium, and his newest ingredient, lime. Charles boiled the thick, black goo for 30 minutes, as the children complained. Then he let it cool, and rolled it out into a thin sheet with his wife's rolling pin.

Now to test its tolerance to temperature extremes. Would tanning finally be the answer to all his dreams and prayers? Charles laid the sheet of rubber on the back porch where the sizzling summer sun could bake it. Then he waited. One hour, two hours, three hours.

"Hey Dad," called Charles Jr., excitement beginning to rise in his young voice. "This rubber hasn't melted like all the others!"

Tanned rubber could withstand heat.

Now the cold test. The whole family gathered around as Charles laid the rubber on a steaming block of dry ice. Again he waited. One hour, two hours.

Little Carolyn couldn't wait any longer. She snatched up the rubber sheet and crumpled it between her hands. Disappointment shown in her eyes. "Oh, Daddy, it doesn't crackle and pop like the other ones."

Both Charles's and Susan's eyes lit up with hope and excitement. The rubber stayed pliable and, well, rubbery, even when cold. It worked! It really worked!

Hope spread out like a cool, refreshing breeze through the stuffy house. The awful smell was forgotten. Tanning rubber was the answer! Even skeptical Charles Jr. broke into an eager smile. Reliable, wearable rubber clothes meant success, family wealth, even new clothes and extra food.

With every penny the family could beg, borrow, or scrape from friends, family, and their meager possessions, Charles Goodyear purchased rubber, turpentine, magnesium, and lime, as well as the thread he would need to convert the tanned rubber into clothes.

Three weeks later, in early September of 1837, the doors of "Goodyear's Rubber Clothes Shop" were flung open to a curious, but very interested crowd of buyers, newspaper reporters, and onlookers. Sales were brisk. The cash drawer filled. There was a strong, steady demand for wearable rubber.

That is, for three days there was a demand. Then the first of the coats was returned with a large, goopy hole drooping down one side. "A few tiny drops of vinegar were splashed on it," announced the irate woman in icy tones. "I will not pay for a coat that disintegrates when a drop of salad dressing touches it!"

Charles was shocked. "Really? A mild acid did that to my rubber? Oh, no!"

By week's end, almost every coat, shoe, and pair of pants had been angrily returned. Any contact with even a mild acid dissolved the bonds holding the rubber compound together. The family was once again destitute and penniless.

"But . . . but who could have dreamed mild acid would destroy the structure of my rubber?" protested Charles when he faced the icy glares of his family. "That batch was *so* close. I know I'm just an inch away from success."

By 1839, Charles had to hide his occasional experiments, even from his wife, for fear that she would explode in anger, and because he couldn't stand to have her watch yet another failure. But no matter what, he could not shake his dream, nor his conviction that ultimate success was only one experiment away.

One morning in early February 1839, while his wife was out shopping and the children were off playing with friends, Charles snuck into the kitchen to try his latest brainstorm. Sulfur. A chemist friend said that sulfur might buffer, or protect, rubber from acids.

Charles had just mixed rubber, turpentine, magnesium, lime, and his newest ingredient, sulfur, into a baseball-sized blob. He was just heating a pot of water to boil the stuff when, out the kitchen window, he saw his wife carrying two heavy shopping sacks up the front walk.

Oh, what awful timing! Charles couldn't let Susan see what he was doing. First, she would be furious. Second, he'd never get to finish and find out if his new idea worked. In desperation, he pitched a blob of the rubber mixture into the firebox of his hot wood stove to hide it. The rubber glob sizzled as he slammed the stove door shut and turned to greet his wife.

Susan's eyebrows arched suspiciously as she sniffed the air. "It smells like rubber in here."

Charles lied sheepishly, "Oh, it must be from that old batch I was examining earlier."

Fifteen minutes later, Susan stepped outside to fetch the children. Charles quickly snatched his charred mess from the family stove. Remarkably, it hadn't hardened. It was still soft and pliable.

"What's this?" muttered Charles with an edge of excitement in his voice.

He grabbed the rubbery mass with both hands and pulled hard. It stretched way out to more than his arm's length. Then it snapped back to its original shape as soon as he let go. "I think I might have something here!" shouted Charles, his heart beginning to pound.

Charles Jr. was the first of the children to get back to the house. "Dad! Are you playing with rubber again?"

Grinning from ear to ear, Charles giggled, "Just pull it, Son."

Charles Jr. stretched the rubber as hard as he could and let go. Snap! The rubber flew back into its original shape. "Wow, Dad! You've never made a batch that could do that!"

"And just what is this?" demanded Susan, standing arms crossed and angry in the door. "Did you make a new batch of rubber?"

"I think I just made my *last* batch," answered Charles with wonder and joy in his voice. "This one works!"

By the end of the day, Charles had tested this burned rubber's tolerance to both heat and cold. Sturdy and firm in heat, flexible and strong in bitter cold, it passed both tests easily. He checked its resistance to both acids and bases, from vinegar to strong household cleaners. Burned rubber survived without a mark! He gave burned rubber every test he could think of. It worked. It always worked!

Sulfur plus high processing heat. Those were the final magic ingredients Charles had searched so hard to find! He had to add sulfur and fire the mixture instead of boiling it in order to create durable rubber. Charles Goodyear named the process *vulcanization* after the Roman god of fire, Vulcan.

Vulcanized rubber has become one of the most important and versatile products of our modern world. One of the largest rubber tire-producing companies is named after rubber's inventor. However, Charles and his family saw neither the wealth nor fame his invention would create. After suffering through years of smelly kitchens and hardships to reach his goal, Goodyear and his wife died poor and unknown, just as they had lived. But that is another story.

Library Link: What are the biggest uses for rubber today?

Topics to Explore: chemistry, physics, scientific method, Charles Goodyear, rubber.

References for Further Reading:

- *In the Children's Library:*

Quackenbush, Robert. *Oh, What an Awful Mess!* Englewood Cliffs, N.J.: Prentice-Hall, 1980.

- *In the Adult Library:*

Regli, Adolph. *Rubber's Goodyear.* New York: Charles Scribner's Sons, 1941.

Consult your librarian for additional titles.

A Research Headache

A story of Charles Gerhardt's discovery of aspirin in 1851

☑ **A Point to Ponder: How do you stop discomfort and pain? How many different kinds of painkillers have you used?**

The tidy Paris office of Charles Gerhardt had the pungent smells of a chemist's office. Each corner of the office seemed dominated by its own unique odor depending on which compounds and chemicals were stored on the shelves lining the walls. Only the corner where a large box of hydrogen sulfide was stored had a recognizable smell, that of rotten eggs.

On this mild June day in 1851, Charles Gerhardt sat quietly at his desk reading a technical paper from a college in Lyons. An acquaintance, Dr. Maurice Duphan, knocked and entered. His brow was furrowed as if he were lost deep in thought as he skirted around Gerhardt's lab table and pulled out the small chair in front of Charles's desk.

After a moment of silence Duphan dove straight to the point of his visit. "I'm tired of ordering patients to chew willow tree bark for aches, pains, headaches, and toothaches. 'Chew on tree bark,' sounds so, so medieval and unprofessional. This is the middle of the nineteenth century! There's got to be something better and more modern for pain."

Gerhardt shrugged. "Prescribe willow leaf tea."

Duphan shook his head. "Too slow."

"Then how about straight salicylic acid?"

Maurice rolled his eyes and slapped the desk. "Awful stuff! Creates brutal mouth and stomach irritation that's worse than the original pain."

Now Gerhardt cupped his chin in his hand and thought. Finally he shrugged. "Sorry, Maurice. But that's all there is for pain."

Maurice Duphan rose and leaned heavily on the desk. "And that's why I'm here, Charles. You're the chemist. Do something!"

Duphan left. But his final words kept buzzing around Gerhardt's here. "You're the chemist. Do something!" Do something . . . Create a modern chemical cure for the world's pain! Could he, an ordinary French chemist, do that? The mere thought was so overwhelming Charles was unable to return to his technical paper for the rest of the day.

Gerhardt's mind swam with a hundred questions. Where to start? What kind of painkiller should he look for? Which way should he turn? Where could he find an unknown miracle? There were a hundred questions, but no answers.

Two days later, Charles was jolted awake in the middle of the night by a beautifully simple idea: Start with what already works, and make it better.

Though it was 2:00 in the morning, Charles hurriedly dressed and rushed to his office. What worked was willow bark. Chemists already knew that the substance in willow that actually blocked pain was an acid, salicylic acid. However, pure salicylic acid, while it did kill pain, also created terrible mouth and stomach sores.

Charles Gerhardt's idea was to take this known painkiller and look for a way to block the side effects rather than to start all over hunting for a new painkiller.

"But how in the world am I going to do that?" he asked himself as he paced his office. Then he smiled and shrugged in answer. "I don't know. But it sure sounds easier than beginning completely from scratch. Besides, there's bound to be an article or study I can find to guide me."

Filled with anticipation and bustling with energy, Charles sifted through his extensive collection of reference manuals and technical papers all that day searching for a clue on how to begin his experiments to prevent salicylic acid's side effects.

He found nothing to steer him toward his goal. But then, neither did he find anything that told him he couldn't do what he sought to do. That night at dinner, Charles was still filled with bubbling enthusiasm. He announced to his wife, Cecile, "I am going to cure the pain of the world! But I'm going to have to do it all on my own. The literature hasn't helped me at all."

Cecile looked skeptically over the top of her glasses. "And exactly how is a struggling chemist who can't even get a decent teaching post at the university going to accomplish that?"

In grand and reverent tones, Charles rose to his feet and answered, "Salicylic acid!"

His wife's face wrinkled up as if she had just sucked on a lemon. "Sally *what?*"

"No, no. Sal-i-cyl-ic acid."

Cecile shook her head with both hands pressed to her cheeks. "Ach. A name like that could give people headaches instead of curing them."

Charles shrugged. "It's what's in willow bark and willow leaf tea."

"Why didn't you say so?" demanded his wife. "Everyone knows about willow to cure pain."

"But I'm going to make it better," announced Charles.

"You're going to make a better willow tree?"

"No! I'm going to make the chemical, salicylic acid, stronger and safer to use."

All through the rest of 1851, Charles struggled to find a way to prevent, delay, or buffer the brutal side effects of salicylic acid. He added and tested over 100 different compounds to the acid. None worked.

In 1852, Charles continued his struggle. He travelled all over France seeking fresh opinions and new ideas. He pored through every medical and scientific library in the country. He tested over 200 additives. Nothing seemed to success-fully block the acid's side effects without also blocking the pain-relieving benefits of salicylic acid.

Cecile said, "Give up this silly quest, Charles. Look at all the time you've wasted on it. If you want to cure *my* headache, spend your time searching for a job with a decent salary!"

Charles answered, "I can't stop now. I must be getting very close to finding something that does work, because it seems I've already tried everything that *doesn't* work."

In early 1853, Charles rushed home early one afternoon. "Cecile, do you have a headache today? If you do, I can cure it!"

Cecile's eyes grew wide with wonder and excitement. "You did it? It works?"

Charles Gerhardt was too excited to play coy or act smug with his longtime skeptical wife. "Yes! I found a way. I heard of a young English researcher who was experimenting with carbon chain molecules, creating them, and adding them to existing compounds. He called the process acetylation. I tried the process with salicylic acid and created acetylsalicylic acid. It works! Pain relief with no side effects."

Cecile's face wrinkled up. "Acidy-salt *what*?"

"No, no. A-cet-yl-sal-i-cyl-ic acid."

"Ach! That's worse than your first name. That name's sure to give everyone a headache!"

Charles reached into his pocket and pulled out a small vial filled with a white power. "Here. Take some of this."

Within minutes, Cecile smiled. "Charles, it worked. I feel much better. This is wonderful!"

Sadly, Charles Gerhardt shook his head. "No, it's not wonderful at all. It works, but it's far too difficult a chemical to produce. The process is far too delicate and slow. I have just this tiny amount from five days' work in the lab. I'm going to have to look for something else that both works, and is practical to manufacture, if I'm going to cure the whole world's pain."

By 1864, Charles Gerhardt sadly abandoned his search, believing that the practical miracle pain killer he sought would never be discovered.

Exactly 30 years later, in 1894, German chemist Felix Hoffman's father lay in bed dying and in excruciating pain. Felix sought a painkiller to relieve his father's suffering. He stumbled upon a short paper by Charles Gerhardt describing his experiments with acetylsalicylic acid, and tried to duplicate Gerhardt's earlier work.

But by 1894, many new processing techniques had been developed. The procedure that was nearly impossible for Charles Gerhardt was relatively simple for Felix Hoffman. He easily created a large batch of acetylsalicylic acid and successfully relieved his father's pain.

It was the hard, steady work of French chemist Charles Gerhardt that gave humanity a powerful painkiller. But it was Felix Hoffman who named the stuff "aspirin," and found a practical way to produce it. But that is another story.

Library Link: How does aspirin, or acetylsalicylic acid, stop pain?

Topics to Explore: biology, medical research, chemistry, scientific method, Charles Gerhardt, aspirin.

References for Further Reading:

- *In the Children's Library:*

Jones, Charlotte. *Mistakes That Worked*. New York: Doubleday, 1988.

- *In the Adult Library:*

Partington, J. R. *History of Chemistry*, London, England: Howe Publishers, 1964.

Consult your librarian for additional titles.

Rod-Wax to Riches

A story of Robert Chesebrough's discovery of petroleum jelly in 1859

☑ **A Point to Ponder: We know that oil and gasoline are "petroleum products." Are they the only petroleum products we use?**

"Excuse me, sir. Is this the train to Pennsylvania?" the bewildered young man asked as politely as he could.

"Read da sign!" snarled a grimy, uniformed train worker, jerking with his thumb back toward the head of the track. Steam, noise, branching train tracks, and rushing bodies stretched out as far as 22-year-old Robert Chesebrough could see. For someone who had never ventured more than 30 blocks from his Brooklyn home, New York's Grand Central Station was overwhelming.

Robert turned round and round, not knowing which way to go. "Excuse me, ma'am. Do you know where the train to Pennsylvania is?" he asked, tipping his soft cap.

"You'll have to read the board, young man. I do not memorize train tables!" And the woman in a bright green bonnet brushed past poor Robert with a snooty "Humph!" and her nose raised in the air.

Robert wove his way against the swirling flood of people back down to the head of the many converging tracks. Above him there was a great notice board he had missed before. And there it was! Buried in the middle of a long list of stops for the train on track 18: Titusville, Pennsylvania.

As his train steamed out of the underground station, Robert Chesebrough settled into his seat with a long, deep sigh. Watching the New Jersey countryside slip by an hour later, the voice of Robert's uncle echoed in his mind. "Kerosene is the future, Bobby. You mark my words!" Robert grunted angrily at the memory.

It was four years ago, in 1855, when Robert had taken his uncle's advice and staked his future on a kerosene shop. But now it was September 1859, and commercial oil wells had been drilled successfully in Titusville, Pennsylvania. Oil was cheaper than kerosene and burned cleaner. As a chemist, Robert knew the future was in oil. He knew *his* future was in oil. Every penny of Robert's savings had gone into this train ticket to Titusville where Robert Chesebrough hoped to find his corner of the booming petroleum industry.

The oil fields of Titusville made Grand Central Station seem quiet and calm. Hastily built wooden oil derricks rose up thicker than trees, each over 50 feet tall. Oil pipe and drilling sections lay in great jumbled stacks like pick-up sticks. The noise of drilling, hammering, steam engines, and pumps was deafening. Men and machinery rushed back and forth yelling angrily for the amazed Robert to "Get out of my way!" "Get out of my way!"

For several days, a stunned Robert Chesebrough wandered aimlessly through this jungle of derricks, rigs, drilling towers, snaking pipes, and pumps. Where was *his* future in this bustling excitement?

By his fourth day in Titusville, Robert found his chemist's curiosity returning over and over to a strange substance the oil workers called "rod-wax."

Rod-wax was a colorless oil residue that caked around the drilling rods as they bored down toward the rich sea of oil below. Robert was fascinated that one minute oil men cursed this pasty gunk when it clogged their pumps and other machinery, yet the next minute they praised the wax-like stuff when they spread it on to soothe a cut or burn.

What was this strange stuff? Where did it come from? The chemist's mind was intrigued by this clear gel that stopped machinery, but healed humans.

Gingerly, Robert approached a busy drilling platform and asked, "Could I have some of that rod-wax that's building up on the drilling rod?"

A burly foreman with oak-beam arms glanced over his shoulder. "What? You burn yourself?"

"No, I just want to study it," answered Robert with an apologetic shrug.

The men all laughed. So Robert added, "I'm a chemist."

Now the workmen laughed harder, shaking their heads. Who but some crazy scientist would want worthless rod-wax? The foreman scraped off a great handful of the waxy goo and smeared it into Robert's outstretched hand.

Robert slid the slippery stuff between his fingers and sniffed hard, searching for a telltale odor. There was none. Robert asked, "Does this stuff really help burns and cuts?"

Exasperated by another interruption, the foreman glared at Robert and rolled up his sleeve. "See this area here?" He pointed at a large, slightly discolored patch of skin on his forearm. "Burned it so bad, the skin turned flaky white two days ago. Smeared rod-wax on it, and it's already good as new."

What was this stuff that crept up out of oil wells? Would it work for regular folks as well as it did for these hearty oil riggers?

Robert found the oilmen gladly gave him all he wanted of this jelly-like rod-wax, since it was mostly an annoyance to them. He filled ten large jars with the stuff, loaded them in cardboard boxes, and headed for the Titusville train station and his home chemistry lab.

Robert's first week of study was discouraging. Rod-wax proved to be a complex blend of oil-based compounds, grease, air, and heat. How could he find its active ingredient when he had not a clue as to what to look for? He finally decided the best thing to do was to eliminate everything he did know couldn't heal a burn or cut.

For six weeks, he carefully tested his rod-wax for every known compound and element. He mixed it with chemicals that turned it green, and with ones that made it glow yellow. He added acids that made it fizz and evaporate. He mixed it with every chemical agent he could find, hoping some test, or combination of tests, would tell him what rod-wax was. During endless twelve-hour days of work that made Robert feel like he was groping blindfolded through a maze, he conducted over 300 separate tests.

In late October, with the glories of fall all around him, Robert Chesebrough finally identified, extracted, and purified the one active ingredient in rod-wax: *white petrolatum*. Robert's white petrolatum was a clear, smooth, sticky cream.

Now that he had isolated it, he had to test his petroleum product to see if it really could heal burns. Rather than wait for someone he knew to be hurt, Robert reluctantly, and with teeth clenched and one eye closed, gave himself a series of cuts, scratches, and burns on both hands and arms. He was careful to always create these injuries in pairs. One of each pair he covered with his white petrolatum. The other he left untreated for comparison.

The cream felt cool and soothing, and seemed to lessen his pain and discomfort as soon as it touched a wound. Three days later Robert declared his test a triumphant success. Every one of the wounds treated with his cream healed faster and with less discomfort, less scarring, and no infection.

His wonder cream needed only a name to be ready for an eager nation. After some thought, Robert chose the name that it still bears today, "Vaseline Petroleum Jelly." Still, it took six more years of work before the product of Robert's new Vaseline Petroleum Jelly Company found its niche as a popular household salve. But that's another story.

Library Link: Besides Vaseline®, motor oil, and gasoline, what other modern products are petroleum based?

Topics to Explore: chemistry, scientific method, petroleum products, first aid, Robert Chesebrough.

References for Further Reading:

- *In the Children's Library:*

Olsen, Frank. *Inventors Who Left Their Brands on America.* New York: Bantam Books, 1991.

- *In the Adult Library:*

No good printed references have been found in the adult section.

Consult your librarian for additional titles.

A Note of Inspiration

A story of Dmitri Mendelyeev's creation of the periodic chart of elements in 1869

☑ **A Point to Ponder: What is a chemical element? How many are there?**

A trim, white-haired woman sat wringing her hands in a small sitting room watching the Tver River flow past her son's comfortable villa on the outskirts of St. Petersburg, Russia. Unaware of her own actions, she repeatedly twisted and wrung a small handkerchief between her hands as she waited for her son, Dmitri, to return from teaching his science class at the University of St. Petersburg.

It was late summer, 1869. In America, the great Civil War was over. In Europe, the great scientific minds had excitedly turned to chemistry and the mushrooming list of natural elements that had been discovered.

Over the sounds of the river and its boats, the woman heard a small carriage stop in front of the villa. She heard footsteps, and then the opening of the front door. And then she heard the long strides of her son, racing to greet her.

"Mama! Such a surprise! Let me look at you. What brings you to St. Petersburg?"

"To see my favorite son, of course," she answered, slowly rising on her 71-year-old legs, and reaching up as high as she could to hug her towering, 35-year-old son, Dmitri Mendelyeev.

Still holding his mother's frail and wrinkled hands, Dmitri stepped back to see her better. "Sit, Mama. Sit, and tell me why you're *really* here. You look worried."

She sank back into her chair and sighed as she dabbed the corner of one eye with her handkerchief. "I am worried, Dmitri, very worried."

"But why, Mama?"

Her face turned hard and serious. "Because of what all Europe is saying about you and your Table of the Chemical Elements."

Dmitri flopped down into a chair, his long arms and legs stretching out from his body like spider's legs. With a harsh grunt and a wave of his hand, he dismissed his mother's concerns. "They are all just afraid of the truth."

"But Dmitri, they laugh and call you 'that crazy Russian.' "

In truth, Dmitri Mendelyeev did look slightly crazed. With long, gangly limbs, round eyes like two great pools of white under bushy black brows, and a wild, untamed thicket of hair that he only cut once a year, Dmitri drew stares even in his home city of St. Petersburg.

Now he reached out and patted his mother's hand. "When they find the three missing elements I have predicted, the laughter will stop. They will all believe and cheer."

As scientists discovered more and more individual elements through the middle 1800s, there was a great rush to bring some order and logic to this growing jumble of chemical elements. Dmitri had found a way to organize and group the 60 known elements into a simple, logical table. Moreover, several gaps in Dmitri's table led him to predict that three new elements must exist, and would someday be found to fill those gaps. He even described what these "missing" elements would look like and act like. All Europe laughed, and said his predictions were the ramblings of a wild fortune-teller.

Mrs. Mendelyeev tried to smile bravely. "I hope you're right, Dmitri. But in the meantime, couldn't you do something with your hair? Just for your mother?"

There was a loud knock on Mendelyeev's front door. One of Dmitri's servants brought in the stylishly dressed, Mikhail Lomonosov, a science professor at the university, and grandson of Russia's first great scientist.

"Dmitri! I just read your paper. Fantastic idea for organizing the elements. But you forgot to include any evidence supporting the design of your Table of Elements."

"What evidence do I need?" asked a surprised Dmitri.

"Well, did you do experiments to prove the relationships in your table?" asked Mikhail.

Dmitri shrugged. "No."

"Then, did you conduct experiments with the individual elements?"

Again Dmitri shook his head. "No."

Mikhail pounded a fist into his palm. "Well what *did* you do? You need some supporting evidence."

"Listen to your friend," cooed Dmitri's mother. ". . . And see how nice his hair looks?"

Dmitri glared at his mother, and then said to Mikhail. "My idea came from the piano. I'll show you."

Mikhail frowned. "A piano doesn't sound very scientific."

Dmitri scooted his friend over to his upright piano and made him sit. "Play middle C. Can you find it?"

"Of course I can find it," replied an irritated Mikhail. One clear note rang out across the room.

"Now move up eight keys," continued Dmitri. "What do you find?"

"Another C, of course," answered Mikhail. "But what does this have to do with chemical elements?"

"So every eight keys a C repeats. After a set *period* each note repeats. I realized nature works in periodic ways, too. In notes, in seasons, in waves at the beach, even in trees: the same characteristics repeat over and over after a set period of time or distance. So I asked myself, 'Why not look at the elements for characteristics that repeat?' "

Dmitri spread out a long list of all the known elements on top of his piano, from the lightest, hydrogen, to the heaviest, uranium. His voice rose with excitement as he continued.

"I made this list of elements from lightest to heaviest and looked for characteristics that repeated after regular periods in that list. And I found so many, Mikhail! Whether the element is a gas, liquid, or solid; whether the metal is soft or hard; whether it melts at a high temperature or low. All of these characteristics repeated regularly on the list.

"Most important, I found that the valence of the elements repeated after a regular period. That was the key for organizing my table!"

Fifteen years before, Edward Franking of England realized that, while each atom of some elements could combine with only one other atom, each atom of other elements could combine with as many as four other atoms. He called this combining power the element's "valence." Some elements, like hydrogen, had a valence of one. Some elements, like oxygen, had a valence of two, as each atom of oxygen could combine with two other atoms. No element had a valence of more than four.

Dmitri now spread a large copy of his Periodic Table of the Elements on top of his list, smiling confidently. The table had seven columns and a number of rows. "Now do you see? In each column the elements all have the same valence. In each row the elements form a family with similar characteristics—all characteristics that repeated. The elements start at the upper left with the lightest, and proceed across and down to the heaviest.

"You see how simple it is? In each square there is a space for an element whose weight, valence, and characteristics are known by its column and row, or family, on the table. These three holes here," Dmitri stabbed dramatically with his finger at three blank spaces on the chart. "These are the three missing elements I know will be discovered someday."

Mikhail shook his head. "It's bewildering, Dmitri. It seems to make sense when you say it. But will anyone ever believe you?"

Gazing at the elaborate table, Dmitri's mother beamed. She leaned close to Mikhail. "My son's a brilliant boy! They'll have to believe. But I do wish he'd do something with his hair."

Three years later, the first of Mendelyeev's "missing" elements, gallium, was discovered in Germany. The scientific community thought it an interesting coincidence. Within eight years, the other two, scandium and germanium, had also been found. All three looked and behaved just as Dmitri Mendelyeev had predicted. Scientists around the world were amazed. Now they called Mendelyeev a great genius who had unlocked the mysteries of the world of elements. They believed and they cheered.

But how, where, and by whom those three important elements were found is, of course, another story.

Library Link: Are chemical elements still being discovered today, or have they all already been found?

Is there anything on earth not made from a combination of the known chemical elements?

Topics to Explore: chemistry, scientific method, periodic table, Dmitri Mendelyeev.

References for Further Reading:

- *In the Children's Library:*

Irwin, Keith. *The Romance of Chemistry*. New York: Viking, 1959.

- *In the Adult Library:*

Asimov, Isaac. *The Search for the Elements*. New York: Basic Books, 1962.

Consult your librarian for additional titles.

A Glowing Discovery

A story of Marie Curie's discovery of radium in 1897-1901

☑ **A Point to Ponder: Uranium is radioactive. What does radioactive mean?**

A gray Paris afternoon faded into damp February twilight. Gas lamps glowed to life through countless city windows. A growing line of eager university professors and students once again snaked across the frozen campus grass. Was it dark enough yet? Could the daily tour begin?

At the head of this long, expectant line stood a dumpy, dilapidated shack. For three years, it had been the laboratory of graduate student Marie Curie and her professor husband, Pierre. Everyone at the university knew by now. Marie had found some new metal buried in a ton of dirt borrowed from Czechoslovakia. And this new metal glowed! Not like a fluorescent glow. No, this new metal glowed all on its own, even at night, a soft, fairy-like glow.

Marie hung test tubes of the stuff from the ceiling of her shack to brighten it up. As darkness fell each evening, an anxious procession of visitors marched through, faces and hands bathed in a warm pastel glow from the radium and polonium compounds. Yellow from one test tube, a faint pink from the next, and luminescent green from a third. Gasps of wonder and delight rose from each person passing slowly through the shed in awe as Marie and Pierre stood proudly by the door.

In 1901, no one knew that radioactivity was deadly, or even the slightest bit dangerous. They only knew that it was new, it was exciting, and it was beautiful.

"How incredible!" gasped a biology professor and his wife, as they peered closely into the test tubes. This was like nothing the world had ever seen before.

Marie Curie, as always, was stunned by the beauty of her radium compounds. They glowed naturally like twinkling fairy lights. Soft luminescent sheens of every hue filled the shed. Each night this ugly shack was transformed into an enchanted, radioactively glowing fairyland.

"How incredible!" murmured another visitor. And Marie remembered back to a warm, summer afternoon three years before when she, herself, had first said those same two words. "How incredible!"

On that afternoon three years before, the front door of Pierre and Marie Curie's Paris apartment burst open without so much as a knock. "Marie! Pierre! Look at *this*!" Monsieur Becquerel, an elderly physicist and good friend of the Curies, stood in the midst of their tiny living room, out of breath and red-faced with excitement, holding out a developed photographic plate. As always, when

Monsieur Becquerel was extremely excited, his little white beard quivered with emotion.

Both Curies scrambled up from their reading and stared at the photograph. It was solid black, except for a large, fuzzy white blotch in the middle.

"*That's* a photograph?" asked Marie, the practical, down-to-earth Curie. She had an angelic face and constant smile of goodwill. "It's not very good."

"What? It's incredible!" blurted Becquerel, hardly able to control himself in his grand excitement.

Pierre, the dreamer of the two Curies, with wavy, amber hair and large, soft eyes, put a hand on his old friend's shoulder. "Calm down before you rupture something."

Becquerel took a deep breath, sank into a chair, and accepted the glass of water Marie offered. "Thank you. As you know, I've been experimenting with natural phosphorescence and fluorescence." The Curies did know that. Since Roentgen had discovered X-rays three years earlier, in late 1895, many European scientists had rushed to see if naturally created phosphorescent and fluorescent light rays were similar to Roentgen's electrically created ones.

Becquerel took another deep breath and continued. "I decided to test uranium ore. No one else had, so I thought to myself . . ."

Marie interrupted. "And what happened?"

"Ahh, that's why I'm here," Becquerel answered, wagging his finger in Marie's face. "My piece of uranium ore had been wrapped in thick black paper for several weeks. So there was no possibility of any fluorescent or phosphorescent activity. I was about to start my experiment when two cousins stopped by for a visit. Well, you know how it is." He paused.

"So what happened?" insisted Marie.

"Ahh. Well, that's why I'm here. As I left the lab to visit, I placed the uranium, which was still wrapped, on top of a photographic plate in a lightless drawer. Several days later I went back to the uranium. There sat the photographic plate. I really don't even know why I did it. I had no real reason to expect anything."

"So what happened?" demanded Marie.

"Ahh, yes. Well, that's why I'm here. I developed that photo plate." And he held out the photograph again. "Here it is."

Pierre stared, dumbfounded. "The uranium did *that* all on its own? Some natural rays came out of your uranium and exposed the photograph? That's just like Roentgen's X-rays, only better."

Marie's practical mind was whirring. "No. Not like X-rays at all. X-rays are created by a strong electrical current, and stop as soon as the current is shut off. Phosphorescence and fluorescence are only created when light strikes a metal. This invisible radiance just naturally burst out of uranium all on its own. How incredible!"

Twenty-nine-year-old Marie, still a graduate student at the university, decided to drop her other studies and concentrate on this amazing natural activity, or *radioactivity*, as she called it. It was new. It was exciting. It was something no one had ever seen before.

But where should she begin to unravel the mystery of invisible rays that flowed out of a metal? She spent a month just trying to pinpoint where radioactivity came from. Over dinner in their apartment, she finally told Pierre, "Radioactive rays seem to burst straight out of the uranium atom itself."

Pierre was stunned motionless, his jaw agape, and a spoonful of soup frozen halfway to his mouth. If Marie were right, it would be a revolutionary finding. It would rumble like an earthquake through the worlds of chemistry and physics. In 1898, an atom was believed to be the smallest thing in existence, the basic building block of the universe. If Marie's radioactivity came out of a uranium atom, then there had to be something inside that was even smaller than an atom.

Pierre realized his wife's research was vastly important and dropped his other projects to join her.

As they had no money to pay for their research, Marie had to scrounge for free lab space. She finally found an abandoned shed at the school on Rue Lhomond. The shed had been used by the biology department to hold cadavers. But its sagging roof, dirt floor, and leaky walls made it unsuitable for the department's needs.

Marie led Pierre to the shed, and his face dropped. "This hovel exceeds my worst nightmares of discomfort! Marie, how can we work here?"

"Cheaply," she answered.

Over the next six months, Marie and Pierre examined each of the 78 known chemical elements to see if radioactive rays could be found in any other substance besides Becquerel's uranium. Most of their time was spent searching and begging for tiny samples of the many elements they could not afford to buy. Their long search uncovered only two elements that possessed this amazing natural radioactivity: uranium and thorium.

Near the end of their search, Marie was given a sample of pitchblend to test. Pitchblend is a weak ore of uranium found in western Czechoslovakia. Marie saw little reason to be interested in pitchblend, but still included it in a group of samples she was testing.

Her wild results convinced her she must have made a mistake. The amount of radioactivity she measured in this pitchblend couldn't be right. Chemically, she recalculated to within .01% of the amount of uranium in the sample. With an electrometer, a very early Geiger counter, she remeasured its radioactivity.

"This can't be right!" she sighed. She must have made another mistake. But where?

Six times Marie tested the pitchblend. Six times she got the same unbelievable result. There was hardly any uranium, and no thorium, in this pitchblend. But she measured massive radioactivity. Something was wrong.

During dinner discussions with Pierre that night, the truth finally hit Marie like a sledgehammer. There must be something *else* in the pitchblend that was the source of this extra radioactivity! That "something" had to be a new, undiscovered element! Marie had stumbled upon the greatest scientific prize of all: the discovery of a new chemical element in the makeup of the earth.

To suspect that a new element was there was one thing. To actually find the new element and prove it to be different from all other elements was quite another, especially when all they had was a leaky, broken-down shed and one ton of donated pitchblend.

The plan they followed was really quite simple. First, by established chemical processes, they would separate out every metal in their pitchblend and measure its radioactivity as they went. When they had finally separated out every known metallic element, whatever was left should be their new mystery element.

They had no money for lab equipment, and so used a large, borrowed iron cauldron to boil solutions of pitchblend during the many phases of the separation process. This they had to do outside; summer or winter; heat, rain, or snow, as they had no other way to vent the noxious fumes that rose up off the bubbling cauldron. Marie spent many days mixing that boiling mass with a long iron rod almost as tall as she was until her arms felt more leaden than the rod she was holding. Between groans, she often giggled at how she must look just like a witch of old, hunched over a foul-smelling, bubbling cauldron. Pierre hauled tons of firewood. They both stoked and tended the crude fire.

Slowly, through 1898 and 1899, they sifted through their ton of radioactive dirt searching for the few grains of the new radioactive metal they knew must be there. Often the chemical reactions Marie performed inside the shed were contaminated and ruined by leaking rainwater, or by the leaves, dirt, and dust that swirled in through the cracks in the walls. Hours of work would be wasted and she would have to start all over with a new batch of pitchblend.

What should have taken weeks dragged into long months because of their dismal working conditions. Still, by late 1899, Marie knew she was getting close. Feverishly Marie worked through freezing rains and bitter cold, sifting, sorting, boiling, hauling, mixing, and testing that ton of pitchblend over and over again.

Finally the pitchblend gave up its secrets to the two hardworking scientists. Marie had found not one, but *two* new radioactive elements in her pitchblend: polonium, named after Marie's native Poland, and radium, so named because it was by far the most radioactive element ever discovered.

Oh, how the compounds of those two elements shimmered and glowed in their darkened shed! They shone like magic. As Marie isolated more and more of these two radioactive metals, she began to hang test tubes of radium salts around the shed to cheer up the place and make it look bright and happy for the long evenings of work.

Soon, others noticed a bewitching glow spilling out of the Curies' shed to wash drab winter snows in rich pastel sheens. Friends began to gather, standing spellbound in the wondrous light. And then the long evening lines started, as everyone wanted a peek into Marie and Pierre's enchanted castle.

For a time, Marie Curie's incredible discoveries were almost lost in the magical glow of her radioactive lanterns. Still, that one ton of pitchblend led Marie and Pierre Curie to two monumental discoveries. First, they found two new naturally radioactive elements.

Second, they shattered the belief that the atom was the smallest thing in the universe. If radioactive rays came from within an atom, there had to be something else inside the atom, something even smaller. That one discovery opened the door to our whole atomic age of nuclear power, nuclear medicine, and nuclear weapons. But that, of course, is another story.

Library Link: Is the radiation from radioactive elements harmful?

We have all heard of "fluorescence" and "phosphorescence." But what are they and how do they differ?

Topics to Explore: chemistry, energy, atomic energy, radioactivity, Madame Curie.

References for Further Reading:

- *In the Children's Library:*

Curie, Eve. *Madame Curie.* New York: Doubleday, 1937.

Fox, Ruth. *Milestones of Medicine.* New York: Random House, 1985.

- *In the Adult Library:*

Conner, Edwina. *Marie Curie.* New York: Bookwright Press, 1987.

McGowen, Tom. *Radioactivity: From the Curies to the Atomic Age.* New York: Franklin Watts, 1986.

Consult your librarian for additional titles.

A Crystal-Clear View of Science

A story of Dorothy Hodgkin's discovery of the structure of a penicillin molecule in 1943

☑ **A Point to Ponder: What is a crystal? Have you ever seen a crystal? When?**

A great, booming echo reverberated through the cavernous room as Dr. Ernst Chain rushed in out of the cold English rain and slammed the museum doors. Colonel Jeffery Stanton marched beside Ernst, the heels of his stiff military boots clicking like slow-motion gunfire on the marble floor. Above their heads, spectral skeletons of ancient whales and dinosaurs hung from the dimly lit ceiling. Collections of dead beetles, moths, and lizards covered the walls.

Dr. Chain led the Colonel to a small side door along one wall of the Oxford University Museum. Opening it, and nodding toward the narrow stairway beyond, he said, "Dorothy Hodgkin's office is down here."

One of five rooms along this little-used basement corridor, Dr. Dorothy Hodgkin's office was a tiny, cramped alcove, hardly big enough for the three of them to sit without moving piles of books and reports and rearranging stacks of test equipment. Dorothy's large brown eyes sparkled with amusement as she watched the Colonel's nose turn up in disgust as he surveyed her jumbled domain.

After preliminary handshakes and introductions, Colonel Stanton rose, standing more stiffly than his starched uniform. His thick, red mustache quivered as he spoke in crisp, precise diction.

"It is 1943, Dr. Hodgkin. The war lingers on. Good English lads, soldiers, are dying every day. Too many of them survive German bullets only to die anyway from battlefield infections. We need a steady supply of those . . ." The Colonel fumbled for the right word, then gestured imploringly to Dr. Chain.

"Antibiotics," responded the doctor.

"Precisely, antibiotics," continued the Colonel. "We need antibiotics to save our soldiers. And we need them now!"

Dorothy Hodgkin shrugged in confusion. "But why come to me? I'm a chemist, not a microbiologist." Dorothy was a tall, slender woman with cropped brown hair. Her desk appeared two sizes too small for her lanky body.

"Precisely. We came to you for your . . . your X crystals . . ." Again he motioned for Dr. Chain to take over.

"X-ray diffraction crystallography," supplied the doctor.

Colonel Stanton looked a trifle bewildered, so Dr. Hodgkin explained. "We shoot X-rays at the molecules locked in a crystal structure and observe how the various atoms bend, or diffract X-rays."

"Ah, precisely!" Colonel Stanton rocked back and forth on his polished heels. "I believe Dr. Chain can better tell you exactly what we want."

Colonel Stanton gestured to Ernst and sat down.

Dr. Chain cleared his throat, smiled, and turned to Dorothy. "What we need is penicillin, the most powerful antibiotic known. Following Dr. Fleming's original work, I have tried to develop a way of producing penicillin as fast as it is needed. But it grows too slowly. The problem is we can't create a synthetic penicillin because we don't know what it is composed of. We don't know which atoms are in a penicillin molecule, and we don't know the arrangement of those atoms. We can grow and use it, but we don't know how to make penicillin."

Dorothy nodded. "And you're hoping I can find out using X-ray diffraction on penicillin crystals."

Stanton fidgeted in his chair, nearly toppling a precarious stack of reports next to him. "What, precisely, is it that you do with crystals? My wife collects them, you know."

Dorothy laughed and leaned back into her chair. "Crystals are all around us, Colonel. Table salt and sugar are crystals. So are snowflakes. Aspirin forms crystals, and copper can form some beautiful blue crystals. Some single crystals are as large as 2,000 tons. Some are microscopic. But, if I could get my hands on a penicillin crystal, I believe I could tell you what's in it."

Dr. Chain smiled and opened his briefcase. "Just what I'd hoped you'd say."

He lifted out a small padded case, much like a jewelry box, and slowly opened the lid. "Will these do?" Inside, on fluffy cotton wadding, sat three tiny crystals. Each shone with the pale, milky translucence of pearls. Very carefully, Ernst lifted one out and set it in Dorothy's outstretched hand.

"The first penicillin crystals ever made. This stuff doesn't crystallize very easily. Took me two months to make a batch crystallize after I ground and boiled it."

Colonel Stanton leaned forward and grabbed Dorothy Hodgkin's shoulder, his eyes filled with harsh urgency. "This is a national top priority, Dr. Hodgkin. We need the formula for penicillin. Do not fail."

Four days later, Colonel Stanton's polished heels again clicked across the Oxford Museum floor and down the narrow side stairway. As he marched into Dorothy's small office, he heard the whir of fans and the whine of test equipment from an even smaller lab beyond. His mustached face poked through the doorway just in time to see Barbara Low, Dorothy Hodgkin's somber research assistant, climb a ladder leaning against one wall.

"What are the new settings, Dr. Hodgkin?" she called over her shoulder as she reached the top.

Glancing at a mound of jumbled notes and scribbled pads of calculations balanced on her lap, Dorothy called back, "Rotate the crystal 15 degrees clockwise and 30 degrees down, please, Barbara."

Stacks of black-boxed test equipment were bolted to the walls and hung from the ceiling. Trays of pungent chemicals climbed up one wall, stacked on top of each other. Cables and cords snaked across chairs and were tacked over the door. Two large adding machines perched on the single table, trailing used paper across the floor.

"Doctor Hodgkin. Hard at work, I see. Do you have a penicillin formula for us yet?"

Dorothy looked up, smiled, and extended her hand. "Welcome, Colonel Stanton. You're just in time to watch us shoot some more film."

"Ahh, good show, Doctor." Colonel Stanton reached over and clicked off the light. "Dark and ready to shoot when you are," he called through the blackness.

"Hey! I can't see! Turn on the lights!" squealed Barbara, still perched atop the ladder.

Dorothy laughed, and reached out to turn the light back on. "X-ray film, Colonel, is not sensitive to visible light, only to high-frequency X-rays. We don't normally darken the room."

"Ahh, precisely, yes." The Colonel's eyes searched the room. He seemed disappointed. "I don't see any crystals, Doctor. My wife wanted me to note the size and kind you use so she could buy the same ones."

Again Dorothy laughed. "The crystals your wife buys in crystal shops are only one kind of crystal. A crystal is any solid whose molecules are locked into a regular, repeating pattern and shape. It is that repeating regularity that lets us look inside the crystal's molecules the way we do."

Colonel Stanton still looked confused. "And what do X-rays have to do with it?"

"X-rays are smaller than visible light waves. They can see things our eyes and visible light can't. X-rays can actually see atoms. They greatly extend what we can look at."

Barbara Low fitted a 10-inch-high, 30-inch-long strip of X-ray film onto a semicircular wooden bracket. Dr. Hodgkin had cut a paper-thin sliver of penicillin crystal with surgical saws. It hung in a glass mount right in the center of that circle. The cone-shaped black nozzle of an X-ray gun stood several inches away, aimed at the crystal sliver.

Barbara climbed back down the ladder. "The crystal's been repositioned. Film's in place. Ready to shoot."

Dorothy reached for a large red button mounted on the wall near her. "All clear?"

"All clear," answered her research assistant.

Dorothy hit the button. Motors whirred. There was a loud "Ka-lunk!" Barbara climbed the ladder to retrieve this new piece of exposed film.

"That was it?" asked the Colonel. "I didn't see anything."

"Sorry to disappoint you, Colonel," laughed Dorothy, "but you can't see X-rays."

Barbara developed the film in the chemical trays stacked on one wall and laid the still wet X-ray negative onto a large lightbox. Dr. Hodgkin turned it on.

As the two women hunched over the film, Colonel Stanton peered over their shoulders at the X-ray. Again he was disappointed. He didn't see a picture of atoms and molecules. Rather, he saw a maze of fuzzy white splotches on a black background. Dorothy and Barbara busily measured the size of, and distance between, each white speck in this pattern of fuzzy white dots.

Numbers were hurriedly punched into the adding machines. The paper tape rolled out across the floor.

"What, precisely, can those fuzzy blotches possibly tell you?" demanded the Colonel.

Dorothy stopped her work and looked up. "Imagine this, Colonel. Forty people stuffed into the middle of a room. One light somewhere along a wall shines onto those people, casting their shadow onto the far wall. Just looking at a picture of their collective shadow, could you correctly identify and place all 40 people in the room?"

"Certainly not," replied Colonel Stanton with an indignant snort.

Dorothy shrugged. "But that is exactly what we are doing. By rotating that penicillin crystal sliver to get different views of the shadow of its atoms, and by knowing what the X-ray shadow of different individual atoms looks like, we can slowly piece together a map of where the atoms must be in each regular, repeating penicillin molecule, and how they are connected—all just from looking at the repeating shadows of the atoms. I suppose it's like finding only a fingerprint on the wall, and trying to figure out the height, weight, and age of the person who made it."

It took over two years of constant work to identify and place the 30 atoms in a basic penicillin molecule and the almost 70 in several of the salts of penicillin. However, that hard-won discovery has saved countless millions of lives, and won Dr. Dorothy Hodgkin the 1964 Nobel Prize. Her work also led to a much better understanding of how crystals function, and to the invention of that now-commonplace electronic crystal, the transistor. But that is another story.

Library Link: Why use crystals to study the molecular structure of a compound?
Why did Dorothy Hodgkin use X-rays to study the structure of a molecule?

Topics to Explore: crystallography, scientific method, X-ray diffraction, chemistry, crystals.

References for Further Reading:

- *In the Children's Library:*

Haber, Louis. *Women Pioneers of Science.* New York: Harcourt Brace Jovanovich, 1979.

- *In the Adult Library:*

Shiels, Barbara. *Winners: Women and the Nobel Prize.* Minneapolis, Minn.: Dillon Press, 1985.

Consult your librarian for additional titles.

Funny Rubber

A story of James Wright's invention of Silly Putty® in 1944

☑ **A Point to Ponder: How many things can you make Silly Putty® do? Would you call it a scientific discovery?**

As it did every day, the half-empty green bus squealed to a stop at Security Gate #3, an "employees only" entrance to the sprawling General Electric Research Facility. With a rush of hot air from the unseasonably warm winds, the bus door swung open and a burly uniformed guard entered to check ID cards. The guard slowly worked his way down the center aisle, comparing ID pictures with the familiar yawning faces before him.

ID check complete, the outer gate swung open and the bus inched forward past security dogs and armed guards to an inner barbed-wire fence. Once the outer gate closed, an inner gate swung open and the green, company-owned bus roared into the top-secret GE research facility with part of the day shift and research crew.

It was the spring of 1944. World War II was in full swing. This GE plant was dedicated to critical War Department research. As the bus squeaked to its second stop, James Wright, a GE chemist, rose from his seat and started down the aisle.

"See you tonight, Jim," waved a neighbor and fellow researcher. James Wright waved back and stepped out in front of Building 242, a two-story cement building housing the War Department's project to develop synthetic rubber. James Wright was one of many chemists who had been assigned to the project at its inception three years before.

So far results had been poor. Both the Army and General Electric top management had begun to pressure these scientists to "produce something, and fast!"

James Wright joined the line of fellow researchers filing through the main Building 242 entrance and past yet another security guard. Finally inside the cozy interior lab he shared with two other chemists, James stepped past an overflowing sandbox just inside the door and plopped down into his desk chair.

A memo from GE Headquarters lay on his desk blotter requesting daily summary reports on all project progress. James was dismayed by this drastic increase of corporate pressure. "Now they want *daily* reports?"

Ernst Gretcher, already heating a test tube over his Bunsen burner, nodded. "The Army must be desperate for new rubber to want daily reports."

Rubber was needed for truck tires, boots, airplane tires, and a host of other war-related uses. The demand far exceeded the available supply. GE researchers had the job of finding a cheap source of synthetic rubber. James and Ernst were part of a group studying sand as a possible source for rubber.

Actually, they were searching for a way to make a rubber substitute from silicon. Silicon is easily refined from sand. If their project worked, there was certainly plenty of sand, and so, plenty of silicon.

"What are you on this week, Ernst?" asked James, rising from his seat and slipping on a white lab coat.

"Still high-temperature silicone alloys," replied Ernst over the roar of his burner. "What about you?"

"I'm just finishing the silicon-acid tests," said James. Adjusting plastic goggles and long rubber gloves, he stepped to a small work area next to the lab sink. From a high shelf he pulled down a series of lab bottles, each labeled with the name of a different acid and partly filled with clear liquid.

He lifted a beaker of pure silicon oil he had refined from sand the day before, and poured a small amount into each of a long row of clear glass dishes. Then he opened his lab book and jotted down a description of the day's setup.

John McCuthy, the third chemist working in the lab, walked in sipping coffee from a heavy paper cup. "Finding anything?"

"Just starting!" called both James and Ernst without looking up from their work.

"Keep at it," said John, settling into his own work area with a deep sigh. "I just came from a staff meeting. Management is screaming for results *now*."

The first of the tests James had scheduled for that day was to try combining his silicon oil with boric acid. He carefully drew a small amount of concentrated boric acid into a glass dropper. One by one he counted and released a dozen drops onto the first dish and its silicon oil. The mixture bubbled softly around the edges. Thin wisps of white smoke rose off the dish. The mixture turned cloudy and solidified as the reaction stopped.

James reached out with a glass stir rod and poked the soft, lumpy goo. It felt springy—like rubber.

For the first time in weeks, the beginning flutters of excitement stirred in James's stomach. He ran a quick pH test to see if his goo was strongly acidic. Whatever it was, it was pH neutral. It was neither acidic nor basic.

James picked up the gooey mass. It held together fairly well, and didn't seem to stick to his gloves. He set it back on the counter and pressed down on it with his thumb. The goo slowly oozed out on all sides. He picked it up and lightly threw it down onto the lab counter. It bounced. Not high, but it bounced.

Excitement and hope beginning to grow, James called, "Ernst, John, look at this stuff!"

Both men dashed over to peer closely at the soft goo in James's hand. "Try to stretch it," said Ernst.

"Try to smash it," suggested John.

James gripped the goo with both hands and slowly pulled. The goop stretched way out like saltwater taffy. But it didn't spring back at all.

He placed the goo on a counter and smashed it with a hammer. The goop shattered into a dozen fragments. Hopes were shattered along with this funny goo. No, it wasn't a rubber substitute. . . . But it was . . . well, *fun.*

The stuff reformed into a single gooey blob as soon as James rolled the individual pieces back together into a ball. He tossed it at Ernst and both men laughed. Ernst bounced it to John. The goo ball bounced off a table and hit John on the chin. All three men laughed.

John pretended to be a basketball player and tried to bank the ball off one wall and into a bucket next to their sandbox. He missed, and the ball rolled across James's sportcoat which lay on his desk.

"Hey look, the goo picks up lint!" exclaimed James, and all three laughed harder.

Word spread quickly through Building 242 of the strange blob James Wright had created. All morning, a constant trickle of engineers and scientists flowed into the lab to take a look.

"Go ahead. Bounce it. Now smash it with a hammer!" Each new person put the new goo through its ever-expanding series of tricks. "Now smoosh it out on the Sunday newspaper comics. Now peel it up. Look! It even picks up Little Orphan Annie!" And everybody laughed all over again.

At 2:00 that afternoon, Dr. William Grayling, the group director, stormed into the lab with an awful scowl on his face. "I hear you've been playing with some new discovery all day."

"Yes, sir," answered James. "Silicon oil and boric acid."

"Is it a possible rubber substitute?" demanded Dr. Grayling.

"No, sir. It isn't. It lacks strength and integrity. But let me show you all it *can* do."

"No!" Dr. Grayling slammed his fist on Wright's desk. "I have to file a report on today's progress in three hours. I do not want to have to say my group spent the entire day playing with some silly toy. Now back to work!"

Over the next few days, James Wright's silly goo was slowly forgotten. Over two dozen learned engineers and scientists had tested and examined the stuff. But no one was able to find a practical use for it. Eventually, even James himself filed it away and forgot it.

Five years later, in 1949, young Peter Hodgson, who had been a student lab tech in Building 242 during the war, finally saw the practical use no one else had found. Dr. Grayling had been exactly right. It *was* a silly toy. Hodgson made a large batch of James Wright's goo, packaged it in plastic Easter eggs, and named it—"Silly Putty®." Within two years, it had become the most popular toy in the Western world. But that's another story.

Library Link: Does science always have to be serious?

Topics to Explore: chemistry, scientific method, physiology, James Wright, Silly Putty®.

References for Further Reading:

- *In the Children's Library:*

Jones, Charlotte. *Mistakes That Worked*. New York: Doubleday, 1985.

- *In the Adult Library:*

No commonly available printed references were found in the adult section.

Consult your librarian for additional titles.

An Ounce of Correction

A story about Bette Nesmith's invention of Liquid Paper® in 1952

☑ **A Point to Ponder: Before computers, self-correcting typewriters, and Liquid Paper®, how would you correct a typing mistake?**

Bette Nesmith slammed her purse shut, rammed her arms into the sleeves of her heavy winter coat, and stomped toward the elevator. Five o'clock could not have come too soon on such a terrible day. Bette, a 34-year-old secretary at the Texas Bank and Trust Company, tried hard to relax and unclench her fists as she rode the crowded elevator down from the eighteenth floor. But when the elevator doors slid open onto the marbled main lobby of the Texas Bank Building, she was still fuming at her boss.

If he had growled at her once today, he had growled twenty times. "Make it neater!" "Type it faster!" "It's too messy!" "Retype it again!"

"It's those new IBM electric typewriters," Bette told herself as she took a last breath of warm indoor air and stepped out into the chilly Dallas street. The single mother, struggling to get by on a secretary's pay, pulled her collar up tight around her stylish pageboy haircut and slender face. "These new electrics have carbon film ribbons. You just can't erase mistakes neatly with film ribbons. And what am I supposed to do if I can't erase mistakes neatly like I always have before?"

On this early December 1952 evening, she paused to watch two painters working on a holiday window scene for the bank's front window. She watched them create bright painted snow mounds and holly branches and begin painting the bright red words "Season's Greetings" as she continued her muttered tirade against her boss. "I'll get positively ill if he tells me one more time that I should be faster with this new electric typewriter. How can I be? With that ribbon, I can't correct mistakes without smearing. So I have to retype the whole page. Of course it's slower!"

One of the painters dabbed over the final red S in "Season's" with the white paint of the snow background. He began repainting the S, readjusting its position. Bette shook her head and thought, "Fixing mistakes is so easy for a painter." Then she sighed and said out loud, "If only I could fix *my* mistakes so easily."

At 7:00, Bette's son, Michael, raced in from high school basketball practice. "What's for dinner, Mom?"

Absentmindedly she answered. "Those new frozen pot pies. They're in the oven now."

"But Mom! The oven's not even turned on!"

Bette apologized and poured out all her troubles with the new electric typewriters.

Michael shrugged in typical teenager fashion and said, "Don't make it so hard on yourself, Mom. There's got to be an easier way."

There it was again. Make it simple. Make it easy. What would be the easy way to fix typing errors? She thought of the painters. What if she could paint over her mistakes just like painters? No retyping whole pages, and no messy, smeared erasures. That's what.

Could it be that simple? Could she literally paint over her mistakes and then type right over them? That night she funnelled some waterbase white tempera paint into a small bottle, and bought a fine watercolor brush. It was certainly worth a try. Her first mistake came just before 10:00 coffee break the next morning. Bette rolled the paper up several lines in her typewriter, slipped the bottle out of her purse, and dabbed some paint over her error with a fine-point brush. Then, she tucked bottle and brush away, and stepped out for a glass of water.

Three minutes later, she was back at her desk. But the paint was not yet dry enough to type over. Two minutes later, her boss found Bette seemingly idle at her desk, fanning the page in her typewriter with a manila folder.

Hands on hips, he glared down at her and growled, "Quit playing, and get busy!"

In an embarrassed rush, Bette typed across her still-soft paint dab and smeared several letters onto the page. The whole page had to be retyped.

Two days later, Bette brought in a new bottle with thicker paint. But it dried grainy and slowly flaked off the page, revealing the mistake underneath to her irate boss. Again Bette had to retype the whole page.

Her next batch of correcting paint turned brittle and cracked when the page was bent or folded. The bank's client discovered the error and a small pile of white paint chips in the fold. Her boss was furious.

The next batch was flexible, but too thick, and left a big lump on the page. Her boss slammed the page back onto Bette's desk with a note, "Stop playing with your paints, and type it right!"

Frustrated, Bette drove straight to the Dallas Public Library to research paint formulas. But no matter where she looked in the card catalog or on the shelves, she found nothing that she could understand that spoke to her special requirements.

Even now Bette still wouldn't give up. She took a vacation day from work and made an appointment with her son's high school chemistry teacher.

"Come in, Mrs. Nesmith. Michael is certainly doing well enough."

Bette interrupted. "This is not about my son. I need your help." She sat nervously on the front edge of a chair, both hands clamped tight around the purse in her lap. "I've tried the library. And I've tried on my own. But nothing works, and I'm tired of being yelled at. I need to make a white paint that will spread very smooth and dry exceptionally fast."

The young chemistry teacher leaned back in his chair. "But Mrs. Nesmith, there are a number of commercial paints . . ."

"*And*," she interrupted, " will not turn brittle or grainy. And will dry as true a white as typing paper."

"I'm sure there must be *some* paint on the market . . ."

"*And*," she continued, now counting off the paint requirements on her fingers, "will allow me to type neatly and cleanly over a mistake, just like the original page. And once dry, it must blend into the piece of paper and disappear. And it must be able to be folded without cracking."

He whistled low and shook his head. "You've got quite a list. Is that everything?"

Bette thought for a moment. "It must also stay liquid in the bottle even with repeated openings, and it must be inexpensive to produce. That, I think, is all."

The young chemistry teacher thought for a long moment, and then dug out two thick reference manuals. He flipped rapidly through the thin pages and scanned several sections, shaking his head as he muttered to himself and jotted some notes. Finally he looked up. "I think I can get you started, Mrs. Nesmith. But I'm not sure *anything* can do all that. If you're going to find it, you'll need better help than me."

Then he spun the book around to face Bette and tapped the page with his finger. "Here are a couple of tests you can start with. And let me give you the phone number of someone at the university."

That night, when Michael got home from basketball practice, he found the kitchen converted into a bubbling chemistry lab. Beakers of brightly colored chemicals were lined up across the counter. Two glass flasks were madly boiling on the stove. Out of one, a long glass tube snaked across to a deep pan. "Mom! What are you cooking for dinner tonight? This place stinks as bad as my chemistry class."

For two years, Bette Nesmith's kitchen was set up as a chemistry lab first, and kitchen second. Her garage became an assembly plant. Two paint-manufacturing specialists worked with her and taught her each step in the paint grinding and mixing process. Bette tried over 100 formulas before she found one that did everything she wanted it to.

By 1956, Bette was selling a hundred bottles of "Mistake Out" a month. In 1960, Bette Nesmith's homemade business became the Liquid Paper Company. A few years later, Bette's son, Michael Nesmith, became a member of the Monkeys, a popular late-1960s rock and roll band. But that is definitely another story.

Library Link: Since 1954 and the invention of Liquid Paper®, what ways have been discovered to correct typewritten mistakes?

Topics to Explore: physical science, chemistry, women in science.

References for Further Reading:

- *In the Children's Library:*

No good references in the children's section have been found.

- *In the Adult Library:*

Vare, Ethlie Ann, and Greg Ptacek. *Mothers of Invention.* New York: William Morrow, 1986.

Consult your librarian for additional titles.

Sticking to Basics

A story of Spencer Silver's invention of Post-it Notes® in 1970

> ☑ **A Point to Ponder: What could make a glue too good to be useful? What could make it too bad to be useful?**

Spencer Silver, a trim, 41-year-old chemist, sighed, slowly shook his head, and poured the contents of his large glass beaker down the lab drain. "Another worthless batch. Why doesn't my concept work?" Then he glanced up at a calendar tacked to the wall of his long, windowless laboratory. July 11, 1970. And he smashed the beaker into the sink in frustration. The beaker shattered. A tinkling shower of glass fragments rained down onto the counter. "I'm out of time. Why won't it work?! It *ought* to work just fine!"

Silver nervously ran his fingers through his neatly combed black hair and fidgeted with his plastic, clip-on ID tag. It read, "Spencer Silver. Staff Chemist. 3M Company." For the hundredth time in the past two weeks, his mind flashed agonizingly back to a bitter-cold afternoon in mid-January when he'd answered his lab phone to the voice of Mrs. Collins, executive secretary to Harris Buell, 3M's Vice-President for New Product Development. "Mr. Silver? Mr. Buell would like to see you in his office right away."

Spencer was amazed and terrified. A senior vice-president had never wanted to see him before. "Now? In his office?"

"Yes, right away, please, Mr. Silver. Third floor, executive wing."

Out of breath from his gallop up from the basement chemistry lab, Spencer Silver pushed through the tall, glass, double doors and onto the plush carpet of Mrs. Collins's office. She looked up from her typewriter and smiled. "Mr. Buell is waiting for you, Spencer."

Spencer nervously smoothed back his thick black hair, and, suddenly embarrassed at his appearance in this elegant office, tried to smooth out the wrinkles in his stained and worn lab coat.

Harris Buell, Vice-President for New Product Development, barely glanced up from a stack of papers on his long mahogany desk as Silver timidly crossed his spacious corner office.

"Sit down, Silver. I read your proposal."

Nervous and excited, Spencer pulled a chair up close to the vice-president's desk, unconsciously rolling and unrolling the hem of his lab coat.

Buell leaned back in his high-backed, leather chair and waved the eight-page proposal casually through the air. "3M makes a full line of glues. What's so different about this one you propose to create?"

"Strength, Mr. Buell. It will be super strong."

Buell nodded. "But a long setup time, right?"

"No sir," assured Silver. "It will set up super fast. That's the one-two punch I want to create. Super strong; super fast."

Buell smiled and dropped the proposal back onto his desk. "A real super glue, eh? Can you do it?"

Excited at this tentative approval, Spencer blushed deep red and answered, "Oh, yes sir! I'm sure I can. Our preliminary tests show great strength promise for several of our new glue molecules. And I think I can mix in a fast hardening agent for almost instant bonding."

Buell tapped his fingers thoughtfully across the lip of his desk. "We could use a glue like that. Do it. You've got six months to present your results. Use whatever lab space you need, and you can have two assistants."

Spencer Silver rose from his chair as if he were floating up on a cloud. "Yes sir, Mr. Buell! I won't disappoint you, Mr. Buell!"

Now on July 11, those words felt like a bitter pill in Spencer's throat. "I won't disappoint you, Mr. Buell." Five months, three weeks, and four days gone, and his new super glue wouldn't even hold two pieces of paper together. The fast-hardening agents somehow inhibited the bonding, sapped its strength. Chemical formula after formula; batch after batch, additive after additive, the results were the same. A piece of paper with this glue smeared on it could easily be pried right back up from anything Silver tried to glue it to. He hadn't made a super strong glue. He had made a super weak one.

For months, Spencer had wracked his brain and pored through every chemistry book on the structure and action of glue molecules. He had methodically tried nearly 100 separate formulas and additives. Nothing worked. He could make it extra strong, or he could make it extra fast bonding. But he couldn't do both. His super glue was a super flop.

Spencer glanced up at his lab clock. 1:30 P.M. His six months were up. He had only three and a half hours left to complete his project and submit his report to Mr. Buell. This was going to be a black day in the history of Spencer Silver.

By 4:00, it was official. Spencer Silver's super glue project was a failure and was cancelled. Spencer was assigned to other duties. But a part of his heart and spirit seemed to get locked away with the one small batch of Super Flop Glue Spencer saved in a storage locker.

Four years later, just before Easter, 1974, Arthur Fry, another 3M scientist, visited Spencer in his lab. Arthur sang in a church choir and was in trouble with the choir director. Arthur marked each week's hymns in his hymnal with small scraps of yellow paper. When he opened the book to a marked page, the yellow scraps often fell out, either fluttering out into the aisle for everyone to see, or floating down to his feet. Either way, the choir director glared at Arthur and shook his head in disgust. When Arthur bent over to pick them back up, the director would tap his baton angrily on the church organ.

Poor Arthur was afraid he would be thrown out of the choir. Then his scientist's mind remembered Silver's flopped glue project. Didn't he create a super weak glue that was the laughingstock of the company for a month or so back in 1970?

Spencer gritted his teeth, blushed, and quietly nodded his head.

Arthur continued. "Could I try some? That is, if you still have any. I know it's lousy glue. But if I smear it on the back of my markers, it might be strong enough to hold them in place when I open the book, and later lift off without ruining the hymnal page."

Resentful of this further wound to his chemist's pride over this most sensitive topic, Spencer angrily shoved his one stored beaker of glue across the lab table at Arthur Fry without a single word.

The glue worked perfectly. It held Arthur's markers to a page until he peeled them off. Even better, he found he could reuse the markers over and over again. The markers with Spencer Silver's Super Flop Glue worked just as well on the second, third, even the fourth use.

Within a month, the entire choir was clamoring for Arthur's self-sticking markers. Within a year, 3M named them "Post-it Notes ®," and sold them as fast as they could be made. Spencer Silver was now a company hero. His Super Flop Glue was renamed as one of the company's greatest super-successes. Failure had turned into brilliant success, and long months of frustration and failure in the lab turned to triumph. But whether or not Spencer Silver ever got his super glue to work the way it was supposed to is another story.

Library Link: How does glue work? What makes it stick?
What won't a Post-it® stick to?

Topics to Explore: chemistry, invention, Post-it Notes®, evaluation.

References for Further Reading:

- *In the Children's Library:*

Jones, Charlotte. *Mistakes That Worked.* New York: Doubleday, 1985.

- *In the Adult Library:*

No good printed references have been found in the adult section.

Consult your librarian for additional titles.

Life Sciences

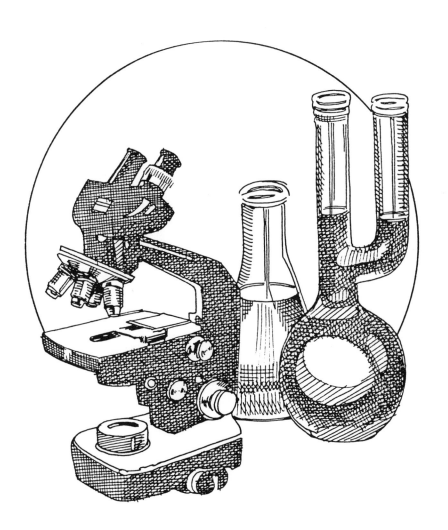

Biology—General

The Evolution of a Voyage

A story of Charles Darwin's discovery of the principles of species evolution in 1835

☑ **A Point to Ponder: Do species stay the same over all time? If not, why do they evolve, or change? When a species changes, how does that change occur?**

With the birds' shrill chirping echoing in my ears, I turned and hurried back as fast as the terrible terrain would permit. I stumbled through a twisted field of crunchy, black lava thrown up into giant, ragged waves. My path was crossed and blocked by great gaping fissures, and by pockets where dense steam and noxious yellow vapors drifted up from deep in the rock. Everywhere, the broken lava was covered by stunted, barren brushwood that looked more dead than alive.

Though I had been told they would not harm me, I still circled wide around the clusters of shiny, black lizards that seemed to love this frightful land. In some pockets, over 100 of them slithered across each other, all three or four feet long with pink, flickering tongues that seemed as long as their tails. They scuttled out of my way on stubby legs, hissing fiercely, as I ran past.

My name is Jason Crum, and, until signing on for this voyage in 1833, I had lived all my 22 years in green, hospitable England. I was assigned the title of second boatswain's mate on the HMS *Beagle*, and set off to see the world. But if I had known this is what the world was going to look like, I'd have stayed at home.

I scurried over the rugged lava under a blazing noonday sun, not on the boatswain's business, but for my other job as assistant to the ship's naturalist, 28-year-old Charles Darwin. I had found some birds I thought he should see.

"Mr. Darwin! Mr. Darwin!" I called as soon as I spotted him studying one of the brittle scrub trees.

Darwin looked up and saw me wave. "Did you find something, Jason?" he called back.

I ran the rest of the way to him, panting to catch my breath. "I think so, Mr. Darwin."

"You think so? Either you did, or you didn't, Jason. Now which is it?" Mr. Darwin studied me with deep-set eyes that always seemed to scowl from under his thick, bushy brows. They held that scowl even when he laughed—which he rarely did—mostly, I think, because he was always seasick, even after three years at sea.

"I think I found a new finch. But the beak's all wrong. So I'm not sure," I answered.

"Really?" he exclaimed. "*Another* new finch. Amazing! Show me where, Jason."

This was our second day ashore on James Island, the fourth of the Galapagos Islands we explored. It was already October 1835. But here, right on the equator in the Pacific Ocean, no day or season seemed any different than any other.

Mr. Darwin hoisted his backpack containing jars and bags for collecting samples, a notebook for recording and sketching, and his nets and traps. He shouldered his rifle and we were off, back across this frightful landscape. Beads of sweat formed on Darwin's balding head and trickled down through his thick, muttonchop sideburns.

The giant lizards and tortured lava that so frightened me seemed to delight Charles Darwin. He must have stopped 30 times to gawk at something and say, "Would you look at that! I've never seen anything quite like it anywhere else in the world."

Up a small rise at the upper far edge of the twisted lava field, we reached a grove of taller trees filled with birds. It was hard to hear each other talk over the noise of a thousand chirping finches.

Mr. Darwin stood entranced, staring first at the birds on one branch and then turning to another like a kid staring at different tubs in an ice cream shop. "They're finches all right, but their beaks are larger and rounder than others we've seen."

Then he froze, staring hard at one small group of bright yellow finches near the end of a long, twisted branch. "Look," he whispered. "Those ones are eating. Can you see *what* they're eating?"

"It looks like small, red berries, Mr. Darwin."

"My word, you're right, Jason. Imagine that! A finch eating berries. We need some sketches and samples."

He dropped to the hard ground and took out his notebook. He ripped out several sheets and handed them to me. "You draw. You're better than I am."

While I carefully drew the birds and their unique beaks, he jotted down quick notes on what we saw. "Done, Jason? Good. Now for some samples."

He lifted his rifle and in two quick shots felled as many of the birds for us to take back to the *Beagle* to study. With a mighty screech and thunderous flapping of wings, a great throng of frightened birds leapt into the air over our heads, darting back and forth like a brightly colored cloud.

Back on board the *Beagle*, Mr. Darwin took his two new finches straight to his crowded cabin, one deck above the captain's quarters. Within an hour he confirmed that these finches seemed to eat nothing but berries. "Think of it, Jason," he said. "Everywhere else on earth finches eat seeds, except in these crazy islands."

"But some of them eat seeds," I reminded him.

He nodded. "You're right. We found those seed-eaters on Chatham Island, wasn't it?" Chatham Island was the first in the Galapagos chain we visited.

But then he pointed at the drawings, notes, and beak samples he had laid out across the floor. "Here on James Island berries are plentiful and the finches have long, rounded beaks. Those that lived on insects had slender, more pointed beaks fit for catching insects. And those from the west side of Chatham Island, who seemed to live off nuts, all have thicker, heavier beaks. Again, just the perfect beak for cracking nuts."

He leaned back against the cabin bulkhead and sighed, swaying slightly with the gentle rocking of the ship.

"The question, Jason, is how did all these specialized finches come to be here, when in all the rest of the world finches have but one standard bill type and eat only seeds?"

We sat in silence through the muggy stillness of evening. The slight breeze seemed only to blow hotter air in upon us. I shrugged and suggested, "Maybe they just grew here."

Again Mr. Darwin nodded. "Each species seems to have adapted to an individual island and its unique food supply. These islands are obviously fairly new. So the original birds must have flown over from South America. But once a flock settled on a particular island, they seem to have begun to change—to adapt—to the unique conditions of that island. Oh, it may well have taken thousands of years for them to evolve this much."

I interrupted. "You mean these birds haven't always been the way they are now? They evolved? Is that what other biologists think?"

"No, Jason, they do not," Darwin answered, his lips cracking into a faint smile that, for him, was the equivalent of a hearty belly laugh. "In fact, every biologist in all of history has always assumed the opposite, that species have always been just as they are now." He shook his head and thinly smiled again. "When you look at it that way, I suppose what we're saying is rather revolutionary. But I can see no other explanation. These birds arrived as one common species. In each succeeding generation, those individuals with beaks best suited for their particular island survived best. So that over a long period more than a dozen separate species have evolved."

That night with the tropical heat bearing down, and the gently rocking *Beagle* beneath us, Darwin's words simply seemed like the obvious truth about the wondrous nature we saw every day with our own eyes. They didn't feel like revolutionary ideas. Who could have imagined the great uproar these simple ideas would create once Mr. Darwin published them in his books, *The Voyage of the Beagle* and *Origin of Species*? But that is another story.

Library Link: Why couldn't Darwin make the observations necessary to discover his principles of species evolution in England and Europe?

Why did he have to go to isolated islands like the Galapagos?

Topics to Explore: Biology, evolution, natural selection, scientific method, data collection, Charles Darwin.

References for Further Reading:

- *In the Children's Library:*

DeCamp, L. Sprague, and Catherine Crook DeCamp. *Darwin and His Great Discovery.* New York: Macmillan, 1972.

Quackenbush, Robert. *The Beagle and Mr. Flycatcher.* Englewood Cliffs, N.J.: Prentice-Hall, 1983.

- *In the Adult Library:*

Darwin, Charles. *The Beagle Record.* Cambridge, England: Cambridge University Press, 1979.

Consult your librarian for additional titles.

Spontaneous War

A story of Louis Pasteur's discovery of microbes in 1858

> ☑ **A Point to Ponder: Why does milk go sour if you leave it out of the refrigerator?**

On a cold, gray, Paris day in early December 1858, Louis Pasteur shifted his chair nearer to the single small window in his tiny attic lab. Satisfied with how the afternoon light shown onto the pages before him, he settled into the chair and continued reading. With first a snort, then a grunt, and finally a low growl, Pasteur's eyes blazed as he marked Felix Pouchet's report, underlining sections, scribbling fierce comments in the margins.

Thirty-eight-year-old Pasteur was Director of Scientific Affairs at the famed Ecole Normale University. It was an honored administrative position. He was supposed to be down in his second-floor office preparing university budgets and program plans. But Pasteur's heart was pure research chemist. He had found a small, abandoned room in the attic and commandeered it for his laboratory. To the university's dismay, he spent more time in that cramped attic nook than in his spacious, carpeted office.

Nearing the conclusion of Felix Pouchet's paper, Louis could feel in his bones that here was the greatest battle, the greatest challenge, of his career. With this paper Pouchet had fired the first shot. The world of science would now wait for Pasteur to either surrender or retaliate. Whether he wanted it or not, whether he felt it was good for science or not, Louis Pasteur had been provoked into a war.

Pasteur drummed his fingers on the arm of his attic chair as he thumbed back through Pouchet's paper. Ah, yes. Here it was, right next to Pasteur's six tall exclamation marks, and underlined so fiercely Pasteur could barely read the words. "The microscopic organisms that appear during fermentation and putrefaction are produced by spontaneous generation. They have no parents. They form spontaneously from the decaying material itself."

"Rubbish!" thought Pasteur. "The experiments he describes don't support that conclusion at all."

For thousands of years, it had been a popular theory that some organisms spontaneously materialized from nonliving matter instead of being born of another living organism. But, by the 1800s, scientists no longer believed that mice spontaneously materialized from old rags and cheese, that eels materialized from mud, or that worms spontaneously generated from rotting meat, as had been believed in previous centuries. But Pasteur's earlier discovery that microscopic live organisms, bacteria called yeasts, were always present during, and seemed to cause, the fermentation of beer and wine, breathed new life into the spontaneous generation theory.

Many scientists now believed that these fermentation microorganisms spontaneously generated from the decaying molecules of organic matter. When something began to rot, yeast bacteria just appeared. Felix Pouchet had become the leading spokesman for this group of scientists. The publication of Pouchet's paper meant that Pasteur would have to either admit they were right, or fight back with a theory of his own.

Repeatedly ducking his head to avoid the low ceiling beams, Pasteur paced the five steps back and forth from end to end of his attic lab, slowly tapping the rolled-up copy of Pouchet's report on his lab bench as he walked. Pouchet hadn't proved his case at all. It was wrong of him to claim that he had. But if fermenting microorganisms didn't generate spontaneously, where did they come from?

Louis Pasteur crumpled the report and slammed it down on his workbench. It was no longer the time for such idle questions. This was a fight. It was time for careful, exacting science. It was time for Pasteur to go to work in the lab.

One month of preliminary experiments crammed in around his administrative duties led Louis to a general theory: Bacteria floated in the air and simply fell by chance onto food and all living matter, multiplying rapidly only when they found a decaying substance to use as a nutrient for growth.

Pasteur released his preliminary theory, just to let Felix Pouchet and the spontaneous generation faction know he had taken up the challenge. Almost immediately, Pouchet fired back a scathing letter. Pasteur's theory was "ridiculous."

"If such an outlandish thing were true," concluded Pouchet, "by now these organisms would form a mist as dense as iron across the whole of the world and blanket every living thing."

Rather than return this hostile fire, Pasteur decided to quietly prove his theory in the lab. Two questions were at the center of the argument. First, did living microbes float in the air? Second, was it really impossible for microbes to grow spontaneously in a sterile environment, one in which all microbes had been cleared from the air? A "yes" answer to both questions proved Pasteur right. A "no" answer to both proved Pouchet right. One "yes" and one "no" meant the war would drag on.

It seemed to Pasteur that, once he had correctly formulated these questions, the necessary experiments were simple and straightforward. First, he heated a glass tube to sterilize both the tube and the air inside. He plugged the open end with a thick wad of guncotton. He used a vacuum pump to draw air from the room through the cotton filter and into the sterile tube.

Pasteur reasoned that any microbes floating in the air should be trapped and concentrated on the outside of the cotton filter as room air was sucked through. Bacterial growth on the filter indicated microbes floating freely in the air. Bacterial growth in the sterile interior of the tube had to mean spontaneous generation.

After 24 hours, the outside of his cotton filter turned dingy gray with bacterial growth, while the inside of the tube remained completely clear. Microbes had concentrated and grown on the filter, but not inside the sterile environment of the tube.

Pasteur examined the gray fuzz under a microscope. The organisms looked exactly like the yeasts that caused fermentation. Pasteur repeated the experiment using an asbestos filter, so that no one could claim the microbes had spontaneously generated from the organic cotton fiber. His results were the same. He repeated this experiment several dozen times to make sure the results he saw were not a fluke. Every time, it worked as Pasteur's theory said it would.

Question #1 was answered. "Yes," microscopic organisms did exist, floating, in the air. Whenever they were concentrated, as on the filter they began to grow and multiply.

Now for question #2. If Pasteur could show that microscopic bacteria really could not generate spontaneously, he would also have proved Pouchet's theory to be wrong, and victory would belong to Louis Pasteur.

To do this, Louis tried to make bacteria spontaneously generate. He mixed a nutrient-rich bullion, a favorite food of hungry bacteria, in a large beaker with a long, curving glass neck. Then he heated the beaker so that the bullion boiled furiously, and the glass glowed. This step killed any bacteria already in the bullion or in the air inside the beaker. Then he quickly stoppered the beaker with a thick wad of guncotton, the same kind of filter he used successfully in his first experiment.

Now, was Pouchet right? Would bacteria spontaneously generate in this ideal, but now sterile and lifeless beaker? If bacteria could spontaneously generate anywhere, they would surely do it here in this bullion. Pasteur had a small incubation warming oven, used to speed the growth of bacterial cultures. Because of his slanted attic roof and limited lab space, he had to crawl on hands and knees to reach the oven door. Almost lying on his stomach he slid the beaker into his incubation oven and noted the time and day in a logbook, 9:00 A.M., Tuesday.

Nine A.M., Wednesday, Pasteur crawled back to his oven and checked the beaker. All was crystal clear. He checked again on Thursday, and on Friday. He carefully checked every day for eight weeks. Nothing grew at all in the beaker. Bacteria had not spontaneously generated.

Pasteur broke the beaker's neck and let normal, unfiltered, unsterilized room air flow into the beaker. Then he put it back in the oven and noted the time. 10:15 A.M., Wednesday. By 6:00 P.M. that same day, lying on his stomach, he saw the first faint tufts of bacterial growth. By 10:00 A.M. on Thursday, the surface of the bullion was covered with the stuff.

Pouchet was wrong. Without the original airborne microbes floating into contact with a nutrient, there was no bacterial growth. They did not spontaneously generate. They fell out of the air and then multiplied like crazy.

Pasteur triumphantly published his findings. The war was over. Pasteur had won. More importantly, a brand new field of study, microbiology, the study of all those microscopic organisms floating all around us, was born. But how the process of removing those microscopic organisms from milk came to be called *pasteurization* is another story.

Library Link: Many of us drink pasteurized milk. What is pasteurization?

Besides discovering the field of microbiology, what other contributions to our health and well-being did Louis Pasteur make?

Topics to Explore: biology, medical research, microbiology, fermentation, scientific method, Louis Pasteur.

References for Further Reading:

- *In the Children's Library:*

Burton, Mary June. *Louis Pasteur: Founder of Microbiology.* New York: Franklin Watts, 1963.

Wood, Laura. *Louis Pasteur.* New York: Julian Messner, 1948.

- *In the Adult Library:*

Dubos, Rene. *Pasteur and Modern Science.* Madison, Wis.: Science Tech Publishers, 1988.

Paget, Stephen. *Pasteur and After Pasteur.* London: A & C Black, 1914.

Consult your librarian for additional titles.

The Dawn of Blood

A story of Florence Sabin's discovery of the origin of blood in 1917

☑ **A Point to Ponder: Everyone has heard the age-old question, "Which came first, the chicken or the egg?" But, if a whole chick develops from one single cell, where, when, and how do blood cells form?**

Often in the world of science, what appear to be setbacks and disappointments turn out to be the necessary and important building blocks that lead to ultimate triumph. The story of biological researcher Florence Sabin is such a story.

On a chilly afternoon in April 1917, with a dull, leaden sky to match their mood, a somber group of medical and research staff and students crowded into the spacious home of Franklin Mall, former professor and department chair of the anatomy department at Johns Hopkins University Medical Center. Even though Professor Mall had died two days ago, and his funeral services had concluded over three hours ago, the dominant feeling was still stunned disbelief that this giant among anatomical researchers could really be gone. What would happen to the department now? Who would carry on?

Two women, both wearing somber black, met near the front door of the house and wept into each other's arms. One was Mabel Mall, Franklin's new widow. The other, wearing wire-rimmed glasses over a square, plain face, was Florence Sabin, an anatomy department associate professor and Franklin Mall's assistant and colleague for over twenty years. These two felt the loss of Franklin Mall more than anyone else.

Hushed conversations around the big Baltimore, Maryland, house slowly turned to the future. Who would become the new department chair? In every group, the answer was the same.

"Why, it has to be Florence Sabin. That's who."

"No major medical facility in the country has a woman as a department chair. Do you really think they'll give her the anatomy department?"

"Just look at all she's done. Her research on the lymphatic system is world-renowned. So is her book on human brain anatomy. She's been the assistant dean for fifteen years. It has to be her!"

"But the anatomy department is the most important in the whole university. Could they really offer the chair to a woman?"

In group after group, this conversation was repeated. In group after group, the conclusion was the same: Florence Sabin was the most qualified person to become the first woman department chair in the country. Even Mable Mall, a medical school graduate herself, agreed. "Only Florence can pick up the work where Franklin left it."

When it was announced three weeks later that a male, former student of Florence Sabin's would become the new anatomy department chair, a shock wave rumbled through the research community as big or bigger than that which accompanied the death of Professor Mall. "How dare they pass over Professor Sabin?"

A public protest was organized. A boycott was planned. It was outrageous to pass over Sabin just because she was a woman! Shy Florence Sabin was undone by all this political turmoil. Science was her one true passion. Politics made her very nervous. So, when she was offered a full professorship and a position as chair of the small histology department, she jumped at it to quiet the uproar.

Of course, histology, the study of blood, was a very small and unimportant department at Johns Hopkins. Everyone agreed it was a cruel slap in the face to a brilliant and deserving researcher. They wanted Florence to resign in protest. Florence said only, "Oh, I couldn't do that. I have research in progress." She hid her disappointment behind dogged dedication, and buried her sense of betrayal deep beneath her new research.

Here is where fate turned a personal setback for Florence into a great gain for humanity. As head of histology, and with the study of blood as her central focus, a new research question occurred to Florence which she had somehow overlooked before. Once she thought of this question, she couldn't imagine why it hadn't occurred to her long before.

Her earlier work showed that the lymphatic system arose as tiny sprouts from blood vessels and grew into lymph glands and canals. The next obvious question was: Where do blood vessels and blood cells come from? What is the origin of our circulatory system? How does it develop and grow?

The problem, of course, was how to do such a study. How can you watch an embryo develop without damaging or destroying it, and halting the process you want to watch? The technolgy available in 1918 required a tissue sample to be stained with special dyes so that the individual cells would be visible through a microscope. However, existing dyes and staining technique altered and often killed living tissue, making it impossible to view the normal function of living cells. You could allow the cells to function normally, or you could observe them through a microscope. But in 1918 there was no way to do both.

New technology came to Florence's rescue one year later, in 1919, in the form of a new live staining technique, developed by a research team in Leipzig, Germany, which used dyes harmless to living tissue. Live tissue samples could now be stained for microscopic observation without affecting the tissue or its normal development in any way.

Florence Sabin could now pursue her research quest. She selected a chicken embryo. The embryonic cells were placed on a glass slide and stained using the Leipzig method. Florence carefully focused her microscope and settled into a comfortable chair to watch. Her wall clock read 9:45 P.M.

At 11:00 P.M., she detected the first tiny blood vessels beginning to form from the thick serum, called the endothelium, which lined the embryo's body cavity. Fascinated by this newly forming and dividing complex life, Florence stared through her microscope lenses as, around 1:00 A.M., the blood vessels spread to form a simple system of interconnecting canals.

At 2:00 A.M., so excited that she was unaware of how cramped and bleary-eyed she had become, she saw them: the first blood cells. Florence watched those first cells separate from the walls of these initial blood vessels to become the new chick's first red and white blood cells. The circulation system was born.

At 5:45 A.M., the summer sun crept through the windows and slowly crawled across her yellow laboratory walls. Florence Sabin never noticed. Her attention was riveted on the chicken embryo. Blood cells now filled a rapidly expanding network of arteries and veins. A tiny heart had formed. And then, before her eyes, just as most people in Baltimore were sleepily stumbling from their beds to start another day, Florence saw the heart make its very first beat. Blood cells streamed down the tiny arteries and flowed back through even smaller veins. Another beat and another. A new life began. Florence Sabin had stayed up all night to watch, so absorbed in this miracle of miracles, with this dawning of a new life, that she was unaware of the passage of time and the dawning of a new day.

More thrilled than on any other day of her life, Florence Sabin hastily jotted down her profound and valuable discoveries. Blood vessels form from the cells of the endothelium. The very first blood plasma cells develop from the liquid portions of the cells that form the walls of the first blood vessels.

Florence's work helped lead to the conquest of tuberculosis and to much of our understanding of the immune system. She was the first woman elected to the National Academy of Sciences and the first woman president of the American Association of Anatomists. But none of those glories were on Florence Sabin's mind that April evening in her bright yellow laboratory on the third floor of a plain brick building on the Johns Hopkins University campus. And, of course, they are all other stories.

Library Link: If each being begins as one single cell, how do different cells decide to specialize and turn into different organs, blood cells, hair, or other body parts?

Why would anyone care how, and from where, the blood vessels and blood cells are formed?

Topics to Explore: biology, medical research, histology, scientific method, Florence Sabin.

References for Further Reading:

- *In the Children's Library:*

Kronstadt, Janet. *Florence Sabin Medical Researcher.* New York: Chelsea House, 1990.

- *In the Adult Library:*

Phelan, Mary Kay. *Probing the Unknown.* New York: Thomas Y. Crowell, 1969.

Consult your librarian for additional titles.

Shark Bait

A story of Eugenie Clark's discovery in 1956 of shark intelligence

☑ **A Point to Ponder: Do you think sharks are smart? As smart as a dog? As smart as a cat?**

Beryl Chadwick shoved the throttles to all stop, and idled the engine. The rumble of twin diesels eased. For the first time in hours he could hear the gentle slap of ocean waves against the hull. Beryl glided the 45-foot trawler alongside the bright red marker buoy before lightly reversing the engines to bring the boat to a full stop.

"We're on station at the first buoy, Dr. Clark," he called down into the main cabin. Beryl scanned the horizon, squinting as he turned west into the early afternoon sun. No other ships in sight and the weather looked good. It was April 1956, not the season for big storms. There would be no problems collecting fish today.

Beryl Chadwick had just been hired by the Cape Hays Marine Laboratory to assist Dr. Eugenie Clark in her collection and cataloging of fish species native to Florida and the Caribbean area. This was his first collection trip and he wanted everything to roll along without a hitch.

Then his eyes widened in disbelief. His face, darkly tanned and leathery from years of exposure to wind, salt spray, and Florida sun, paled. Eugenie Clark walked onto the rear deck wearing a scuba-diving suit. "I don't like the look of this," thought Beryl. "She must be crazy."

He leapt down from the flying bridge and landed, "thunk!" behind Eugenie as she checked the air pressure on her tanks and adjusted her weight belt. "Oh, no, no, no, Dr. Clark. You don't want to dive here. These are shark-infested waters!"

Eugenie Clark laughed and tucked her shoulder-length brown hair under her neoprene diving hood. "Of course they are, Beryl. That's why we're here."

"But Dr. Clark!" he protested. "We might have already caught a shark on one of those hooks down there." He pointed with his thumb over the side of the lab's boat.

Dr. Clark, Genie to everyone who knew her, just nodded. "Better have. I need three new live specimens for Dr. Gilbert at Cornell."

This was not going at all well, thought Beryl. It was bad enough that his first trip for the lab was a shark-collecting expedition. It was unthinkable to him that anyone, *especially* a woman, would want to dive with the sharks. Beryl had been a fishing boat captain and local fishing expert for over 30 years. He knew the waters. He knew the fish. And he knew the sharks.

Above all else, he knew this was a very bad idea. After all, how would it look if he had to report to the lab that his boss had been eaten by sharks on his very first trip?

He tried again. "But Dr. Clark, those are *big* hooks. It might have gouged the shark. It could be bleeding. 'When there is blood in the water, don't dive.' It's an old—and very wise—local saying."

Genie broke into a wide, friendly smile, and patted Beryl's shoulder as she hoisted her tanks. "The very reason I have to dive down there is because the shark might be hurt and bleeding. I have to protect it."

"But what will you *do* down there?" demanded Beryl, turning angry at this seemingly senseless, stubborn woman.

Genie Clark held up a pressurized can, like an aerosol spray can. "I'm going to spray some of this MS-222 down its throat. It knocks a shark unconscious and makes it much easier to bring in."

Beryl's face wrinkled up with fear. "You're going to reach out right next to its jaws and spray that stuff down its throat? Oh, no, no, no! This is a *very bad idea!*"

"Just remember the signals on the line," directed Genie as she adjusted her face mask and dropped into the warm, blue waters off the Florida Keys.

As the sun dipped below the western horizon like a shimmering red ball, Eugenie and Beryl were back on the cement walkway surrounding the Cape Hays Marine Lab shark pen. The lemon shark they had caught that afternoon wallowed drunkenly back and forth, trying to shake off the effects of Eugenie's well-aimed dose of MS-222.

"She'll pull through," said Genie with a satisfied nod. "I think I'll name her Rosie." Rosie would be the fourth lemon shark in the pen.

Beryl Chadwick gruffly crossed his arms tightly across his chest, still angry at what he thought was an unnecessary and dangerous dive that afternoon. "You shouldn't have gone in the water with vicious, senseless killers."

Genie paused to think hard about Beryl's comment. "They *can* be killers. But are they really senseless?"

"Oh, yes," he reassured her. "Sharks act only on primal instinct."

"I wonder . . ." said Genie, realizing that no one had ever bothered to challenge that popular belief and test shark intelligence. "I wonder . . ."

Genie Clark's mind raced through the many shark studies she had read. They all dealt with shark behavior. No one had ever thought to test shark intelligence, or to find out whether sharks were capable of learning. "Beryl," she said. "It is high time we tested your theory."

But how could she test a shark's intelligence, or learning ability? She couldn't ask sharks to take a test, or answer questions. So Genie studied as many animal intelligence studies as she could find, from graduate student projects with rat mazes to the Russian Doctor Pavlov's famous studies using dogs.

Genie decided that if Pavlov could test a dog's learning ability, she could test her lemon sharks the same way. Genie attached a piece of food to a bright white wooden target. When one of the sharks came for the food, it had to bump the target with its nose in order to get its mouth on the food and pull it free. This bump set off a bell. Once one shark took some food, Genie quickly reloaded her target with a fresh piece.

Time and time again, as the four lemon sharks drifted in lazy circles, one would veer off and rush at the target for its tasty reward. "Clang!" went the bell. First the female Genie named Rosie, then Hazel, then one of the two males, drove at Genie's white board. "Clang! Clang!"

Now, were the sharks learning to associate the clanging bell with food, or just sensing the food anew each time? Genie Clark moved the reward a few feet to one side of her target board and put it behind a sturdy iron mesh fence. Either she or Beryl would lift the fence if one of the sharks set off the target bell.

At first the sharks hungrily attacked the iron fence, bashing long dents into it, twisting and bending individual bars. But none of the lemon sharks could break through to the food behind. Then Hazel seemed to give up and to glide slowly out to the middle of their pen. She hesitated, as if thinking. Up on the walkway Genie Clark actually held her breath. Would Hazel figure it out?

Yes! She drove straight at the target. "Clang!" Genie raised a section of the fence and Hazel swam off with a large hunk of tuna. An amazed Beryl Chadwick slowly shook his head. "I would have bet a thousand to one a shark could *never* have thought of ringing the bell. Maybe they're not so senseless after all."

Rosie was the second shark to figure out that only by hitting the target would she be able to reach the food. "Clang!" Genie actually cheered before she entered careful notes in her journal.

Genie now wondered how far she could get her sharks to go with their learned behavior. For two days she slowly inched the iron fence and reward farther and farther from the white target. None of the four sharks cared. "Clang!" They had learned exactly what to do and nosed into the target every time before turning to rush for their reward.

Within two weeks, the sharks had learned to ring the bell and then swim all the way across their pen to wait for a treat thrown in by one of the staff biologists. "It's amazing," said the lab director. "Remarkable work," said marine biologists all over the world. "I still can't believe it," groused Beryl Chadwick.

But Eugenie Clark still worried about her results. Had the sharks merely memorized a pattern of movements, or did they really understand the individual steps as a necessary sequence of deliberate actions? How would she ever tell?

On a bright afternoon three days later, Rosie gave Genie her answer. Paul, one of the males, drove in hard at the target for a snack. He slammed viciously into the target board. The bell clanged wildly. Paul's hit was so hard, it knocked the bell cord loose from the target. But no one noticed until Rosie glided over and nosed the target for a treat of her own. No bell. Rosie turned to streak across the pen for her reward. Then she pulled up. Something was wrong. She hadn't heard the familiar bell. She spun around and nosed the target again. Still no bell.

Rosie hovered there before the target board for a few seconds before ramming it again with her nose. Genie rushed over and clanged the bell by hand. Satisfied by the familiar sound, Rosie swam off for her reward.

Eugenie Clark was ecstatically happy! The sharks *did* understand. They *were* intelligent, every bit as intelligent as many of the smarter land animals. They could learn complex actions and really understand what they were doing. Rosie's insistence on ringing the bell before expecting a treat proved it.

Beryl slowly shook his head in awe. "I guess maybe they are pretty smart. But they're still vicious killers."

Eugenie Clark just laughed on that clear, May afternoon and entered detailed notes in her experiment journal. Those notes not only revolutionized shark research worldwide, but led marine biologists to rethink their basic approach to research on many other oceanic species. But that's another story.

Library Link: Are sharks in captivity dangerous?
How do sharks find their prey?

Topics to Explore: Biology, scientific method, ichthyology, sharks, Eugenie Clark.

References for Further Reading:

- *In the Children's Library:*

Emberlin, Diane.—*Contributions of Women—Science*. Minneapolis, Minn.: Dillion Press, Inc., 1977.

- *In the Adult Library:*

Clark, Eugenie. *Lady with a Spear*. New York: Harpers Publishing Co., 1953.

McGovern, Ann. *Shark Lady: True Adventures of Eugenie Clark*. New York: Four Winds Press, 1978.

Consult your librarian for additional titles.

Biology—Heredity

Green Pea, Yellow Pea

A story of Gregor Mendel's discovery of dominant and recessive genes in 1865

☑ **A Point to Ponder: After all the centuries that people have been living and reproducing and mixing on this planet, why don't all people look alike? Why don't you look just like your parents?**

On a bright, spring morning in early May of 1865, the Bishop of Prague's open-top carriage pulled leisurely up the dirt road to the main gate of the Austrian Monastery of Bruun. The Abbot and his monks were eagerly assembled to meet this high dignitary. It was a rare opportunity for the monastery to show its efforts and to promote its programs to the Church hierarchy for more support and funding.

By midafternoon, the bishop's tour of the monastery led him to the gardens and fields, including the small plot used by Father Gregor Mendel, for his experiments on heredity.

Strolling beside the neat rows of pea plants in the bright, soothing sun, the bishop smiled. "Ah, peas for dinner, I see."

"Oh, no, Your Grace!" exclaimed the plump monk, Gregor Mendel, nervously wiping his small round glasses. "No one eats these peas. They're my experiment in heredity, that is, a study of how individual traits are blended from an individual through successive generations into a population."

"Pity," mused the bishop, and then added, "Heredity experiment, you say? I thought that English fellow Darwin settled all that."

As the bishop rocked back and forth, hands clasped behind his back, his face turned to soak in the sunshine, Mendel patiently explained that Darwin's work had, indeed, explained much about evolution. But it hadn't successfully addressed how characteristics are passed down through the generations, some to dominate in every generation, some to pop up seemingly at random every now and then. Why and how did this happen? That was what Mendel wanted to study.

"Yes, I see," droned the bishop. "And how does it happen?"

Mendel shrugged his shoulders and turned his eyes to the rows of plants just beginning to stretch their vines up and around the supporting trellises. "The answer, Your Grace, is somewhere in my new crop of peas."

Continuing on his official tour, the bishop grunted over his shoulder. "Peas. Such an odd place to look for heredity."

On a hazy August day that same year, Church business brought the bishop back to Bruun. Near the end of his stay at the monastery, he found Gregor Mendel diligently weeding in his garden plot. "Ah, Father Mendel," he smiled. "Have your peas whispered any secrets to you this summer?"

Mendel bristled at the sarcastic tone of the bishop's voice. But he said only, "I will show you, Your Grace."

Pointing at a row of tall, straight pea plants Mendel said, "I crossed a strain of tall pea plants with one of short pea plants. What do you think I got?"

The bishop maintained his thoroughly bored pose. "Medium-size plants, I suppose."

"Wrong!" corrected Mendel eagerly. "I got all tall plants. And when I planted the seeds of those tall plants what do you think I got next?"

The bishop waved his hand in a dismissive, careless way. "More tall plants, I suppose." Then he added, "This really isn't very interesting work, Father Mendel."

"Wrong!" shouted Mendel triumphantly. "I got mostly tall with a few short plants. The short trait returned in the second generation."

"Really?" asked the bishop, somewhat interested in spite of himself. "How many short ones did you get?"

But Mendel was already pointing at the next row and the next demonstration. "And now guess what happened when I crossbred yellow peas with green peas?"

"Yellow-green peas, I suppose," answered the bishop.

"Wrong!" exclaimed Mendel. "I got all yellow peas. But in the next generation I got mostly yellow with a few green peas. But never a yellow-green. The traits don't mix."

"Really? Never?" The bishop was fascinated. "And how many green peas do you get?"

"How many, Your Grace? Well, let me see." Mendel adjusted his glasses and flipped through the pages and careful notes of his ledger. "Why it's exactly three yellow peas to one green."

"Ah," answered the bishop, nodding his head. "And which one tastes better? That is the point, I assume: to produce a tastier pea?"

But Mendel was lost in the pages of his ledger. "Yes! In the second generation there were also three tall plants to every short one. Three to one again . . ."

"Really? Both the same? Exactly three to one?" asked the bishop with considerable alarm, finally finding something in Mendel's work more important than dinner. "That would seem to defy the very laws of nature."

The mathematician's wheels were spinning inside Gregor's head as he flipped through the notebook records of his plants. "Yes, here again. Three smooth-skinned peas to one wrinkled-skin pea in the second generation . . . Always three to one . . . But why? Why always the same?"

That night, pacing his small room, the answer came to Gregor Mendel. Six year's work in his garden plot crystallized in his mind into one simple mathematical principle. "How odd," he thought. "It took six years to uncover the obvious. Three to one. It doesn't defy nature. It defines nature!"

For each characteristic, he knew, a plant inherited one gene from each parent plant. But what if, in each pairing of traits, one trait were always stronger, or dominant, and one always weaker, or recessive? Then, when the traits mixed, a first-generation plant would always show the dominant one.

But three to one. That happened in the second generation. Mendel realized simple mathematical probability said there could be four possible combinations of traits given to a second-generation plant: dominant-dominant, dominant-recessive, recessive-dominant, or recessive-recessive. Three of those combinations had at least one dominant gene, and that would be the trait the plant would exhibit. Only one combination had nothing but the recessive genes, which would allow the recessive trait to show. Three to one.

Peas, mathematics, and a seventh year of testing in the garden gave Gregor Mendel his answer. Traits do not mix. They are inherited from generation to generation and appear only when they are dominant in an individual organism. Traits from countless ancestors flow in each of us through our genes, unblended for us to pass on, even if the traits don't show in our generation.

In the fall of 1866, Gregor Mendel presented his findings to the Bruun Society for Natural Studies. "Inherited traits follow simple mathematical laws, either dominating or recessing in any given generation according to simple mathematical probabilities," he told them, expecting the light of understanding to fire in their eyes.

He got only blank stares. "Father Mendel, mathematics and botany have absolutely nothing to do with each other. What, in Heaven's name, are you talking about?"

No amount of explaining and lecturing made Mendel's generation understand. It was not for 34 years that the Dutch scientist, Hugo de Vries, in 1900, realized Mendel's great gift to the world with his insights on heredity. But that is another story.

Library Link: Why do geneticists study plants, when we really want to know about heredity in humans?

Topics to Explore: biology, botany, heredity, Gregor Mendel, scientific method, observation.

References for Further Reading:

- *In the Children's Library:*

Sootin, Harry. *Gregor Mendel: Father of the Science of Genetics.* New York: Vanguard, 1959.

Webster, Gary. *The Man Who Found Out Why.* New York: Hawthorne, 1963.

- *In the Adult Library:*

George, Wilma. *Gregor Mendel and Heredity.* Wayland, England: Howe Publishers, 1975.

Olby, Robert. *Origins of Mendelism.* New York: Schocken Books, 1966.

Consult your librarian for additional titles.

The Fly Room

A story of T. H. Morgan's discoveries in the field of heredity in 1910

☑ **A Point to Ponder: What is a mutation? Have you ever heard of something being a mutant, or mutated form?**

Three old ceiling fans fought to move enough air around the stifling lecture hall to make the late September day bearable. Flies lazily buzzed from desk to desk, from notebook to notebook. Few of the students in the packed room had enough energy to shoo them away.

It was a cruel, late-summer New York heat wave in 1910. Just when eager students at Columbia University should be diving into their new classes, the heat had sapped any interest beyond seeking the cool shade of a tree and praying for a hint of breeze.

The biology lectures of T. H. Morgan, the 44-year-old, lanky Kentuckian with a great booming voice and the permanent scowl of a skeptic, didn't help any. He was famous for putting as little energy into his teaching as possible. All his energy and time he saved for his research.

The subject of this class was how different species evolved, changed, and adapted over long centuries. It was an important concept for all biology students to learn. Morgan paced and droned on. His deep, monotonous voice seemed to blend perfectly with the buzzing of flies. In the heat, precious few of the students were really listening.

"Professor Morgan. Isn't evolution really a matter of survival of the fittest?" asked one student hoping for a simple, straightforward answer.

"What? Survival of the fittest?" Morgan stopped in midstride, surprised by the interruption. In truth, his mind was also far from the lecture hall. As his mouth rambled on about the flaws in existing theories of evolution, Morgan's mind was on his latest experiment, commonly called "The Fly Room."

T. H. Morgan scowled and boomed out in his deepest, most intimidating voice, "Put a plate of various bacteria on the table. If there is food, they all eat and multiply. When the food is gone, they all die. Where is the survival? Where's the fittest?"

A second student bravely came to the aid of his friend. "But Professor Morgan, didn't Gregor Mendel prove that all changes in any species—peas, porcupines, or people—are controlled by genes passed on from one generation to the next?"

Morgan scoffed and glared at the poor student, who began to sweat under his fierce gaze. "Have *you* seen a gene? Do you know anyone who *has* seen a gene? No, you don't. Because no one ever has. Therefore, I don't believe they exist. If Mendel's genes existed, why wouldn't you look just like your parents, from whom you got all your genes? Genes are a convenient myth to explain what fools do not understand. If you can't see it or demonstrate it in the lab, don't ever believe it. Remember, ideas are a dime a dozen."

A third student joined in, thinking Morgan was at least more interesting and entertaining when agitated by persistent student questions. "Then how *do* species change and evolve, Professor Morgan?"

"Mutation! Random *mutation!*" Morgan's voice echoed off the overheated plaster walls, causing two napping students to bolt straight up, tumbling notebooks and pens noisily to the floor. "If you had read the chapter on De Vries's work with primroses you'd know that! Class dismissed." And Morgan stomped out of the hall even though there were twenty minutes left in the period.

An hour later, Morgan climbed to the second floor of the Columbia University Biology Building and down the long corridor to the door marked "The Fly Room."

Morgan's Fly Room laboratory was a small, messy room with the overpowering reek of rotting bananas. Two walls of the room were lined floor to ceiling with rows of corked glass milk bottles containing hundreds of thousands of tiny fruit flies. Swarms of escaped flies, cockroaches, and mice scurried between hanging bunches of bananas. The constant buzz of countless flies was hard to talk over.

Morgan's two hardworking assistants, cocky but quick and accurate Calvin Bridges, and the quieter, steady Alfred Sturtevant, were bent over microscopes along the lab's back wall.

"When you have classes of your own, always neglect your teaching, boys," bellowed Morgan as he threw open the door. "Research is more important and your lectures will be boring anyway, just like mine."

Morgan peered over the young men's shoulders as they painstakingly examined fly after fly in the newest generation. "Any luck?" asked Morgan, hoping against hope that at long last they would have found one of the random mutations he was searching for.

T. H. Morgan had decided long ago to dig to the bottom of the evolutionary process. Believing the answer lay in a long series of random mutations, Morgan set up a lab to identify mutations and then follow their effect over many generations of a species.

He chose fruit flies to study for three reasons. First, they were only one-quarter inch long. Second, they lived their whole life very happily on nothing but mashed banana. And third, they created a new generation in less than two weeks. Morgan could study almost 30 generations a year.

For two disappointing years, generation after generation had been carefully tracked with no mutations at all. It had been a mind-numbing effort for Morgan and his assistants. Each month, thousands of new fruit flies had to be carefully examined under the microscope for mutations, one by one.

Morgan sighed and turned back to gaze at several milk bottles housing the newest generation. Suddenly Calvin Bridges gasped and slid back his chair. White-faced, he bolted to his feet. He was almost too excited to speak, his voice a tiny squeak. "Found one."

An electric shock sizzled through Morgan. He spun around with his boomingest voice. "*What?*"

After looking at 25,000 normal fruit flies, it was all Bridges could say. "Found one."

In two long strides, Morgan was across the room and had his eye glued to the microscope. And there it was. A male fruit fly with clear, white eyes instead of the normal deep red. They had found a mutation at last!

But would this mutation spread into future generations to change and evolve the fruit fly species as Morgan believed it would?

The white-eyed male was carefully segregated into its own bottle and mated with a normal red-eyed female. Now Morgan had to suffer through two long weeks of waiting for a new generation.

The September heat wave finally broke. October rolled in cool and wet. Morgan's lectures continued to bore his students. But Morgan didn't care. His mind was on the Fly Room. Finally the call came to his office from Calvin Bridges. The next generation had hatched.

Morgan rushed up to the second floor. All Morgan's hopes and beliefs rode on the color of these flies' eyes. If they were white, off-white, or even rose-colored, as he was sure they would be, then the random mutation Bridges found would have changed and evolved the species. That was the theory of evolution De Vries presented. That was the theory Morgan believed.

It took three days to examine the 1,237 new flies. Each and every one had normal red eyes.

T. H. Morgan was crushed. The mutation hadn't held. It had disappeared. It hadn't affected the species at all. Morgan was wrong.

By October 20, with fall colors still blazing across the Columbia University campus, the second generation, the grandchildren of the original white-eyed male, were hatched. There were over 4,000 flies in this generation to be counted. When Morgan saw the results, his face paled and his knees turned rubbery. White-eyed flies were back. There were almost exactly three normal, red-eyed flies to each white-eyed fly.

Three to one. That was Mendel's ratio for the interaction of a dominant and a recessive trait. T. H. Morgan's own experiment had just proved himself wrong and Mendel's gene theory right!

Over the next two years, more than 300,000 fruit flies were examined in the Fly Room. Morgan found that Mendel's theory of genes and the traits they carried consistently predicted the way characteristics appeared in each generation.

Genes *did* exist, just as Gregor Mendel had claimed 40 years before. In trying to disprove the gene theory in his messy, smelly Fly Room, T. H. Morgan actually proved it to be true. But what he did with 200 pounds of leftover, mashed bananas is another story.

Library Link: How would you examine 1,000 tiny flies?
Name as many traits we inherit through genes as you can.

Topics to Explore: biology, experimental process, scientific method, T. H. Morgan, genes, heredity, evolution.

References for Further Reading:

- *In the Children's Library:*

Edey, Maitland, and Donald Johanson. *Blueprints: Solving the Mystery of Evolution.* New York: Penguin Books, 1986.

- *In the Adult Library:*

Sturtevant, A. H. *Thomas Hunt Morgan.* Washington, D.C.: National Academy of Sciences, 1959.

Consult your librarian for additional titles.

What the Mold Told

The story of George Beadle's discovery of the function of genes in 1934

☑ **A Point to Ponder: Make a list of the differences between you and the others in your class. Now make a list of ways in which you are all the same. Where do your differences come from? Why aren't we all the same?**

Mrs. Lillian Fremont slowly worked her way down the long corridor of laboratories on the third floor of the University of Chicago's Chemistry Building. Before her, she pushed a small, squeaking cart loaded with rags, brooms, a mop, and a large bucket of ammonia water. Her rich, gray hair framed a round, pleasant face as she puffed from lab to lab, giving them each a good cleaning.

This was Mrs. Fremont's first Saturday cleaning the Chemistry Building after six years of cleaning the Math Building. She would rather still be in the Math Building, but with the Great Depression still on, she was glad to have any job at all.

As she entered one of the large labs near the end of the hall, she found 35-year-old Dr. George Beadle hunched over a lab table intently reading a thick book.

"Oh, sorry to bother you," smiled Mrs. Fremont. "I'm the new custodian. I'll just sweep up and, empty the wastebaskets. Oh, and I'll clean out those filthy, moldy test tubes for you."

George Beadle's head snapped up. "Don't you *dare* touch those test tubes!" he bellowed. Then, realizing how harsh he must have sounded, he apologized. "I'm sorry I snapped at you. But I am growing the mold in these test tubes for an important experiment."

Lillian's mouth dropped open in surprise. "You grow mold *on purpose*? I mean, that's actually part of your job?"

"It is part of an important experiment on heredity," he said defensively.

Lillian Fremont slowly shook her head in amazement. "Science professors. They get paid to grow what the university pays me to get rid of!"

George Beadle laughed, glanced down at the cleaning woman's name tag, and flipped his book shut. "All right, Mrs. Fremont . . ."

"Call me Lilly," she grinned and stuck out her hand to shake.

"All right, Lilly. Let me explain what we're doing here." He paused for a moment to decide where to begin. "The question is: 'How do genes work?' "

Lilly frowned and thoughtfully thumbed along her feather duster. "My boy has jeans. What's to know besides you zip them up?"

"Not jeans you wear," corrected Beadle. "These genes are tiny codes built into the cells of every living organism that determine what that organism is. Genes direct every cell and organ in the body and tell them how to look, act, function, grow, and change. We know that all of our physical traits, like height, color of hair, and every characteristic that makes each of us unique, are passed from generation to generation through our genes. But we don't know *how* they do it. And that's the thing we need to figure out before we can fully understand the human body and fight hereditary diseases. Are you with me so far?"

The foggy look on Mrs. Fremont's face told George she didn't. "Okay, look at it this way. Genes are like the blueprints of a house; they are the plans. The body is the house. What we are trying to discover is how written blueprints become a finished house. How do the coded signals in genes direct growing cells to become arms, or organs, or fingers? How do genes tell one human body to create brown eyes, straight teeth, and black hair that will fall out at an early age; and tell something very different to another body?"

A light slowly dawned in Mrs. Fremont's eyes. "I see what you're after. But if you want to learn about heredity, why not look at people? That's where heredity is."

"People are too complex," answered George. "They have too many genes and very complicated systems. We get hopelessly lost. We have to start with much simpler organisms untilwe understand how genes do what they do, then we can begin applying that knowledge to more complicated organisms. For example, I started out by growing and studying flies . . ."

Lilly interrupted, "You grew flies? On *purpose?*"

"Yes," he answered, "for four years in Paris."

Lilly chuckled and shook her head. "Science professors. You never know what crazy thing they'll do next."

Beadle was becoming irritated. "Fruit flies are an excellent way to study heredity. But even they are too complex for *this* experiment. We needed to find a life form that's incredibly simple, with so few genes that we can see how individual genes work and what they do." Then he smiled and gestured to the many rows of moldy test tubes. "And here, I think we have found just the organism. The bread mold in those test tubes."

Lilly was surprised "Bread mold? You mean that nasty mold that spoils my loaves of bread in the summer?"

"That's the stuff," answered George. "And I hope the mold in these test tubes will tell us how genes work."

Again Lilly Fremont laughed and slowly shook her head. "How's a moldy test tube going to tell you that? Only thing they tell me is that it's time to clean!"

Smugly, Beadle folded his arms and leaned back in his chair. "Good question, Lilly. And in the design of this experiment we finally have an answer. You see, this bread mold has only four genes, and they are all essential to its basic survival, to its reproduction and the processing of basic nutrients to survive. We'll use X-rays to alter, or mutate, a gene in this mold and then see what ability, or talent, the mold loses or gains. That, we hope, will tell us how individual genes direct any living cell."

Lilly shook her head hard as if to clear her senses of this clutter of mind-boggling concepts, and shuffled to the door. "Science professors sure have funny ways of spending a weekend."

"We should be more respectful of lowly molds," George called after her. "Molds have only four genes. We have millions. Still they can all do something we can't. They can take the basic chemicals of the earth and *create* vitamins. You have to get your vitamins from oranges and other foods."

He heard her chuckle from the hallway, "Science professors. Who else could find a reason to be jealous of a mold?"

By noon, Edward Tatum, George Beadle's partner, arrived at the lab. "Everything ready, George?"

George nodded. "Ready and waiting."

While other heredity researchers had always tried to determine how traits are passed from generation to generation, Beadle and Tatum designed their experiment to find out how genes actually direct the body to grow and change.

Their experiment seemed simple enough. First they had to grow small batches of bread mold in each test tube. That part was done. Next they had to create a change, or what scientists call *mutations,* in one gene of the living bread mold. Finally, they would try to see how the genes of the mutated bread mold acted different than those of normal mold. That, they hoped, would tell them how all genes work.

It sounded simple. But no one had ever worked with bread mold. Beadle and Tatum weren't even sure they could force the bread mold genes to mutate. To be safe, they prepared 1,000 test tubes, each with a starting colony of mold spores and an ample supply of food.

Today they were going to blast all 1,000 tubes with high-energy X-rays in the hope that the genes would mutate.

One at a time, George placed square trays of 100 test tubes each on a counter under the X-ray machine's long focusing lens. Then he leaned back to avoid the rays, and called, "Tray one, all clear."

Edward stood by the switch, stopwatch in hand, notepaper before him. "Tray number one," he repeated and turned on the X-ray machine and stopwatch. Inside the machine a cathode ray tube (CRT) flashed bright blue-green. Fan motors hummed.

After a brief time, Edward stopped the machine and the stopwatch simultaneously. "Number one's done."

They exposed each tray for a different amount of time, ranging from a few seconds, to a full minute. They just weren't sure what X-rays would do to the mold.

Now to wait and see if they had had an effect. George went back to his book, but Edward paced back and forth like an expectant father. Every few minutes he'd stop and peer anxiously at the long rows of test tubes.

"It won't help to stare at the test tubes, Edward," said Beadle. "A watched pot never boils, and that mold will take five or six hours to grow."

Edward groaned and went back to his pacing. Finally, with a deep sigh, he gave up and went out for an early dinner. When he returned at 7:00 in the evening, the two men began a careful inspection of all 1,000 test tubes. A normal, light, reddish-blue bread mold fuzz was happily growing in each of the test tubes, just as if they hadn't been zapped with X-rays at all.

That is, in all but one tube. In tube number 299 no mold was growing. But why not? This tube started with the same mold spores and food supply as all the others. Why was it different?

Eagerly George and Edward carried test tube 299 to their microscope to make sure the original mold colony was still alive. It was quite alive and patiently waiting for a food supply it could grow on. Both men knew something important had happened inside that test tube. In number 299 the mold had mutated. For some reason, it could no longer grow on the food it used to love.

Here was the key to their experiment. This mold could no longer grow on its own. It could no longer process, or eat, the food supply normal mold could. Why not? One of its genes had mutated. Because of that mutation, the mold could no longer convert basic nutrients into the chemical compounds it needed. In a similar way, our digestive systems convert the food we eat into the chemical compounds our cells need. If our digestive systems changed and created different compounds, or if they were suddenly unable to perform that conversion at all, our cells would starve.

This mutated mold needed extra help in processing food. But what kind of help?

The scientists quickly broke the mutated mold sample into individual spores and placed each in a different test tube with a normal supply of food. Then they added a different amino acid enzyme to each test tube, to see if this was the help the mutated cells needed to process the available food.

Now they had to wait again. George went back to his book. Edward went out for coffee.

By 2:00 in the morning, Beadle and Tatum both stared excitedly at a happy and healthy crop of reddish-blue mold fuzz growing in one of the new test tubes. This was the test tube to which they had added an amino acid enzyme that controls the production of vitamin B6. Before being X-rayed, the mold could produce B6 on its own and grow successfully. After the mutation, it had lost the ability to make vitamin B6. Beadle and Tatum had to add an amino acid enzyme to direct the mold's production of vitamin B6. Before it had been mutated, the mold's gene must have provided that enzyme.

Mrs. Lillian Fremont probably wouldn't have been impressed with a little bread mold growing in one test tube, and would have muttered something about science professors. But the two weary scientists had the answer they sought. Genes produce enzymes. These amino acid enzymes direct a body's cells to do what they are designed to do. They had proved it by mutating a gene in a simple mold and discovering that what the gene was no longer able to do was produce an enzyme. Genes must direct and control body functions by producing different enzymes for each function. That's how genes controlled body activity. Beadle and Tatum had found their answer.

As is true with most research, one answer leads straight to at least two new questions. That was certainly true of George Beadle and Edward Tatum's Nobel Prize winning experiment. The questions that grew out of their answer opened the door into a whole new field of research: biochemistry. But that is another story.

Library Link: What is mold? Where does it come from, and how does it grow?

Topics to Explore: biological science, experimental process, scientific method, George Beadle, Edward Tatum, heredity, genes, molds.

References for Further Reading:

- *In the Children's Library:*

Edey, Maitland, and Donald Johanson. *Blueprints: Solving the Mystery of Evolution.* New York: Penguin Books, 1986.

- *In the Adult Library:*

Davern, Cedric. *Genetics: Readings from Scientific American.* San Francisco, Calif.: W. H. Freeman, 1981.

Consult your librarian for additional titles.

Jumping Genes

A story of Barbara McClintock's discoveries about the function of genes in 1950

☑ **A Point to Ponder: Do new technologies, new developments in equipment design, and new research methods always make for better science?**

When they named the place Cold Spring Harbor, they named it right. Biting winds whistled off Long Island Sound, New York, even as far into spring as late April. Marcus Rhoades pulled his jacket tight around his neck and wished he'd brought a heavy coat as he stepped from his rental car. The chill wind sliced straight through to his bones.

Marcus folded the map that had led him out to this isolated spot on northeastern Long Island and shaded his eyes from the glaring sun. Off to the left, beyond the gate and fence, tucked in between the trees and waving coastal grasses, he spotted the small cornfield he sought.

With hands jammed down deep into his pockets for warmth on this afternoon in 1950, Marcus Rhoades jogged under the "Carnegie Institute Cold Springs Harbor Research Facility" sign and headed through the gate, into the wind, and toward the corn.

Marcus stopped at the edge of the plot, watching the lone woman carefully planting corn seeds by hand, row after row. Barbara McClintock, a 90-pound, self-confident, frustratingly independent scientist was one of Marcus Rhoades's former professors. The locals in Cold Spring Harbor called her "odd" and a "loner." Scientific contemporaries of the 48-year-old genetic researcher called her a "relic of the old ways." Marcus Rhoades called her "friend." He was one of the very few who still did.

This was 1950, and research into the structure, function, and genetic codes of a cell was a bustling world of new technologies such as electron microscopes, X-ray crystallography, and radioisotopes. There was no room for an old-fashioned fool who divided her time between cornfield and ordinary microscope.

Marcus stepped out into the soft dirt, careful to stay between the neatly planted rows, waved, and called Barbara's name. She burst into bright laughter at the sight of her friend and colleague. She wiped the dirt off her knee socks and thin sweater, seemingly immune to the wind's icy spell, and bounded across to greet her former student.

"I had trouble finding you, Barbara. It's as if you dropped off the face of the earth, way out here all alone."

Barbara's eyes twinkled and she laughed a loud, horsey laugh, bending over to slap her knee.

They stood looking across her small field to the choppy waters of Long Island Sound beyond. Marcus asked, "Why *are* you out here?"

Again Barbara laughed. "Marcus, being here in this field is a tremendous joy. The careful process of finding an answer where none existed before—it's just pure joy." Then her face clouded. "Besides, you know perfectly well there are no university professorships for women. Where else could I go?"

Marcus looked at her freshly planted rows. "You've dug around in corn-fields for almost 30 years. Twenty-five years ago you discovered the corn chromosomes for the world to study. What's still to learn from ordinary corn?"

"This isn't ordinary corn," explained McClintock. "It's wild indian corn with the bright blue, brown, and red kernels. It makes studying color heredity easier." Then Barbara grew serious. "Really, we know so little about how heredity really works. Why do some corn kernels turn out blue while others are red? Why do dark mutation spots appear in some generations, and not in others? What really controls how genetic information is passed from generation to generation?"

Now Marcus sounded surprised. "But that's already so well known. First Mendel said it, and then Dr. Morgan at Cornell. Everybody knows genes carry heredity information, are fixed like tiny strings of pearls onto chromosomes, and pass in the same fixed order from generation to generation. Everyone knows that, Barbara."

Barbara just grunted.

Barbara McClintock was known for her humor and mischievous pranks. Marcus began to feel that his leg was being pulled. "What are you saying? Surely you can't disagree with every genetic scientist in the world. They all agree that genes are fixed in place along the chromosomes and never move."

Barbara grunted again.

"Can you really disagree with every scientist in the country?" he asked, eyes wide with wonder. "All right, where's your proof?"

Barbara pointed into her cornfield. "For ten years I've studied each and every plant in this field. I've tracked their color mutations and patterns and changes. Here's what I've found. Genes are not fixed along chromosomes as everyone thinks. They can move. They *do* move. Some genes seem able to direct other genes, telling them where they should go and when they should act. These genes act like genetic directors, controlling the movement and action of other genes."

Marcus Rhoades laughed and shook his head. "Good one, Barbara. You had me going there. That's quite a joke."

"But I'm serious. And I'm right. Everyone else is wrong. Sooner or later, they'll see."

Now Marcus was amazed. "But . . . but that's scientific heresy. How can you refute the best minds and research equipment of the twentieth century using only a microscope?"

Barbara led him back to the two rooms she lived in up over the lab's bright green garage and pointed at two bulging file cabinets. "There's ten years of careful notes, data, and observations. My corn plants don't lie. Genes *do* move along a chromosome. They jump almost randomly from spot to spot, generation to generation. That's why everyone else's research is stalling and falling apart. Look at all the trouble other researchers are running into. They aren't accounting for gene movement."

Marcus Rhoades left just after sunset, still laughing and shaking his head, still convinced this must be a grand Barbara McClintock prank. How could one woman working all alone in a remote cornfield be right and the greatest universities in the country all be wrong?

Late that night, Barbara paced back and forth across her two-room flat, carrying on both sides of an internal debate. "We look at genetic control all wrong. Genes aren't fixed. They move, they jump."

She reached the windows and spun on her heel for another lap across the well-worn rug. "But if I can't even convince Marcus that I'm serious, let alone that I'm right, how can I hope to convince anyone else?"

Reaching the wall next to the file cabinets, she turned back for her next lap. "If I write it compellingly, forcefully, if I make it vivid and impassioned, I'll make them see." Turn. "But am I absolutely sure? Could I be wrong?" Turn. "I've got ten drawers of data. How much surer can I be?" Turn. "Maybe one more year of study. Then I'll write and present my findings at the 1951 symposium." Turn. "Why can no one else see what is so clear to me?" Turn. "Will anyone ever listen to me?" Turn. Turn. Turn.

At the September 1951 national symposium on genetic research, Barbara McClintock nervously presented her carefully documented research, hoping for excited questions and looks of sudden understanding, secretly expecting argument and attack. But, as so often happens with radically new ideas, she got neither. She was simply dismissed by the audience with a bored and indifferent shrug. She was ignored. They simply couldn't understand the implications of what she said.

Still, what she said was exactly right. The 1983 Nobel Prize Committee called Barbara McClintock's pioneering work on how genetic information is controlled, stored, and transmitted "one of the two great discoveries of our time in genetics." Her work has become the basis for a dozen major medical and disease-fighting breakthroughs. But for over twenty years after that first presentation of her research in 1951, the scientific world dismissed and shunned Barbara McClintock as a silly and foolish relic. But how this brave, feisty woman survived those twenty long years is another story.

Library Link: Why did genetic researchers use pea plants, corn plants, and fruit flies to study heredity instead of looking at people?

Topics to Explore: biology, botany, heredity, Barbara McClintock, scientific method, observation.

References for Further Reading:

- *In the Children's Library:*

Keller, Evelyn. *A Feeling for the Organism: The Life and Work of Barbara McClintock.* San Francisco, Calif.: W. H. Freeman, 1983.

- *In the Adult Library:*

Dash, Joan. *The Triumph of Discovery.* New York: Simon & Schuster, 1991.

Consult your librarian for additional titles.

Medical Research

AB or Not AB

A story of Karl Landsteiner's discovery of different human blood types in 1897

☑ **A Point to Ponder: Do you know what blood type you have? Do you know what that blood type designation means?**

A postmortem lab, where medical researchers examine a deceased body to find the cause of death, is always a grisly place. Even now, with all our knowledge and modern facilities, it is a grim place. But it was much worse in 1897. Many thought it was a truly awful place to work.

But life often comes from death. And, at least once, vital, life-giving information came from a postmortem lab.

Vienna, Austria, in 1897, was a busy, glamorous city where opera, symphonies, and theater flourished, where great universities, like the University of Vienna, were as modern as any in the world. But even here, in this shining center of culture, the postmortem lab was a dreary, poorly ventilated, poorly equipped rat trap. The university seemed to try to pretend the lab didn't exist by tucking it away in the far corner of the Medical Center basement.

It was a delightfully warm, early spring day in late April that seemed to draw out every iris, crocus, wildflower, and chirping bird in Vienna. It seemed a shame to waste this day in a dreary, windowless basement, but Dr. Karl Landsteiner sighed, took one last breath of sweet fresh air, and pushed open the double doors leading to the postmortem lab where he worked.

In the lab office, he checked in with the director, Dr. Weichselbaum. Weichselbaum sat, stuffed into his chair behind a small desk sorting through a jumbled pile of government and hospital forms.

As always, Karl Landsteiner walked timidly toward his boss's desk and softly knocked on the wall, as there was no door separating Weichselbaum's desk from the entryway.

The director looked up at the sound of the apologetic knock, still chewing on a monstrous bite of muffin he had crammed into his mouth. "Ah, Landsteiner. You're *finally* here." His words were barely recognizable around the thick wad of food.

Karl's eyes turned down to the floor and his voice was almost too soft to be understood. "Actually, Herr Weichselbaum, I'm ten minutes early."

The director gulped down his bite and gestured at the pile of paperwork in front of him in frustration. "Who cares what time it is? Get busy! We've got six postmortem examinations to do today."

Karl gulped. "Six? All for today?"

"We'll split it," concluded Weichselbaum. "I'll do two, and you only have to do four."

By 2:30 that afternoon, Karl had finished three of his examinations. The cause of death in two of these cases was the same: blood agglutination, or clotting, during surgery. Both patients had received blood transfusions, and both patients died when their own red blood cells clumped together into thick clots with red blood cells in the blood they were given.

Landsteiner had seen this so often during his thousands of examinations of patients who died during, or just after, surgery. Yet it didn't always happen. In most cases, a patient had no problems at all with donated blood. But far too often, there were deadly problems. As Karl finished his fourth patient early that evening, he was still wondering, "Why?"

That night, Karl Landsteiner played piano for his wife and several friends. It was the one thing Karl felt he did well. Most who heard him thought he was so gifted he should give up medicine for a brilliant career as a pianist. Karl always blushed and shook his head.

But in the middle of a familiar piece that night, Karl missed two chords back to back. Karl's face turned red. His friends gasped. His wife winced. When he missed yet another note, his wife asked, "Karl, what's wrong? Don't you feel well?"

Deeply embarrassed, Karl looked down at the keys as he mumbled, "I'm so sorry. It's all my fault. I wasn't concentrating. It's just that it suddenly occurred to me that it must be something in the blood . . ."

"What's in the blood?" asked his wife.

"In whose blood?" asked a friend.

Karl continued apologetically. "I'm sure this is boring for all of you. But I was thinking about how many people die from blood transfusions during surgery. What if different people have different blood? What if all blood is not the same as everyone supposes? What if all those people died because their blood couldn't mix with the blood they were given in surgery?"

"What can this possibly have to do with your piano playing?" asked a friend.

"Did he say someone's bleeding to death?" asked another.

The next morning, Karl Landsteiner summoned up enough courage to ask Dr. Weichselbaum if he could be excused from postmortem duty while he pursued a theory.

"No!" bellowed the director. "Do frivolous experiments on your own time. And get me another muffin on your way into the lab."

It took a week for Karl to secretly collect enough blood from twenty different patients to begin his tests. He wanted to see if he could find a way to predict which blood samples were safe to mix with each other.

Karl waited in the lab late one night until Dr. Weichselbaum left for home. He gathered his blood samples and a large tray of test tubes, and snuck into a back lab where no one would notice the lights. There, he mixed a few drops of the blood he had collected from each patient with a few drops of blood from each other patient in separate test tubes. Before him stood a forest of 380 test tubes, each with a few drops of two different people's blood.

He carried the tray of test tubes to a microscope and checked to see which red blood cells clotted with which others, and which did not. Before he had checked half the test tubes under a microscope, Karl was stunned to find that there was a simple pattern. He could easily divide the blood samples into two distinct groups.

By looking only at one person's blood, he was able to make a group of samples that clotted with it, and a group of samples that didn't. Landsteiner named these groups "A" and "B". The blood from a person of group A could be safely mixed with blood cells from any other person in group A. The blood samples were compatible and would not clot. However, when the blood of any group A person was mixed with the blood of anyone in group B, the red blod cells viewed this new blood as a foreign invader, and attacked it. In Landsteiner's test tube, the red blood cells clotted with each other harmlessly. But when it happened during an operation, the clotting blood killed the patient.

Not all blood was compatible. Different people's blood *was* different!

If a person with type A blood were given type B blood, the red blood cells would clot and kill the patient. However, if the donor was also type A, no problems would arise.

Excitedly, he shared these early findings with two coworkers, Doctors Desactello and Sturli. They instantly saw the value of his work, and offered to help check more samples against his A and B groups.

Within ten minutes, both doctors found blood samples that didn't agglutinate, or clot, with either type A or B red blood cells. Landsteiner's face dropped. The excited luster drained away from his cheeks. His theory didn't work. He must have made a mistake. Dejectedly he sank into a chair.

Then he realized. "No. There must be a *third* group." People in this group could safely donate blood to anyone since their blood wouldn't agglutinate with either A or B. He named this third blood group type "O."

All three doctors were now very excited by their findings. Here was an easy-to-do test of blood type that could save many thousands of lives every year. Then Dr. Sturli found a blood sample that agglutinated with *both* type A and type B blood.

Again Karl Landsteiner was dismayed. His bright smile evaporated. His theory was a flop after all.

"No," cried Sturli. "There must be a *fourth* group, who react to both A and B blood, just as type O blood reacts to neither."

Karl instantly named this fourth group type "AB."

Blood was not all the same. There were four distinct types. Safe mixing of a patient's blood required that a doctor know the blood types of both patient and donor. It seemed like such a simple, obvious idea to Karl that he didn't think he deserved any of the fame and awards heaped upon him. Yet it was an idea no one else had thought of, and it has saved millions of lives.

The day that Karl Landsteiner's results were published, blood transfusions became a much safer part of surgery. A patient's chances of being sent for a postmortem examination in Dr. Landsteiner's windowless, cheerless basement lab were greatly reduced. But how Dr. Karl Landsteiner finally made it out of the postmortem lab, and whether or not he became a concert pianist, are both other stories.

Library Link: What does it mean to have different blood types? How are they different?

Topics to Explore: biology, medical research, scientific method, physiology, Karl Landsteiner, blood types.

References for Further Reading:

- *In the Children's Library:*

Showers, Paul. *A Drop of Blood.* New York: Thomas Y. Crowell, 1989.

White, Anne. *Secrets of Heart and Blood.* Champaign, Ill.: Garrard, 1965.

- *In the Adult Library:*

Race, R. R. *Blood Groups in Man.* Oxford, England: Blackwell Scientific Publishers, 1975.

Consult your librarian for additional titles.

The Sweet Juice of Success

A story of Frederick Banting's discovery of insulin in 1920

☑ **A Point to Ponder: Is it ethical to use animals, or parts of animals, to cure human diseases?**

Frederick Banting slumped gloomily in his squeaky swivel chair and propped his feet on the desk. Bored and depressed, the slight, delicate featured, 28-year-old doctor thumbed through a small stack of medical journals and thoughtfully chewed on the end of a pencil. The sign on his office door read "Doctor and Orthopedic Surgeon." But sitting all alone in his small western Ontario office, Frederick certainly didn't feel like a doctor. Apparently no one else in town thought of him as a doctor either. His practice had been open eight months, and he only had four patients.

But then, he thought, why should people flock to him for care? Because of the start of World War I, his class had been rushed through medical school and into the Canadian army. He had missed one whole year of classes and had had no residency or internship. One day he had been a bewildered medical student. The next, he was a captain in the army, and stationed in Belgium as a front-line doctor.

Then the war ended, and Frederick Banting was discharged. Now, here he sat in 1920 with no real experience, no income, no patients, and, worst of all, absolutely no self-confidence.

There was a knock on his door. Frederick's heart leapt. Could it be a new patient? No, it was just the ten-year-old boy from next door, a redheaded bundle of motion and energy named Billy Harken. Billy held out a paper sack with one hand, and stuck the forefinger of his other hand toward Frederick. "Mother said I should give you this," he nodded toward the sack, "so you'd take out this." He nodded toward his extended forefinger.

Dr. Banting spun around in his chair with a look of total surprise. "Your mother wants me to take off your finger, Billy?"

"Nooo. The splinter."

Frederick sighed. That was the story of his life, nothing more exciting than a splinter. "Okay, Billy. Bring it over under the light."

Billy marched to the desk and plopped down his sack. "The biscuits are fresh today." Then he held out his finger for Banting to examine. Payment in food wasn't quite as good as cash. But it was much better than the IOUs he had gotten from two of his patients recently.

Billy looked at the cluttered books and journals on Banting's desk. "What were you doing when I came in?"

"Studying for the physiology course I teach at the college. Now hold out your finger."

"*What* kind of course?" asked Billy.

"Physiology. That's the study of how the different parts of the body function. Hold your finger still."

Billy hesitated, staring at the needles and knives on Dr. Banting's instrument table. "Why are you studying if you *teach* the course? I wouldn't."

"Because I skipped physiology in med school. You see, we graduated early because of the war, and. . . . Never mind. Just hold your finger still!"

Frederick could sense the boy's fear, and decided to keep Billy's mind off the splinter with more talk. But the only subject that came to his mind was tomorrow's lecture that he had been struggling with all evening. He was convinced many of the sophomores in his class knew more than he did. "Billy, would you like to hear about my class? It's on how the pancreas controls carbohydrate metabolism. *Metabolism* is how our bodies turn starches and sugars into energy."

"Mom says I have too much energy," said Billy with a thoughtful nod. "Maybe I have too much pan grease."

"That's *pancreas*, Billy. Here, I'll show you what it looks like." Banting thumbed through one of his thick textbooks. "There. That's a pancreas." He tapped a finger on the picture of a small, oblong organ lying just behind the stomach. "Now, the important thing about a pancreas is that it has two kinds of cells. Do you know what cells are, Billy?"

As the boy thought, a sly movement by Banting's tweezers had the splinter out without Billy ever feeling it. "Isn't a cell where you keep prisoners?"

"That's not the kind of cell I mean. I'm talking about cells in the body, Billy."

"Oh, yeah!" Billy interrupted. "Our teacher told us about those."

"Now, the outer cells of the pancreas," continued Frederick, "produce strong, acidic digestive juices. But the inner cells . . ."

Billy interrupted again. "Are we ever getting back to met-a-bo-lism?"

"That's metabolism. And we're almost there. The inner pancreatic cells produce a delicate juice that flows straight into the blood. When a muscle needs energy, it gets it from sugars traveling in the bloodstream. *But*," and Banting paused to let the importance of his next statement sink in. "But, a muscle can't pull sugar out of the blood without that juice from the inner cells of the pancreas.

"When the inner cells of the pancreas stop making that juice, the muscles starve and shrink because they can't *metabolize,* or get energy from the blood. The blood becomes overloaded with sugar and struggles to get rid of it through excess urination. This dehydrates the body, and the entire condition makes the person very sick. The disease is called *diabetes*."

"Wow," whispered Billy, wide-eyed. "That sounds awful."

"It is," answered Frederick. "And it's deadly. Today we know of no cure for diabetes. It is always fatal."

Billy stammered. "Why can't you borrow some inner-cell juice from someone else?"

"Ah, if only we could," answered Banting. But he wasn't at all sure why you couldn't grind up the pancreas of an animal and inject its juice into a diabetic human. Similar techniques were used for many other diseases.

After Billy left for home, Banting searched his medical books for an answer. And there it was. Others had had the same idea. But when a pancreas was ground up, the digestive juices from the outer cells destroyed the delicate juice from inner cells before it could be used. It seemed that there was no way to use the pancreas of another animal to cure diabetes. But still, Billy's question haunted Frederick. It would save so much suffering if it could work.

Again depressed, Frederick thumbed back through his stack of journals. One article by Dr. Moses Barron caught his eye. It described the fate of several patients in whom a blockage had developed in the ducts carrying pancreatic outer-cell digestive juices to the stomach. These strong acids had been trapped in the outer cells of the pancreas and had destroyed those cells. The cells had literally shut down and dried up.

Frederick thought it was mildly interesting, nothing more.

An hour later, in that drowsy half-in, half-out state, just before Banting fell asleep, *Wham!* Billy's question hit him again like a sledgehammer. Why not intentionally close the outer-cell ducts on a test animal, destroy those cells, and then retrieve the rest of the pancreas? There should only be inner cells left, and Billy's suggestion might be possible. It seemed worth a try.

Full of hope, fear, and uncertainty, Frederick Banting travelled to see the famous Dr. John MacLeod, who was the head of the Physiology Department at Toronto University. Would this great researcher listen to a proposal from an inexperienced, young doctor who barely knew enough to teach a sophomore physiology course?

No. He would not. MacLeod threw Frederick out, saying, "It's been tried" and "You don't know what you're talking about!" A month later, Frederick asked again, and was tossed out again. In March, having heard that MacLeod would be visiting Scotland for most of the summer, Banting asked once more. Could he please use MacLeod's lab and a few test dogs, just while MacLeod was gone?

The answer this time was, "Alright. *If* you promise to be gone before I return, and to never bother me again!"

In early July, Frederick Banting packed everything he owned into his old Ford truck and drove to Toronto. He now had access to an excellent lab, six dogs, and one lab assistant. He also had only six weeks and less than $50 to work with. Within a week he had spent all $50 on supplies and had been forced to sell his last real possession, his truck, to keep the experiment going.

His plan was simple enough. He would operate on the dogs to tie off the ducts from the pancreatic outer cells to the stomach. Then he would wait eight weeks, which was the time Dr. Barron had mentioned in his article. Finally, in a second operation, he would see if the outer cells had dried up and died, leaving only life-giving inner cells and their precious juice in each dog's pancreas.

With dread, Banting read that several famous European physiologists had tried exactly the same procedure. All had failed. Banting's old depression sank back in. How could he, an inexperienced orthopedic surgeon, hope to succeed when the best Europe had to offer had failed? Was he fooling himself and wasting his career? The only force that kept him going was the echo of young Billy Harken's innocent question, "Why can't you borrow some inner-cell juice from someone else?"

The surgery was simple enough. Now Banting had to wait and watch. Late in the first week, he realized he had two big problems. First, he wasn't sure how to tell if the experiment worked. Second, he didn't have eight weeks to wait. He had only six before MacLeod returned.

Banting stewed over both these problems as week one rolled into week two and then into week three. Frederick and his young assistant, Charles Best, decided the only way to test their success was to give one of the dogs diabetes and see if the juice from the others would keep the diabetic dog alive.

Early in week six, the sick dog slid into a common diabetic coma. This was the last stage before death. Banting couldn't wait any longer. He operated on one of the other dogs, successfully removing its pancreas. He ground up this tissue and extracted the juice by dissolving it in a chloride solution.

But had he waited long enough? Would there still be enough digestive acid to destroy the inner-cell juice? More practically, how much juice should he give to the diabetic dog? Banting and Best started by injecting only a small amount into the dog. Within 30 minutes, the dog woke from its coma. Within two hours, it was back on its feet. In five hours, the dog began to deteriorate again. With another injection, it perked up enough to bark and wag its tail.

Frederick was ecstatic. Somehow, it had worked! His hunch had been right! He *could* save thousands of diabetics. But why? What had made *him* successful? He could think of no reason why his experiment had worked when those of other, more qualified scientists had failed.

Eight months of careful research went into unlocking a simple answer. The lucky magic of Banting's experiment was that he didn't wait too long. In eight weeks, both outer and inner pancreatic cells died. By waiting only six weeks, only the outer cells had dried up. Inner cells still functioned, and Banting had succeeded where others had failed.

But many more tests were needed to solidify the research and to find sources of pancreatic juice that wouldn't sacrifice lab dogs. Banting still had much to do.

Dr. John MacLeod was four weeks late returning from Scotland. In amazement, he found Frederick Banting, eight bustling lab assistants, ten diabetic test dogs, six large notebooks jammed with test results, and three extra rooms used for testing new sources of pancreatic juice. MacLeod stumbled from room to room, slack-jawed, unable to believe his eyes.

Finally, Dr. MacLeod recovered his gruff composure. He snarled and grumbled about Frederick Banting still being in his lab. He groused about the mess. But, grudgingly, he also had to admit that unsure Frederick Banting, who had staked every penny he had in the world on his experiment, had done some remarkable work.

It was John MacLeod who named the juice "insulin," as he and Dr. Banting searched for a way to create this precious juice without harming any more lab dogs. But how that was done is another story.

Library Link: Are there other well-known human diseases treated with tissues extracted from animals?

Topics to Explore: biological science, medical research, chemical research, scientific method, physiology, Frederick Banting, insulin.

References for Further Reading:

- *In the Children's Library:*

Fox, Ruth. *Milestones in Medicine.* New York: Random House, 1985.

- *In the Adult Library:*

Levine, I. E. *Discoverer of Insulin, Dr. Frederick Banting.* New York: Messner, Inc., 1959.

Consult your librarian for additional titles.

Miracle Mold

A story of Alexander Fleming's discovery of penicillin

☑ **A Point to Ponder: What is a mold? Have you ever seen one? Where do they come from?**

It happens so often that one day looks pretty much like all its neighbors, that it's hard to believe any one particular day could turn out to be very different. Once, a tall Scotsman in his late sixties named Alexander Fleming looked back on his life and said, "When I woke up just after dawn on September 28, 1928, I certainly didn't plan to revolutionize all medicine by discovering the world's first antibiotic, or bacteria killer. But I guess that's exactly what I did."

In 1928, Alexander Fleming was a quiet, steady 47-year-old biochemist with a laboratory in the basement of St. Mary's Hospital in London. September 28 of that year dawned damp, cold, and drizzly, just as it seemed the whole month had. This had been a chilly, damp September even for London.

As he had every month, every week, every workday for over a decade, Alexander Fleming rose that Tuesday, ate a simple breakfast, and walked eight blocks to his long, low-ceilinged lab tucked away next to the boiler room in the St. Mary's Hospital basement. There, as the one and only staff bacteriologist, he grew, or "cultured," bacteria in small round plates for hospital study and experiment. He would take a microscopic amount of a bacteria (often collected from a sick patient) and try to grow enough of it to determine why the patient was sick and how to fight the infection. Small dishes of deadly staphylococci, streptococci, and pneumococci bacteria were lined up across the one long lab bench that stretched the length of the room. Each was tagged with the name of a patient suffering from staph or strep infections, from pneumonia, or even from diptheria. In 1928, each of these diseases could prove deadly.

Fleming's lab alternated between drafty cold and stuffy hot, depending on the weather outside and how hard the boiler was working next door. When the lab got hot, he had to open the single window for ventilation. But when the London afternoon breeze kicked up, it blew leaves, dust, and, especially when it was damp out, a great variety of airborne molds through this window and into the lab. During a damp September like that of 1928, when the London air was far better suited for molds than for people, it seemed impossible to keep molds from drifting into, and contaminating, almost every bacteria Fleming tried to grow.

Molds were the one greatest hazard to Fleming's lab operation. Luckily, the good-natured Scot was easy-going, and only grumbled for a moment when some mold settled into a pure bacteria culture and ruined it. He would wash the contaminated culture down the lab sink, saving only a tiny speck of the bacteria he was sure hadn't been contaminated by mold with which to start the culture growing all over again in another dish.

As Alexander Fleming stepped into his lab on that chilly morning and hung up his raincoat and hat, he groaned at the almost stifling heat in his lab. The boiler must have been going full-steam all night to hold the chill out of the hospital wards above. Alexander sighed, and opened his one window wide to bring in fresh, cool air, and turned to inspect the plates of bacteria cultures on his lab table.

Several dishes of streptococci were developing nicely. They would soon be ready for testing. Then Fleming's heart sank as he realized that a prized dish of pure, and deadly, staphylococci bacteria next to them had been completely ruined by a strange, green mold. The mold must have floated into the dish sometime early last night and had been multiplying since then. Greenish mold fuzz now covered half the dish.

Fleming grunted and sighed, "Oh well. Almost every day this month some culture has been ruined by mold." He casually slid the dish over to the sink, and continued down the line to finish his morning inspection tour of culture plates. Fortunately, the staph culture was the only one ruined by molds that night.

Alexander turned on the water and casually reached for the staph plate to wash the spoiled culture down the drain. The plate was only inches from a strong stream of cold water, moments from being washed away and lost forever.

But in that last possible moment, Alexander happened to glance down. He glanced at that staph culture, and he froze. Something very odd had happened. Where this strange green mold had grown, the staphylococci bacteria had simply disappeared. Even bacteria more than an inch from the mold had turned transparent and sickly.

Fleming slammed off the water and jerked the plate back to protect this unknown green mold. What was this? What kind of mold could destroy one of the most hearty, tenacious, and deadly bacteria on earth? No other substance then known to man could attack staphylococci so successfully.

Questions raced through Fleming's mind. What kind of mold was this hungry, green bacteria-killer? What other bacteria would it attack? Was it dangerous to humans? Each question summoned a series of experiments into the biochemist's mind.

He was not nearly as excited as you might think, since he had not yet imagined the wondrous life-saving power of this mold. On September 28, he was simply curious. He simply felt this mold was worth a little study.

It took two weeks for Fleming to isolate and culture enough of the tough green mold to complete an identification: *Penicillium notatum*. Few biochemists had bothered to work with molds, and so, with precious little guidance, Alexander had to grope along at a snail's pace to protect his precious mold.

Within a month, he discovered that the mold secreted a substance that killed bacteria. He began to call this substance "penicillin." He waited until a healthy crop of penicillin mold covered a culture plate. Then he simmered it for two weeks in a broth and filtered off the liquid. What remained on the filter paper was the world's first test batch of penicillin.

Through culture-dish experiments that winter and early spring he discovered that penicillin could easily kill all the common deadly bacteria such as staphylococci, streptococci, pneumococci, even the toughest of all, the bacilli of diphtheria. The only bacteria penicillin fought but did not destroy was the weak, sensitive bacteria that caused influenza (flu). What sort of mold easily conquered all the tough bacterial-killers, but was unable to destroy the simplest, weakest of disease-causing bacteria? It seemed like wild fiction. Instead, it was the simple truth of this strange penicillin mold.

One question now remained before Fleming could release his miraculous findings and consider using penicillin to treat needy patients in St. Mary's. Was it dangerous to the patient as well as to the bacteria that infected the patient? What good was an antibacterial agent if it killed the patient along with the infecting disease? First he injected penicillin broth into two healthy rabbits. Nothing happened to either. They were unaffected by penicillin. Good.

Next he injected penicillin broth into two rabbits he had infected with streptococci bacteria. The rabbits recovered. Great! Penicillin not only didn't harm a patient, it killed bacteria as well in a patient as it did on a culture plate.

Finally Alexander Fleming was ready to publish a paper on his miracle mold. The complete conquest of so many dreaded diseases seemed imminent. But dreams of rapid conquest turned into years of tedious work. It took another twenty years of testing, and the research efforts of a dozen scientists, before Elizabeth McCoy at the University of Wisconsin and Margaret Hutchinson with the United States government developed a method of producing penicillin fast enough to meet the world's demand for the miracle mold. But that is another story.

Library Link: Are there other molds we now use to cure or prevent disease? What molds are we most likely to encounter?

Topics to Explore: biology, medical research, antibiotics, molds, scientific method, Alexander Fleming, penicillin.

References for Further Reading:

- *In the Children's Library:*

Rowland, John. *The Penicillin Man*. New York: Roy Publishers, 1957.

- *In the Adult Library:*

Hughes, William. *Alexander Fleming and Penicillin*. Sussex, England: Wayland, Hove, 1974.

MacFarlane, Gwyn. *Alexander Fleming, the Man and the Myth*. Cambridge, Mass.: Harvard University Press, 1984.

Consult your librarian for additional titles.

Skin Deep Success

A story of Jewell Cobb's discovery in 1982 of a link between skin pigment and resistance to cancer treatments

☑ **A Point to Ponder: Are there color pigments in your skin, or in parts of your skin? Are those pigments good or bad?**

"Is it true that women aren't as good at science as men?" The sixteen-year-old high school junior asked the question nervously, looked down at her notepad, and checked her tape recorder for the twentieth time to avoid the powerful gaze of the woman seated at the wide desk before her. As one of the writers for the Santa Ana High School 1982 yearbook and the school weekly newspaper, Adriana Compalo had jumped at the chance to interview the first black woman to become the president of a major university in the country, a black woman who had come to the university presidency through a career in science.

But now, Adriana's face flushed with nervous embarrassment. In this plush office, under the powerful gaze of the woman before her, Adriana felt that her questions were amateurish and inadequate. She looked down and nervously smoothed the white dress, her best, that she had worn on this scorching southern California October day for the interview. She suddenly knew her real motive for coming was not to write an article for the high school newspaper, but to have this important woman tell her it was all right for her, an Hispanic high school junior, to dream of a career in astrophysics. This wasn't just a writing assignment; Adriana felt her whole future hung in the balance with this answer.

"Is it true women aren't as good at science as men?" The question seemed to linger, to echo in the air. Adriana's heart pounded. How would a university president answer?

Jewell Cobb, the stylishly dressed, 58-year-old woman in the president's chair of California State University, Fullerton, leaned back with a soft, wide smile. She recognized the pleading nervousness in Adriana's voice. She had heard it many times before from other minority women. She had even asked the question herself, when she was a high school sophomore.

There was a moment of silence, broken only by the constant drone of window air conditioners, as Jewell Cobb flashed back to her own high school years of science discovery and struggle. Then she took in a deep breath and smiled at Adriana, and said, "Is it true? Let me tell you how I got into science."

Adriana glanced down at her notepad and wiped a light sheen of nervous perspiration from her upper lip. Then she rushed to interrupt with another question. "When did you first know you wanted to be a famous scientist?"

Jewell laughed and shook her head. "I never wanted to be a *famous* scientist. I was a sophomore when I fell in love with science—Ms. Hyman's biology class at Englewood High School in Chicago in 1939. It was a mostly black, ghetto school. The school only had a couple of microscopes. We had to take turns. I waited in line thinking that little bit of leaf laid out on the glass plate wasn't worth our time. Then I lowered my right eye down to the microscope. I gasped and jumped back, and looked at the leaf again. To my naked eye it looked like an ordinary, smooth leaf. But through the microscope it was a completely different world of sharp ridges, valleys, and cells.

"I stayed in at recess, and then at lunch to look at everything I could get my hands on. Up close through the microscope nothing looked at all like it did to my eye. It's as if our eyes see only whole buildings. Through the microscope I was able to study each brick and nail. For the first time I could look at the level at which our bodies really work, the cellular level."

Adriana struggled to keep up, furiously jotting notes as fast as she could. "Is cell biology why you went to Michigan State University?" she asked.

Once again Jewell smiled her broad, easy smile. "No. I loved football. It was 1942 and Tom Harmon was the star at Michigan State. He was a kind of hero. Also I had a number of friends who all were going to Michigan State."

Adriana asked, "Is that where you became a molecular biologist and worked on cancer cures?"

"Not a molecular biologist," corrected Jewell. "I'm a cellular biologist."

Adriana flushed red at her mistake. She checked her tape recorder for the twenty-first time.

Jewell Cobb continued. "Just as millions of molecules make up each cell, millions of cells make up a living, functioning organism. The actions, processes, and interactions of cells make bodies function."

Dr. Cobb paused and looked at Adriana. "Have you ever heard of *melanin*?" The student shook her head.

"Melanin is the pigment that gives skin cells their color. Have you ever heard of a *melanoma*?"

Adriana brightened at finally being able to show that she knew something. "It's a kind of cancer. My grandmother died of a melanoma."

Dr. Cobb nodded. "A very nasty cancer, one that starts in pigmented skin cells. In my early research I wanted to track down the origins of melanin. It emerged in Africa to protect bodies that didn't have a protective coating of hair from the dangerous ultraviolet rays so strong in the harsh tropical sunlight. Melanin in the skin cells blocks UV rays and protects the tissue underneath."

Adriana interrupted. "Is melanin only found in black people?"

"Oh, no," answered Jewell. "Any coloration of the skin is caused by protective melanin. But then doctors noticed a curious thing. In the '60s and '70s chemo- and radiation therapies for cancer were developed. But consistently doctors noted that blacks did not respond to radium and X-ray treatments nearly as well as whites."

"Was it something in their diet?" asked Adriana, trying to sound scientific and intelligent.

"No one knew," continued Dr. Cobb. "I was able to get the funding to find out. We created tumors in mice."

"Mice? You had to work with mice?" asked Adriana, crinkling up her nose.

"Yes. Working with mice gave us the control over our study. We could let some go untreated, and treat others with a wide variety of doses and treatments."

"You really worked with *lots* of mice?"

Dr. Cobb smiled. "Yes. Many hundreds of them. Once the tumors developed, I operated on the mice and removed thin sections of tumor to treat and study. I suspected that there was a connection with melanin. So we sought out cells that contained different amounts of melanin for detailed study. I wanted to see if cells with melanin responded differently to X-ray and radium treatment than did cells without melanin."

Jewell paused for a moment. Adriana leaned forward in her chair. "And?"

"And I was right. Melanin blocks both X-rays and radium radiation, just as it blocks UV light. The more melanin in the skin cells, the more complete the blockage. My research helped revise and improve the use of these important cancer treatments for blacks."

Again Jewell paused and studied Adriana for a long moment. "So you ask me if it's true that men are better at science than women? Absolutely not. In fact, women just might be better. Women have never had equal access to science classes, equipment, and top-grade scientists. Women have had to fight their way into science hindered by this inequality. Still, once they get there, they are every bit as effective as men. Who knows, with equal access to training and resources, women might have been the ones to write the history of science."

A wave of relief, hope, determination, and enthusiasm flowed over Adriana Compalo. "Thank you, Dr. Cobb! I'm going to be a scientist, too. The first female Hispanic scientist ever."

"No, you won't be the first," answered Dr. Cobb. "But there haven't been very many. Certainly not enough."

"But is it okay if I don't want to touch a bunch of mice?"

"That depends on what you want to do, Adriana."

Adriana excitedly rose from her seat and started for the office door. "I'm going to be an astronomer, an astrophysicist, and find the origin of the whole universe!"

Jewell Cobb nodded and picked up the still-running tape recorder Adriana had forgotten on the desk. "But first, don't you want to take this and write your article?"

Of course, whether or not Adriana Compalo created a successful career for herself in astrophysics is another story—a story that has not yet been written.

Library Link: What is the purpose of color pigment in human skin? How did it develop? Why don't we all have the same amount of it?

Topics to Explore: cellular biology, cancer research, scientific method, skin pigment cells.

References for Further Reading:

- *In the Children's Library:*

Turner, Joseph, ed. *Black Women Achievements Against Odds*. Washington D.C.: Smithsonian Institute Press, 1989.

- *In the Adult Library:*

Cobb, Jewell P. "A Life in Science: Research and Service." *Sage: A Scholarly Journal on Black Women* 6, no. 2 (1989): 39-43.

Smity, Jessie Carnie, ed. *Notable Black American Women*. Detroit, Mich.: Gale Research, 1992.

Consult your librarian for additional titles.

Earth Sciences

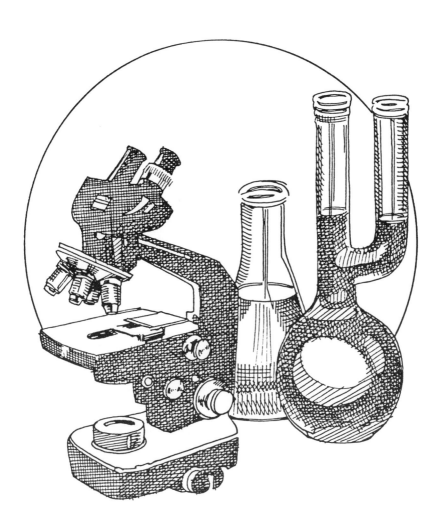

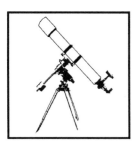

Astronomy

Circles in the Sky

A story of Nicolaus Copernicus's discovery in 1499 that the earth is not the center of the universe

☑ **A Point to Ponder: How can you measure the location, or placement in the sky, of a star? Do stars ever appear to move? Do they really move?**

"Step aside and let me see if you've set them correctly." Domineco Novara pushed past his student and squinted along the quadrant, which was an early kind of sextant, really little more than two slender, hinged, pointing sticks.

Novara, one of the most famous astronomy teachers in all Europe, stared up at the Bologna, Italy, night sky to twinkling stars above. Then he carefully sighted along the quadrant his pupil, 26-year-old Nicolaus Copernicus, had set.

"Sloppy work, Nicolaus. Look here! You're off."

"Impossible!" exploded Copernicus. His large eyes had a stern and dreary look as always. His long, exclamation-mark nose exaggerated this sour expression.

"Not impossible at all, Nicolaus. Learn to be more careful, more exact. What good is an astronomer who can't make accurate measurements on the stars? What do we really know besides our measurements of the nightly angles between stars and planets, or between stars and points on the earth?"

Copernicus shook his head angrily. "But what good are accurate measurements if they never match our *predictions* of where planets and stars are supposed to be?"

Novara completed his adjustments on the quadrant and stepped back for Copernicus to see. "There. Readings are always important. The predictions of Ptolemy's model can always be corrected."

Copernicus held up his hands in disgust. "Oh, please! No more circles on circles. That model already makes no sense!"

"*Epi*circles," corrected Novara with a sigh. "And don't argue with your teacher! What else can we do but take careful measurements and try to correct the model?"

The world of astronomy in 1499 still relied on a model of the universe created by the Greek scientist, Ptolemy, over 1,400 years earlier. According to Ptolemy, the earth was the center of the universe and never moved. The sun and planets revolved around the earth in great circles, while the distant stars perched way out on the great spherical shell of space.

The problem was that the actual movement of the planets, as measured by astronomers from the night sky, didn't match the movement they would make if they really did travel in neat circles around the earth. Sometimes the planets moved too fast, sometimes too slow. Sometimes they jumped rapidly against the background stars. Sometimes they actually moved backwards across the sky for a few days. Sometimes they hardly moved at all.

So astronomers modified Ptolemy's universe of circles by adding more circles within circles. The model now claimed that each planet traveled along a small circle, or *epicircle* that rolled along its big orbital circle around the earth. Century after century, the errors in this model grew larger and larger. More epicircles were added to the model so that there were epicircles within epicircles, as astronomers tried to make the actual measurements match the model.

Copernicus shook his head. "Something must be wrong with Ptolemy's model. Nature just wouldn't move in such a complicated way."

"The only thing that's wrong," said Novara, sternly tapping the quadrant, "is the care some astronomy students take with their measurements! What will your uncle, Bishop Waczenrode, think? Now take a reading on Venus, and this time do it carefully!"

Copernicus grumbled under his breath as he snatched up the quadrant and turned to find the evening planet low in the western sky. "Something's wrong with Ptolemy's model of the universe, and I'm going to find out what it is."

Copernicus graduated, was ordained as a priest in the Catholic Church, and returned to Poland to work for his uncle, Bishop Waczenrode, at the Frauenburg Cathedral. Copernicus was given the top rooms in the east tower so he could continue his astronomy measurements. For almost twenty years, he spent his nights measuring the stars, and his days trying to understand what was wrong with Ptolemy's model of the universe. But it made no sense.

Sitting in his window one afternoon, waiting for sunset, Copernicus watched two riders gallop along the dusty road below the cathedral wall. The long afternoon shadow of one of the men fell across the other. And that shadow caught Copernicus's eye. Because the two men rode at exactly the same speed, it didn't move forward or back on the second rider. It merely bounced up and down across his chest.

With a start, Copernicus realized that to each of the riders, the other rider would not appear to move forward or backward at all. He would only appear to bounce slightly up and down, just as the shadow did. Further, the earth itself would appear to move *backward* to the riders, while to Copernicus, it seemed that the earth stood still and it was the riders who were moving.

Of course, everyone could see that this was true. But had an astronomer ever taken the time to think about what it meant? "Probably not," thought Copernicus. As he watched those riders, Nicolaus could not help but ask himself one very important question: "What if the earth moved?" What would the movement of other planets look like from a moving earth?

A moving earth. Copernicus actually trembled with the enormity of the thought as he sat on his windowsill. For all his life he had believed the earth sat still. Why? Because the Church said that mankind was God's premiere creation, and that the earth was the center of the universe. Besides, Ptolemy's model said that the earth was at the center, and remained still. "But something is wrong with Ptolemy's model," said Nicolaus out loud. Could that something possibly be that the earth really moved through space?

Copernicus was far too excited to take any measurements that night. He paced across his wide chamber and flung out questions to bounce off the walls and spin across the room. If the earth moved, *how* did it move? How could he ever prove that it did since it *appeared* to stand still? What would the movement of the other planets look like from a moving earth? Could he find a model for the earth's movement that would get rid of epicircles on epicircles and have the other planets follow simple, regular orbits?

For over a year, Copernicus studied his twenty years' worth of measurements, searching for a new model of the universe: one that had a moving earth and simple orbits for all the other planets. When he finally found the one model that worked, the great excitement of his discovery was balanced by an equally tremendous fear.

Copernicus's new model of the universe put the sun at the center with all the planets orbiting around it in simple circles. The earth's orbit lay between Venus and Mars. It made perfect sense, and the measurements Copernicus had taken for two decades fit this new model perfectly. But, would anyone ever believe him? The Church taught, and the world believed, that the earth was at the center of the universe. The Church's word was law. What would they think of Nicolaus Copernicus if he stood up and said everyone else was wrong? Was he strong enough and brave enough to stand all alone? Did he dare face the consequences of of his boldness? If he could not convince the world he was right, besides the ridicule, he could be defrocked, imprisoned, excommunicated, or executed.

Copernicus scarcely dared mention his finding to even his closest friends. Still, secrets were almost impossible to keep in the confined walls of the cathedral. Nicolaus was still debating with himself about what to do when his uncle burst into his chambers one hot afternoon. The Bishop's face was beet-red and full of fury. "Do you hate me, Nicolaus? Didn't I get you this prestigious appointment? Why do you now attack me and our Church?"

Nicolaus began to tremble. Word of his discovery had somehow leaked out. Now he would find out if he was brave enough to hold onto his beliefs in the face of an angry world. "I'm not attacking anyone, Uncle. I am merely searching for the truth."

"The truth," bellowed Bishop Waczenrode, "is that the great Ptolemy and the Church both say the earth does not move and is at the center of the universe!"

"Ptolemy is wrong," explained Copernicus. "If you *separate* the apparent motion of the planets, which is really the motion of the earth, from their *actual* motion, you don't need complex epicircles."

The Bishop slammed his fist on Copernicus's table. "That's ridiculous! The earth doesn't move. When a bird moves, I see it move. When a cloud moves, I see it move. When I move, I feel my motion. If the earth moved I would see it or feel it!"

Patiently Copernicus tried to both calm down, and reason with, his uncle. "You can't feel the earth's motion because you, the bird, and the cloud all move with the earth."

Still red-faced and flustered, the Bishop blurted, "But how can the earth move if it is at the center of the universe?"

Copernicus gulped. This was the part he feared to say the most. Nicolaus took a deep breath and answered. "The truth, Uncle, is that the earth is not at the center of the universe. The sun is."

The Bishop's eyes grew wide. "*What?*" he exploded. "Do not utter such nonsense. It is blasphemy!"

"Please, Uncle. Just look," pleaded Copernicus. "See how much more sense my measurements make if the sun, which has the largest mass, is at the center, and the earth orbits around it between Venus and Mars? Look how *this* model of the universe improves the accuracy of our predictions!"

In a perfect rage, Bishop Waczenrode swept out of the room. "Utter rubbish! I forbid you to talk of it. Why not make the moon the center, and have the earth rotate around Mars?" And he slammed Copernicus's door.

Copernicus sighed and answered very softly, "Because my measurements do not support a moon-centered universe."

For fear of more reactions like that of his uncle, Copernicus did not dare have his findings published until after his death in 1543. Even then they were consistently scorned and ridiculed by Church, astronomers, and universities alike. His thoughts lay dormant for another 70 years, waiting for first Galileo and then John Keppler to pick them up, validate them, and use them to further our understanding of the universe. But that is another story.

Library Link: Does the earth travel in a circle around the sun? Do the planets travel around the sun at a constant speed?

Topics to Explore: earth science, astronomy, Copernicus, scientific method, observation, evaluation.

References for Further Reading:

- *In the Children's Library:*

Knight, David C. *Copernicus: Titan of Modern Astronomy.* New York: Franklin Watts, 1965.

- *In the Adult Library:*

Adamcyewski, Jan. *Nicolaus Copernicus and His Epoch.* Philadelphia: Copernicus Society of America, 1976.

Kesler, Hermann. *Copernicus and His World.* New York: Roy Publishers, 1945.

Consult your librarian for additional titles.

The Orbit of Truth

A story of Galileo Galilei's discovery in 1619 that Copernicus was right

☑ **A Point to Ponder: How can you tell that the earth orbits around the sun, rather than the sun orbiting around the earth?**

"I don't believe it," he groaned, pulling back from his telescope. "Not Aristotle again!" Galileo Galilei sighed and wearily peered back through the eyepiece of his new telescope, fixing his gaze on the far-off surface of the moon. His eye saw craters, valleys, mountains, and a surface that gave off no light of its own, but merely reflected the sun's light. Galileo's mind, however, saw only Aristotle. Aristotle had said that the moon was very different from what Galileo saw.

This was not the first time that what Galileo saw contradicted what Aristotle had taught. But Europe in 1610 believed in Aristotle. Aristotle's words were the very foundation of scientific belief. How could Galileo challenge Aristotle again?

It had happened first eleven years earlier when Galileo's experiments disproved Aristotle's theory that heavier objects always fall faster than lighter objects. Galileo dropped two balls of very different weight from the Tower of Piza. Thud—thud! They smashed to the ground 200 feet below at almost the same instant. Galileo was right. Aristotle was wrong. The evidence was clear. All objects fell at the same rate regardless of weight. Galileo had descended the tower and expected congratulations, fame, and recognition. He was to be disappointed.

That was in 1598, and the many supporters of Aristotle bitterly denounced and disputed Galileo's demonstration. Aristotle could not be wrong. Galileo must be stopped. Quietly, but quickly, the University of Piza had withdrawn Galileo's teaching appointment. For his scientific discovery, he was fired.

So now, in 1610, Galileo gazed warily at the moon through his telescope and thought of Aristotle. Aristotle said the moon was a smooth disk shining by its own light. Through his telescope that he had invented the previous year, Galileo saw that Aristotle was wrong again. But should he announce his findings? Would anyone believe him this time? "But the evidence is clear and compelling and speaks for itself," Galileo thought. But then, he had thought the same thing twelve years earlier when he faced the Italian scholars and priests who supported Aristotle at the Leaning Tower of Piza. The only evidence they had been willing to hear was that Aristotle could not be wrong.

Galileo waited. He would look and chart some more in private before revealing what he had learned. He dared not face the ghost of Aristotle again. Not yet.

Through the instrument that he had named a *telescope* by combining the Greek words meaning "distant" and "looking," Galileo saw a magnified view of the heavens that no human eye had ever seen. He saw Jupiter clearly, and discovered the first three of its moons. He saw Saturn well enough to detect that it was oddly misshapen. Fifty years later, with a better telescope, the Dutch astronomer Christian Huygens would identify Galileo's "misshapen" planet as the rings of Saturn.

Then Galileo turned his lens on earth's nearest neighbors, Venus and Mars. He studied them very carefully night after night, plotting the position, size, and phase of each planet over months. What he saw dismayed and excited him. Aristotle was wrong yet again! The planets did not move as Aristotle said they would.

In 1610, all Europe accepted as fact that the earth was the center of the universe.

Aristotle and Ptolemy had both said so. Every university agreed. Only one man, a little-known Polish astronomer, Nicolaus Copernicus, had claimed, 70 years before, that the sun was at the center, and that the earth rotated about it with the other planets. But Copernicus's book was banned. His theory was thoroughly discredited.

Still, there it was, plain as day on Galileo's charts. The movements of Mars and Venus that Galileo observed and carefully plotted supported the theory of Copernicus. They did not move the way they would have to if the earth were really at the center of the the universe. Could everybody be wrong? Could all the scholars and priests of Europe, *and* Aristotle, *and* Ptolemy be wrong, while only Galileo and a banned, dismissed Polish astronomer were right? Did Galileo dare to report such findings and challenge the whole world? What would happen to him from such a bold act?

Galileo sought counsel from one of the few professors he could trust with such explosive information, Cardinal Bellamine.

"Ah, my friend," beamed the Cardinal as Galileo entered his study. "It has been too long. Why do you look so burdened and perplexed?"

Galileo cleared off a long table and rolled out his charts. "As a trusted friend and ally, please look at these."

The Cardinal gazed at the chart of the solar system Galileo held open with his hands. Then Bellamine roared with laughter and slapped Galileo on the back. "This is a good joke, my friend. Your chart is a child's fantasy. It has the sun at the center."

Galileo face was tense and serious. "That is because the sun *is* the center."

The Cardinal's laughter evaporated. His face paled. "You can't be serious. Everyone knows that the earth is the center!"

Laying out his notebooks of careful readings, Galileo said, "Through my telescope I have been able to watch the heavens as never before possible. Look at these plottings. Look at my data. I have mapped the way the planets actually move. It is not a theory, not a guess. It is fact. The only way to explain the motion I have seen is for the sun to be the center of this system, and for the earth to rotate around it along with the other planets."

Bellamine's face grew red with anger. "How dare you contradict Aristotle, Ptolemy, the Church, and every university in Europe?"

Quietly but firmly Galileo said, "Because they are wrong."

Fearing the wrath of the world would crush his brilliant friend if such findings were released, Cardinal Bellamine advised caution. "Say it is only a suggestion, Galileo. Say your findings are still an untested theory. Don't call it *proof* or *fact*. Give the world time to adjust. Maybe you should take more time, yourself, to study, Galileo. Perhaps you will find some slight error."

Galileo gazed down at his chart of the universe, so sure it was correct. He thought of what had happened last time he announced that Aristotle was wrong. But over and over Galileo came back to one central thought, "The truth speaks for itself. If I show them the evidence, they'll have to believe." His evidence was irrefutable. His methods and procedure had been exact. Copernicus had been right. The sun was the center.

"I thank you for your counsel," Galileo said quietly. "But I must tell the truth. That Aristotle was wrong about the moon I can ignore. But I must publish these findings as they are."

Still, old beliefs do not die easily. Opposition and dislike quickly gathered and strengthened like iron filings drawn to a magnet. In 1616, the Council of Cardinals forbade Galileo ever again to teach or promote Copernicus's theories.

When Galileo ignored their warning, he was summoned to Rome by the Church's all-powerful Inquisition. A grueling trial followed. Galileo presented his findings. But the world in 1632 was still not ready to hear what Galileo called *fact*, or *truth*.

Galileo was condemned by the Church and forced to publicly recant his views and findings. Instead of prison, he was placed under house-arrest for the rest of his life. Galileo died in 1640 without ever hearing even one voice outside his own heart proclaim that his discoveries were true. The condemnation of Galileo and his discoveries was not rescinded by the Church until October of 1992, 360 years after Galileo stood before the Inquisition, 382 years after he had correctly, accurately charted the motion and structure of our solar system.

But like Copernicus before him, Galileo's careful, exacting scientific work opened the door to the modern study of astronomy, and laid the foundation upon which scientists like John Keppler and Isaac Newton would begin to unravel the orderly mysteries of our universe. But that is another story.

Library Link: Galileo was persecuted for his scientific findings. Has that happened at any other time in history?

Topics to Explore: earth science, astronomy, Galileo, scientific method, observation, evaluation.

References for Further Reading:

- *In the Children's Library:*

Fisher, Leonard. *Galileo*. New York: Macmillan, 1992.

- *In the Adult Library:*

Parker, Steve. *Galileo and the Universe*. New York: HarperCollins, 1992.

Consult your librarian for additional titles.

A Gold Medal Speck of Light

A story of Maria Mitchell's discovery of a comet in 1847

☑ **A Point to Ponder: What is a comet? What is its "tail" made out of?**

In 1847, there was no place on Nantucket Island where you couldn't hear the constant creak of wooden decks, the clanging of the channel buoys, and the screeching of gulls. Flat, marshy ground stretched away from the town of Nantucket on three sides. On the fourth side, a busy harbor led out to an endless, flat sea. The masts of the ever-present whaling and cargo ships were the tallest points for miles in any direction.

Nantucket Island sits off the southern shore of Massachusetts. The island's one town, Nantucket, was a bustling ocean port. With most of the men at sea, Nantucket always looked like a town where the only residents were women, children, and dogs.

Everyone in Nantucket learned to tell time by the stars, and every house had a sextant, which is a device used by ships at sea to navigate by the stars. The lifeblood of the town beat with the ebb and flow of the tides.

But there *were* some things in Nantucket that ran according to the clock rather than the stars, tides, or a sextant. The public library was one of these. It opened at noon each day, and closed precisely at 5:00 in the afternoon. Except for Saturday, when the library stayed open until 8:00, and Sunday when it remained closed all day.

At five minutes to twelve each day, Maria Mitchell, the Nantucket librarian, walked through the front gate of her family's house at the west edge of Nantucket and made the short walk downtown to open the library. Maria loved her job at the library. In part, this was because she loved books and had read every book in the library. In part, this was because she thought reading was important, and wanted to influence what the children of Nantucket read. But she especially loved her job because it let her stay up most nights studying the stars.

Studying the stars at night had been a part of Maria's life since she was five. One of her father's jobs in Nantucket had been to check the chronometers (early timepieces) on whaling ships before they put out to sea. To do that, he made a series of precise observations over the course of an evening while his assistant, usually Maria, recorded and checked the chronometer's time for each event. Maria was able to use a sextant when she was six. She got her first telescope when she was eight.

The daily pattern of her life had changed little by the fall of 1847, when Maria was 29. She still lived at home with her father and three brothers. She still worked each day at the library. She still studied the stars every evening, if it was clear, and if the moon wasn't out to obscure faint stars with its great wash of reflected sunlight.

October 1, 1847, was a busy day for Maria Mitchell at the library. The annual inventory of books by the library trustees would begin tomorrow. In addition to all her normal duties, Maria had to check and straighten all the shelves of books, and sneak her secret stash of secret "lost" books back into the children's area. Whenever Maria saw the children going after a book she deemed inappropriate, she would conveniently lose the book. All these lost books had to reappear on the shelves before the trustees' examination.

When she closed and locked the library doors at 5:15 that evening, Maria was dead tired. As she trudged home toward the setting sun, with the first hints of coming fall chill in the air, her spirits were buoyed by the realization that it would be a crystal-clear night. Better yet, the quarter moon was already on its way down toward the western horizon. It would set before midnight. From midnight on, the sky would be perfect for stargazing.

Maria ate dinner with her family and lay down for a short nap, setting an alarm for 11:45. She rose, washed the sleep from her face with cold water, and carried her telescope into the backyard. The sky was crisp, clear, and pitch black. The stars seemed to leap out of the heavens at her.

She began her usual slow sweep across the constellations, noting and recording the position and reflectivity of each major star. Mars and Jupiter were both plainly visible. Through her telescope she could clearly see the famed canals on Mars, and could even make out some detail on Jupiter's distant surface. She turned past the planets to her favorite celestial formations: nebulae. She carefully noted the spectrum of reflected light, and paused to glory and wonder at these phenomenal formations.

About 1:00 A.M., she turned toward the last of the constellations in her normal sweep, and began to wonder what she would choose to study in greater depth this sparkling evening. She scanned past Cassiopeia, and . . . what was that? She almost missed it because it wasn't supposed to be there. A faint white dot where there was supposed to be only black, empty space.

Fine-tuning her telescopic focus, she stared at the distant dot of light. Her heart began to pound. Her breath came more rapidly. This was something new. This something wasn't there two nights ago when she had last looked in this quadrant of the sky. What was it?

Maria dashed inside for her father's telescope. It was more powerful than hers, not as good for general sweeps of the sky, but better for detailed study. Excitedly, she set up her father's telescope next to her own. Her hands trembled with anticipation. It made the telescope wiggle slightly and blurred her vision.

It seemed an eternity before she correctly aimed and focused her father's powerful telescope. And there it was. A heavenly body she had never seen before, a faint tail scattered out behind it. She could already tell the body had moved relative to the stars near it. This was a comet. It could only be a comet.

But there was no record, no listing for this comet. Was it some conveniently "lost" star the heavens snuck back into place before a celestial inspection? Could it possibly be a *new* comet? Could she be the first human to gaze at this chunk of rock hurtling through space toward to the earth? Now her heart truly pounded. Was it possible that a simple librarian in Nantucket, Massachusetts, with only a high school education, could be the first to discover a new comet?

As had all astronomers around the world, Maria had read the report some years before that the King of Denmark was offering a gold medal to the first person to discover a new comet. Could this be Maria's gold-medal comet?

Maria stared through her father's telescope until dawn, tracing her new comet's progress across the sky. As a new day's light hid the stars, and her family awoke, Maria rushed in to share the news with her father. Far too excited to sleep, she immediately wrote letters to William Bond at the Harvard Observatory and Joseph Henry, director of the Smithsonian Institute in Washington.

However, Nantucket mail had to wait for the twice-weekly mail boat to leave the island. Maria's letter did not leave Nantucket until October 4. On October 3, two other astronomers, one in England and one in Rome, found and claimed the discovery of Maria's new comet.

A flurry of letters, claims, and charges sped back and forth for over a year before the Danish gold medal was officially awarded to Maria in early 1849. But as grand as the trip to Denmark and her shiny medal were, neither could compare with the thrill of that crystal-clear night of October 1, 1847, when Maria Mitchell realized the secret dream of almost every amateur astronomer. With the medal came fame and important offers to pursue her astronomy while teaching at a university. But that is another story.

Library Link: Can you see the differences between planets and stars with the the naked eye?

How do comets look different from planets and stars?

Topics to Explore: astronomy, scientific method, Maria Mitchell.

References for Further Reading:

- *In the Children's Library:*

Baker, Rachel. *America's First Woman Astronomer: Maria Mitchell.* New York: J. Messner, 1960.

- *In the Adult Library:*

Oles, Carole. *Night Watches: Inventions on the Life of Maria Mitchell.* Cambridge, Mass.: Alice James Books, 1985.

Consult your librarian for additional titles.

Geology

The Sands of Time

A story of James Hutton's discovery in 1792 of the forces building up and tearing down the earth

☑ **A Point to Ponder: Have you ever actually seen the earth's surface change? Where? How?**

For the Scottish coast, where even the middle of summer can be chill and damp, this was a balmy July day in 1792. The lanky, 67-year-old, more-or-less retired physician and farmer, James Hutton, walked with long, swinging strides across the steep, green hills. The rhythmic sound of the pounding surf softly filled the background. Huffing and puffing, short, round William Grayson struggled to keep up with his neighbor and friend.

"James. Stop a moment while I catch my breath!"

White-haired James Hutton glanced back over his shoulder. "Don't be too long, Will. I don't want to dawdle out here and miss supper."

Grayson stopped, resting both hands on his knees to help ease his pounding heart and aching lungs. "You said you wanted to come out for a talk about geology, not for a race, James!" William Grayson was a noted geologist teaching at the university in Edinborough.

"Aye, that I did," replied Hutton, chuckling at his red-faced and sweating neighbor. "And I thought a geologist would be in better shape, Will. You spend too many hours sitting in lecture halls."

Then James became more serious. "Maybe if you got out more you'd realize the way you teach geology can't be right."

Caught completely by surprise, Grayson stammered, "What on earth can you mean, James? I teach only the latest theories of geology to my students."

Hutton grunted and shook his head. "Latest theories. Call them what they are. They're wild guesses, Will." James pointed at the smooth rolling hills that surrounded them. "Where are these catastrophes you say shaped the earth?"

"Catastrophic events," corrected Grayson. "And that *is* what shaped the earth. Great floods carved out valleys in hours. Great wrenchings formed mountains . . ."

"Overnight, I suppose," interrupted Hutton.

Feeling defensive, William stood his ground. "Yes. Quite possibly, overnight."

"And have you seen any of these great catastrophes with your own eyes, man? Do you know of anyone who has?"

Grayson dropped his voice. "No."

Some pent-up frustration seemed to erupt inside James Hutton. "Well, it's just not right, Will!" he exploded. "Why can't geology be more systematic like astronomy? Astronomers carefully measure the stars, build up great volumes of data, and *then* draw conclusions from that knowledge, not from random guesses."

Grayson tried to defend his teachings. "I assure you our guesses are far from random."

But Hutton's booming voice cut him off. "But you have no proof, no data, no basis for your theories."

"The valleys and mountains are here," answered Grayson. "What more proof do I need? How would you make the study of geology different?"

Hutton almost trembled as he struggled to put words to the vague ideas tickling the back of his mind. "I don't know yet. But mark my words, Will, the answer is out here in the hills, not in your classroom. If I tramp about long enough, I'll find it."

The subject was dropped. The two men continued their walk through stiff westerly breezes in thoughtful silence.

But at night, James Hutton couldn't sleep. It was true. Something itched at the back of his awareness, just beyond his grasp, tormenting him day in and day out. What gnawed so terribly at James Hutton was the feeling that he already knew the answer, that he had already seen it with his own eyes. He just couldn't recognize what it was.

It was his restlessness that drove him out on long walks, hoping that something in the Scottish hills would jog his memory, his understanding.

August 1 of that year, 1792, rose cloudy and cool with a strong wind howling down the valley from the west, and the smell of rain just over the hills. Still, James Hutton was out hiking. He stopped at a small stream tumbling out of a steep canyon in a tall ridgeline. Without thinking he bent down and picked up a handful of tiny pebbles and sand from the streambed. As he sifted the sand between his fingers, that nagging itch crashed through to his conscious mind. He found a corner of that vague idea he could grab hold of and pull.

These sands and pebbles had drifted down this small stream, tumbling, crashing, and breaking into smaller pieces as they went. This sand *used* to be a bigger rock. And it had come from the ridge above him.

He scooped up a handful of water and could see tiny flecks of dirt and sand suspended in it. This stream was carrying dirt and rock from the hilltop to its base.

This stream was reshaping the entire hill, slowly, grain by grain, day by day. Not catastrophically as Grayson claimed.

Hutton's mental fog cleared just as the sheets of rain swept down onto his back. He *had* seen the answer. He had seen it a hundred times on every walk. It was everywhere, all around him. But like not seeing a forest for the trees, no one had noticed this obvious answer because the William Graysons of geology were looking for something big and earth-shattering, not small and ordinary.

The earth, Hutton realized, was shaped slowly, not overnight. Rain pounding down on the hills pulled particles of dirt and rock down into streams and then down to the plains. Streams gouged out channels, gullies, and valleys bit by bit, year by year, always washing the hills down into valleys and plains below.

The wind around him tore at hills in the same way. Ripping off grains of dirt from hilltops and depositing them at the base of other hills. Waves tore at coastlines, always pulling them down into the sea. Gravity pulled boulders from mountaintops, forcing them to tumble down to lower perches.

The forces of nature were everywhere tearing down the earth, leveling it out. Nature did this not in a day, but over countless centuries of relentless, steady work by wind and water. Everyone had searched for catastrophic single events. Hutton now saw that there were none. Just the slow, steady grinding work of wind and water. Soaked to the skin by the summer rain, elated beyond his wildest dreams that he finally saw the truth, James Hutton cried out, "The steady assault of nature is the force that shapes the earth!"

Then he stopped. If that were true, why hadn't nature already leveled out the earth? Why weren't the hills and mountains worn down? There must be a second force, one that builds up the land, just as other forces of nature tear it down.

But what? Was this second force as obvious, and yet as hard to recognize, as the tearing-down forces had been?

For days, James Hutton walked and looked and pondered. What built up the earth? When finally it hit him, James was so excited he ran straight to William Grayson's house to show him his vision of geology.

"Will, I've found it! Geology should be the study of *two* great opposing forces: the wind, water, and gravity of nature which constantly tear down the land, and the heat of the earth's core which steadily builds up the land through volcanoes. Look at the evidence. Rocks are either sedimentary, being deposited during tear-down, or volcanic, created during a building-up of the earth.

"Mountain ranges are forced up by the heat of the earth. Wind and rain slowly tear them back down. With no real beginning and no end, these two great forces struggle in dynamic balance. Over eons they cancel each other out. This is the time scale for geologic study, eons rather than hours and days, and these are the processes geologists should study."

Hutton stood flushed with triumph over his shorter friend. Grayson slumped, stunned into a chair, his mind whirring. In one great flash of understanding, James Hutton had changed the way geologists would forever look at the earth and its processes. Almost more importantly, he completely changed mankind's sense of the scale of time required to measure these changes.

While tramping over the Scottish hills as a more-or-less retired farmer and doctor, James Hutton created a vision of the modern field of geology, and an understanding of the time scale over which natural forces act. It would take over ten years and the work of dozens of scientists to discover ways to actually understand how these two great forces have shaped and reshaped the surface of the earth. But that is another story.

Library Link: How fast are mountain ranges pushed up by the shifting plates of the earth's crust?

Have the continents of the earth always been where they now are?

Topics to Explore: geology, scientific method, erosion, continental drift, plate tectonics, volcanic activity, James Hutton.

References for Further Reading:

- *In the Children's Library:*

Clayton, Keith. *The Crust of the Earth: The Story of Geology.* Garden City, N.Y.: Natural Museum Press for the American Museum of Natural History, 1967.

- *In the Adult Library:*

Gould, Stephen. *Time's Arrow, Time's Cycle: Myth and Metaphor in the Discovery of Geological Time.* Cambridge, Mass.: Harvard University Press, 1987.

Consult your librarian for additional titles.

Putting the Truth on Ice

*A story of Jean Louis Agassiz's discovery
in 1837 of the ice ages*

☑ **A Point to Ponder: How do glaciers shape the earth's surface?**

The night settled in hard and black around the two men, seeming to push the meager light of their campfire back in toward the glowing coals. A bitterly cold wind rolled off the glaciers and drove them deeper into their blankets. Above them, countless stars, scattered across the summer sky like sparkling jewels, seemed close enough to reach out and grab.

Far below, at the base of these jagged Swiss Alps, bright summer flowers splashed across meadows. Families took evening strolls without even a sweater.

But up here, with massive, snake-like rivers of ice curving down from the highest peaks on either side of them, it felt more like perpetual winter. Twenty-eight-year-old Alexander Braun groaned as the cold seeped through his clothes and slid an icy finger down his back.

"I'm tired of this, Louis. Camping with you is nothing but work, cold, and misery. Let's go home."

Twenty-nine-year-old Jean Louis Agassiz, known to his friends as "Louis," and to his students at the Neuchatel, Switzerland, college as the demanding "Professor Agassiz," shook his head. "I need more data."

What?" cried Alexander, "You already have a mountain of data big enough to last a lifetime. Why would you possibly want more?"

"I can never have enough data," answered Louis. "While it is true that at some point each scientist has to stop collecting data and guess at its meaning, more data means a better guess. I intend to gather more data before I make mine."

Above them, on the steep mountain slopes, long, screeching groans, fierce grinding, and an occasional sharp "pop!" echoed from deep within the glaciers. Ice pushed and ground against ice as gravity pulled the glacier slowly toward the valley. Glaciers were never quiet, but the noise always sounded more eerie and dangerous at night.

Still, Alexander, four inches taller and 45 pounds heavier than Louis, pleaded. "It's miserable up here. Let's collect data someplace warmer."

Louis Agassiz frowned and pointed his finger. "Back in college you were my friend. But this summer I hired you as an assistant. This is 1837! These are modern times, and geology has become a serious science. I will decide when there is enough data. You will stop complaining and do your job!"

Early the next morning, both men huddled around a flickering campfire searching for enough warmth to thaw their numbed fingers and toes. "Eat quickly, Alexander. We have a busy day ahead."

Just as a bright, yellow sun swept over a sawtooth ridge of craggy peaks along the eastern side of their small valley, Louis Agassiz and a grumbling Alexander Braun hoisted heavy packs and started their day's trek toward the front edge of Berinina Glacier.

"Don't daydream, Alexander! Keep your eyes and mind sharp. These marks won't jump off the rocks at you. You have to hunt for them. There! To your left. You almost missed one."

Agassiz pointed at a twenty-foot-high wall of granite hidden behind thick bushes. The rock face was marred by deep gouges and scrapes as if giant fingers had scratched along its surface. "Mark its location relative to the glacier in the logbook while I sketch those markings," he directed.

As they returned the logs to their packs, Alexander asked, "Why do you get so excited by scratched rocks? We've seen them almost every day on this trip."

Louis nodded. "But think of *where* we have seen them. Always along the edges, and especially near the leading edges, of glaciers. Those scrapings must have been caused by ice, or more likely, by rocks trapped in the ice, scraping along the valley wall as a glacier passes."

Alexander grunted in exasperation. "Of course they were. We're right next to a glacier!"

"*But*," continued Agassiz sternly. "I have also seen these markings in England, in the plains of Germany, even in the coastal lowland countries. That must mean that glaciers were once there, too. But the only way to *prove* it is to gather data on the distribution of these markings all over Europe."

Half an hour later, they rounded a small ridge and gazed down into a wide, U-shaped valley beyond the leading edge of the glacier. "Look at this valley," commanded Agassiz. "Tell me what you see."

Alexander paused and shrugged. "I see a glacier, a small stream running down from its base, a pasture."

"No!" interrupted Agassiz. "You see the footprint of an ancient glacier. You see history."

Alexander squinted as he gazed down, searching for some clue he had missed before. "History? Where?"

"Streams and rivers make V-shaped valleys," said Louis. "Only glaciers gouge out rounded, U-shaped ones. And see those huge boulders way down the valley? How do you think they got there? A glacier carried them there and left them as it melted and shrank back up the valley. Once this whole valley was covered by a glacier. *That's* history."

Agassiz paced back and forth excitedly on the ledge. A pleasantly warm breeze rippled into their faces. "I have seen this valley shape before, too. Such valleys are all over Europe. At some time in the ancient past, all Europe must have been covered by glaciers! The earth must have been much colder then. It was an age of ice—an *ice age*."

Agassiz reached back and tapped the thick notebooks in his pack. "This is why we have to keep such careful notes. We can't actually see what the earth used to be like. But, like a careful detective, I can sift for clues, footprints, and fingerprints that tell me what used to be here. The notes and drawings in these books are my clues. They prove the existence of an ancient ice age on earth. Without this data I would have only uninformed guesses. Come, Alexander. It is time to present my findings to the world."

Six months later, at a European scientific convention, Jean Louis Agassiz proudly presented his research and conclusions. After presenting volumes of field data and drawings, he loudly concluded, "My comparisons of rock markings and regional geological structure across Europe prove the existence of ancient ages of ice, with thick glacial blankets, covering this entire continent."

"I believe that these ice ages and their colder temperatures were created by God, and that there has been more than one such ice age—maybe as many as twenty. I further believe that all flora and fauna are destroyed during an ice age. The living periods between, and all of their individual species, are completely isolated from each other."

Reaction to Agassiz's bold presentation was swift. Geologists were stunned. Never before had a researcher collected such careful and extensive field data. Never before had anyone attempted to create such a grand theory as to include all of Europe. Never before had anyone been able to use current geological structure, markings, and other clues to actually prove what happened in the ancient and barely imaginable past. Geologists instantly recognized that Agassiz had shown them a more accurate and thorough way of conducting their science.

Biologists, such as the British scientists Darwin and Lyell, studying the evolution of living species were delighted with Agassiz's report, even though they knew his conclusion about the isolation of life between ice ages was wrong. What excited them was Agassiz's proof that amazingly different periods, such as the ice ages, existed in the earth's past at all. It was the first time scientists understood that our world hadn't always been as they found it.

Biologists saw that the changing temperature patterns of the ice ages explained something that had puzzled them for years. Many European plant species grew in regions where they didn't belong. The temperatures in these regions would normally be too hot for these species. But there they were. Suddenly, it made perfect sense. The plant species must have migrated south into new regions with the colder temperatures of an ice age, and now were trapped there, struggling to survive the heat of a modern world. But that's another story.

Library Link: How do glaciers shape the earth's surface?

Topics to Explore: geology, scientific method, Jean Louis Agassiz, glaciers, ice ages.

References for Further Reading:

- *In the Children's Library:*

Tallcott, Emogene. *Glacier Tracks.* New York: Lothrop, Lee & Shepard, 1970.

- *In the Adult Library:*

Tharp, Louis. *Adventurous Alliance: The Story of the Agassiz Family of Boston.* Boston: Little, Brown, 1959.

Consult your librarian for additional titles.

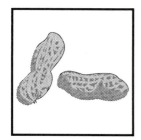

Other Earth Sciences

Nutty Science

A story of George Washington Carver's discovery in 1921 of more than 300 uses for the peanut

☑ **A Point to Ponder: How many uses can you think of for an ordinary peanut? George Carver thought of over 300. How many did you think of?**

Occasionally in science a moment of shining glory actually occurs in the bright spotlights on center stage rather than off in the wings. This is a story of one of those moments.

On an afternoon of bone-chilling drizzle in late January 1921, United States Senators Howard Fordney and John Garner paused in the long marble hallway outside the "Ways and Means" Committee meeting room on the Senate side of the capitol building. Hurried footsteps of staff and spectators echoed noisily off the polished walls.

"What's left, Howard? I'm bored stiff with these hearings. When can we go home?"

Senator Fordney, committee chairman, scanned his agenda sheet. "Just one more this afternoon, John. Let's see, some peanutman from somewhere in Alabama."

Garner groaned with a laugh. "Peanuts? Is this a joke, Howard? Why would the U.S. Senate include a two-bit, worthless crop like peanuts in the Tariff Protection Bill?"

Fordney shrugged and shook his head. "Beats me. Maybe he's really a circus man. That's the only place I ever saw peanuts. Maybe it *is* a joke."

Five minutes later, Senator Fordney pounded his gavel to begin the final round of public testimony on which crops were important enough to the American economy to be included in the new Tariff Protection Bill. "Order please. Order! At this time, the Senate Ways and Means Committee would like to call on Mr. . . . ." Fordney shuffled through his agenda notes searching for the name he was convinced was some kind of joke. "Oh yes. Mr. George Washington Carver from the circus . . . er, the peanuts."

"From Tuskegee Institute," corrected the trim, 56-year-old black man in an old, rumpled suit, with clear, brown eyes, who stepped to the witness table carrying a heavy cardboard suitcase. "I'm here representing the United Peanut Growers Association."

Many of the senators on the committee groaned or chuckled. Two tossed their pencils lightly into the air and leaned back, crossing their arms with disgusted looks that said their time was being wasted. Up and down the line of seated senators, the muttered words were repeated. "Peanuts? Why are we wasting our time on peanuts?"

Fordney tapped his gavel again for order and shrugged apologetically to his fellow senators. "According to the committee rules, Mr. Carver, you have ten minutes. Begin."

Carver smiled with a confidence few of that time could understand. Cotton was king in the South. Peanuts were at best a sideshow, an amusement for the circus or the county fair. "Gentlemen," he began in his high-pitched, quiet voice. "I am especially interested in southern crops and their potential for our regional and national economy. In my 25 years of research at Tuskegee Institute, I have found the peanut to be the most amazing, versatile, and promising of all crops."

Senators arched their eyebrows in disbelief. But George Washington Carver had 25 years of careful science to back him up. Like a skilled magician, he began to pull jars, bottles, bags, and vials from his bulging cardboard suitcase.

"Gentlemen, I apologize for not bringing all that peanuts offer. But I have identified over 300 valuable products that can be made from the simple peanut. This is only a small sample."

One jar held facial cream made with a peanut oil base. A bag held peanut-based cattle feed. There was peanut breakfast cereal, and peanut coffee. A bottle was filled with milk made from peanuts. "This peanut milk, gentlemen, has been fed to starving children in regions of Africa where animals are scarce, and where peanuts are much easier to grow than cows. It has saved thousands of lives in one region alone."

Other jars held dyes, butter, soap, wood stain, and meat sauce. Bottles were filled with oils, ink, and shaving cream. On the table was a stack of paper made from peanut shells. Carver picked up a strip of peanut-based plastic and tossed it to one senator. To another he tossed a synthetic rubber made from peanuts.

The great magician Houdini, himself, could not have dreamed of a more amazed reaction from his audience. All along the table, senatorial mouths dropped open, hands thoughtfully stroked chins, pencils scribbled notes, and hurried instructions were whispered to staff members.

Newspaper reporters who had watched all three long days of the hearings said that the peanutman was the only witness to get a reaction out of the Committee, to *really* get their attention.

All along the Committee hands began to rise. "Mr. Carver, are you telling us this amazing variety of things all come from *peanuts?*"

"Mr. Carver, if peanuts will do all this, why haven't we been producing them all along?"

"Mr. Carver, I don't think you told us what the brown stuff is in that large jar to your left."

Carver smiled. "My mistake, Senator. That one is peanut butter."

Chairman Fordney tapped his gavel and recommended they extend the peanutman's 10 minutes to 30, and the whole Committe nodded agreement.

To all appearances, George Washington Carver was calm as he answered questions and smiled. But inside, he was bursting with waves of satisfaction and joy. While his mouth quietly explained the research techniques he had used to isolate and study the oils, starches, proteins, and other elements in peanuts, peanut skins, and peanut shells, his mind flashed back to 1896 and his long-ago beginning at Tuskegee Institute.

Booker T. Washington, Tuskegee Institute's first president, had talked Carver into coming to Alabama from his graduate studies in Iowa. On a hot, muggy August morning, Booker showed George around the campus.

"Where's my research lab?" asked Carver.

Washington hesitated. "Where would you like it to be?"

Carver groaned. "You mean to tell me I am supposed to conduct agricultural research with no laboratory?"

"I'm sorry, George. This is a poor, black college. We barely scrape by as it is."

In frustration, George scanned around the south end of the campus where they stood. "What's that small barn?"

Washington smiled and clapped Carver on the shoulder. "It *was* a rundown eyesore. Now it's your new Agricultural Experiment Station."

For months, Carver struggled to stock his lab with even the most basic equipment. He rummaged through the county dump for bottles he could use as laboratory beakers. He found an old tin cup to use as a mortar for grinding stems, shells, or grains for his experiments. He adapted metal parts from an abandoned, rusting wagon into storage shelves and burners.

But by far the hardest thing for Carver to endure was not the crude working conditions or lack of financial support. It was the scorn of the local farming community. Regularly doors were slammed in his face when he asked for a bushel of a crop to test or for the use of old farm equipment. Carver often heard comments like, "We got folks starvin' on farms all over this state. Why doesn't that school do something to help instead of wasting time and money on high-falootin', do-nothin' science?"

By early May, 1897, Carver felt desperate to do something, anything to quiet the angry accusations as he slumped glumly into an overstuffed arm chair in Booker T. Washington's office. "Booker, I have to show the farmers that science is their hope, not their hindrance. Science is a process, a systematic way of doing things. I have to make it work to their benefit."

Booker only halfheartedly listened as he shuffled through stacks of papers spread across his desk. "Now George, you've already found and tested new and cheaper ways for them to fertilize the soil. And you're well on your way toward isolating several major cotton diseases and ways to fight them. I'd say that's pretty good for the first year at your science post."

"But it's not enough. I want science to make their lives better."

Washington laughed. "To do that, George, you would need to find a new crop to replace cotton. Cotton's in real trouble around here with the boll weevil infestations and soil depletion being as bad as it is."

Something about the way Booker said "new crop" blasted like a thunderbolt in Carver's mind. "No! Not new crops. New *products* from old crops!"

A great picture of southern survival and prosperity flashed vividly into Carver's mind. He was already in the midst of a study on how to replenish a vital plant nutrient, nitrogen, in the soil by planting peanuts in nitrogen-poor fields. Peanut plants replaced nitrogen.

Carver rose to his feet with eager excitement dancing in his eyes. "*Peanuts!*" he shouted, his voice rising from merely high-pitched to squeaky. "I'll find new products for them to make from peanuts!"

"Peanuts?" asked Booker, as if he hadn't quite heard right.

"Peanuts?" exclaimed the county farmers, as if this confirmed their belief that all scientists had lost their minds.

But here stood George Washington Carver, 24 years later, facing fifteen excited U.S. senators. "Peanuts, gentlemen. My research shows it is a crop America needs."

When the Tariff Protection Bill of 1921 reached the Senate floor two weeks later, peanuts were prominently included, while many better-known crops were not.

It was a shining moment of triumph for the scientific process and for the steadfast determination of one lone scientist working in a rundown barn with little equipment and less funding but with a vision of how science could serve his community. It seems the only successful peanut combination George Washington Carver did not invent was "peanut butter and jelly." But that is another story.

Library Link: Which parts of the peanut did George Washington Carver use to create his many peanut products?

Topics to Explore: life sciences, botany, agriculture, George Washington Carver, scientific method, observation.

References for Further Reading:

- *In the Children's Library:*

Adair, Gene. *George Washington Carver*. New York: Chelsea House Publishers, 1989.

- *In the Adult Library:*

Hayden, Robert C. *Seven African American Scientists*. Frederick, Md.: Twenty-First Century Books, 1970.

Consult your librarian for additional titles.

Library Link Answers

From "Teetering at the Beginning of Knowledge":

Question: How can someone very light lift someone very heavy on a seesaw? Why does this work?

Answer: A teeter-totter, or seesaw, is a good example of a lever at work. A light person cannot lift a heavy person on a seesaw—unless the heavy person scoots closer to the fulcrum than the lighter person. In this way, you are balancing the force pushing down on each side of the seesaw. Force is equal to the weight times that weight's distance from the fulcrum. Moving the lighter person farther out on the seesaw, increases the distance from the fulcrum, and increases the force exerted on that side of the lever, or seesaw.

From "The Fall of Galileo":

Question: Before laser guns, digital watches, and clocks, how would you time a falling brick?

Answer: With your own pulse.

From "A Weighty Matter":

Question: Can you feel the weight of the air pushing down on you?

Answer: You're not aware of this pressure. But, yes, you feel it. If earth's atmosphere were suddenly to evaporate, you would be aware of the absence of its weight.

Question: Do you know anyone who can feel changes in air pressure?

Answer: Many people have a "trick knee," elbow, or other joint that is sensitive to changes in atmospheric pressure. Some people even have a tooth that aches when air pressure changes. These people often say they can feel changes in the weather in their joints. What they really feel is changes in air pressure.

From "Apples, Moons, and Questions":

Question: Put two rocks on the ground. If gravity attracts all objects to all other objects, why don't the two rocks slide or roll toward each other?

Answer: Gravity is proportional to the mass of the two objects. Rocks are very, very small compared to earth, so the force of gravity attracting them to each other is small. Other, much larger forces overpower the attraction of gravity, including: friction, drag, air resistance, and the gravitational pull of other objects on the two rocks.

Question: Why do planets closer to the sun travel faster than planets at the outer edge of the solar system?

Answer: Gravity decreases with distance. Since Pluto is far away from the sun, its gravitational pull is much lower. Thus the rotational force trying to pull each planet away from the sun must also be smaller. Since this rotational force is proportional to speed, the same size planet would have to travel much faster in a close-in orbit, like Mercury's, to counter the strong gravitational pull of the sun.

Question: If the planets stopped traveling in their orbit around the sun, would they fall into the sun?

Answer: Yes. There would be no force to counter the gravitational pull of the sun.

From "Compressing the Truth":

Question: Have you ever compressed air? When?

Answer: Everyone has compressed air, and used Boyle's Law without knowing it. Two common examples are when you blow up a balloon, and when you squeeze the plastic bubbles in bubble-wrap packaging to make them pop. A third, even more common example happens when you exhale. The muscles in your chest squeeze and slightly compress the air in your lungs, forcing it to flow out through your nose.

From "Boring in on the Flow of Heat":

Question: Rub your hands against each other very fast. Did that motion create heat? What do we call this kind of heat?

Answer: Friction.

Question: Name as many sources of heat as you can.

Answer: There are many sources. The long list includes: friction, exothermic (or heat-producing) chemical reactions, nuclear reactions (fission and fusion, including the sun), resistance to an electrical current flow (light bulbs, electric heaters), burning (gas, matches, candle, wood), and biological activity (intracellular activity to convert matter to heat energy), among others.

From "The Truth About Monsieur Le Blanc":

Question: Do you think the sort of discrimination Sophie Germain faced has disappeared from science?

Answer: Gender discrimination still exists in science. But it is slight compared to that which existed at the beginning of this century and seems to be on a steady decline. Slightly less than 20% of all working scientists in the United States are female. While that percentage is far less than the 52% of the general population that is female, it is a far higher percentage than existed only a few years ago.

Question: Where do you think ideas like "women can't do science" ever got started?

Answer: While a number of good theories exist, and it is most likely tied to very early male/female role separation, no one knows for sure how it started. Certainly the notion that science and schooling were for males only existed by the time of the Greeks—around 3,000 years ago. From that perspective, it is remarkable that most of the discriminatory barriers that have blocked women from science for so long either have been, or are being, torn down in well under one century.

From "Faster Than a Speeding Bullet":

Question: What travels at the speed of light?

Answer: Only light.

Question: Name some common tools you use to make your everyday measurements more accurate.

Answer: The list is very long indeed. Some very common measurement tools include: clocks, digital watches, thermometers, rulers, scales, and speedometers. How many more can you name?

From "A Beeline to Physics":

Question: What do physicists study now?

Answer: With a whole world to study, physicists look at a great variety of topics. However, the greatest single area of current study is the motion and characterization of subatomic particles, those particles that are smaller than, and components of, protons, neutrons, and electrons.

Question: Have we always known that matter and energy were so closely related, that matter and energy are really different forms of the same thing?

Answer: No. The matter-energy relationship was first made clear by Albert Einstein's famous equation, $E=mc^2$. It has only been in this century that matter and energy have come to be viewed as interchangeable.

From "A Spark of Genius":

Question: Electricity is a powerful and dangerous form of energy. If you were beginning to experiment with electricity, how would you protect yourself from harm?

Answer: By avoiding contact with conducting surfaces, like metal or water, around electric currents, and by surrounding yourself with nonconducting insulators, like rubber and glass.

Question: Why was a Leyden Jar filled with water?

Answer: Water is an excellent conductor and can efficiently store an electric charge.

From "The Thread of Invention":

Question: Why do we have to have a glass bulb around the filament in a light bulb?

Answer: The glass bulb holds a vacuum environment around the filament. If oxygen got to the filament, it would immediately burn up.

From "A Ray of Insight":

Question: A Crookes Tube is an early example of a well-known type of electronic vacuum tube. Can you think of any modern uses for this type of tube?

Answer: The best-known uses of this type of tube, now called a cathode ray tube, or CRT, are televisions, video games, and computer terminals.

Question: Why do you have to wear a heavy, lead-filled vest when you get a tooth X-rayed at the dentist's office?

Answer: Exposure to too many X-rays over the course of your lifetime can cause any one of many very serious diseases. It is, therefore, important to expose yourself to as few as possible. The lead vest protects your body from stray X-rays produced by the machine that is taking a valuable picture of teeth, roots, and gums.

From "The Code for Success":

Question: Do we still use an electromagnetic telegraph system in the United States?

Answer: No. All commercial telegraph systems in the United States have converted to digital, computer-driven systems.

Question: What is a patent, and how can it protect an inventor's work?

Answer: The federal government grants a patent to acknowledge that an inventor has truly developed something new and different. Granting a patent to one person makes it illegal for anyone else to make the same or very similar thing without the inventor's permission.

From "The Call of Greatness:"

Question: Why was it easier to send Morse's telegraph dots and dashes through an electric line than voice?

Answer: Telegraphs send only two signals: "on" and "off." Changes or variations in electric current flow didn't matter. Either there was an electric current, or there wasn't. Voice transmission required creating, sending, detecting, and reproducing small, rapid changes in the flow of electric current. This was much harder to do.

Question: What happens when you talk that allows others to hear?

Answer: As you talk, you push a stream of air out of your mouth. The vibrations of your vocal cords causes this stream of air to vibrate. These vibrations travel through the air just as waves travel across the ocean. The louder you talk, the bigger these waves are. As you raise the pitch of your voice, the distance between waves shortens. The human ear feels these pressure changes and interprets them as the sound of speech.

From "A Signal to His Father":

Question: How does an antenna pick up a signal from the air?

Answer: A radio transmitter sends a powerful electrical current into a transmitting antenna. This stream of electrons literally leaps off the antenna and flies out through the air in all directions. A tiny fraction of these electrons run into some distant antenna. Most electrons, of course, run into the ground, or into trees, houses, rocks, or fly off into space. A radio antenna merely collects those electrons that finally run into it and channels them into a radio receiver.

Question: What were the first uses of radio signals?

Answer: Radio signals were first used for ship-to-shore communications, so that ships at sea wouldn't be completely isolated from the rest of the world. Next, they were used to pass official information from one governmental center to another. In both of these cases, the radio signal went from one specific point to another specific point. At each of those points there was both a radio receiver and a transmitter. It wasn't until almost three decades after Marconi's invention that someone thought of broadcasting signals that many people would pick up on small, individual radio receivers, or what we would call a modern radio station.

From "All Steamed Up":

Question: How does a steam engine work?

Answer: Some fuel (wood, coal, or oil) is burned to create heat. The heat boils water which turns to steam. This steam expands, pushing a piston up and down to do work.

Question: Name the most common uses of steam engines in this country.

Answer: Water and industrial pumps, steam locomotives up to the mid-1950s, industrial plants, and the Stanley Steamer, a 1911 automobile.

From "The Drive for Perfection":

Question: Virtually all components and systems in an automobile have been redesigned and improved many times since the time of Karl Benz. But have any completely new systems been invented for cars since his day?

Answer: Really very few. Karl Benz's cars contained virtually all the same major components you find on modern cars. Some exceptions include the hydraulic system for power steering and brakes, emission control systems, temperature control systems, and electronic ignition systems.

From "Launching a Scientist":

Question: What forces pull a rocket back to earth?

Answers: Only one: gravity.

Question: Why does a space shuttle get so hot as it rises through the atmosphere or as it reenters the atmosphere to return to earth?

Answer: It's the same reason your hand gets hot if you rub your hands together quickly: friction. For the space shuttle, heat comes from friction with the air.

From "A Warped Idea":

Question: Birds have always been our model for the design of flying machines. What about birds would be hardest to copy in a pair of man-made wings?

Answer: Bird wings move and bend in so many independent ways. It would be almost impossible to make mechanical wings move as freely. Also, bird wings are very large compared to the size of a bird's body. Wings for a human would have to be well over twenty feet long and thus very heavy.

Question: What holds an airplane up in the air?

Answer: Airplane wings are curved. The top is slightly convex. The bottom is slightly concave. As air flows over the wing it must go faster over the top. This creates greater pressure on the bottom of the wing than on the top. That greater pressure actually pushes the plane up.

From "An Explosive Idea":

Question: Why does an explosion create a sound?

Answer: When something explodes, it is really burning very rapidly. This burning creates tremendous heat, causing the air around the explosion to rapidly expand. The expansion of the air around an explosion rolls outward as a pressure wave and sounds like thunder to our ears.

Question: What is alchemy?

Answer: Alchemy is a medieval branch of chemistry that tried to account for many more than just the physical properties of a substance, and is best remembered for attempts to turn common base metals into gold.

From "The Measure of His Success":

Question: In what way is a burning candle the same as a rusting hunk of iron?

Answer: They are two examples of the same chemical process: oxidation, or the combining of a substance with oxygen. The candle combines with oxygen quickly. We call it "burning." The iron combines more slowly, just as Lavoisier's tin did. We call it "rusting," but it is exactly the same process.

Question: What is the air around us made of?

Answer: Nearly 80% nitrogen and 20% oxygen with some water vapor and a great many trace elements and environmental pollutants.

From "A Breath of Fresh Air":

Question: Why do people feel good when they breathe pure oxygen?

Answer: Oxygen is that part of the air we breathe that our bodies need. Oxygen is an essential ingredient in converting sugars and fats into useful energy. Normal air is only 20% oxygen. Breathing pure oxygen lets the lungs absorb much more oxygen than usual, and gives the body a rush of energy.

Question: Priestley started with a solid metal and wound up with liquid mercury and oxygen gas. What kind of a metal compound must the original metal have been?

Answer: It had to be a combination of mercury and oxygen, or an oxide of mercury. This oxide layer on the mercury is similar to a common layer of rust on iron, which is also an oxide compound.

From "A Liter of Mystery":

Question: What's the difference between an atom and a molecule?

Answer: Atoms are the smallest particle of each pure chemical element. When you subdivide an atom into protons, electrons, and neutrons, you can no longer tell which element they came from. Molecules are the smallest particles of any material substance on earth, such as water, bread, steel, or rubber. When you divide a molecule into separate atoms, you can no longer tell what substance the atoms were part of.

From "The Smell of Success":

Question: What are the biggest uses for rubber today?

Answer: Over 60% of rubber used in America goes for tires and inner tubes (car, plane, truck, etc.). Another 10% is used for mechanical and manufacturing belts, gaskets, seals, and rollers. About 14% goes into waterproof aprons, boots, hats, clothes, swimwear, and as a component in other fabrics. The other major uses of rubber include: hard rubber, medical rubber, toys, rubber bands, foam rubber, and so on.

From "A Research Headache":

Question: How does aspirin, or acetylsalicylic acid, stop pain?

Answer: Until very recently, no one knew. We just knew it worked, just as Charles Gerhardt did. Recent studies indicate that aspirin blocks the action of a hormone that is used to transmit pain signals to the brain.

From "Rod-Wax to Riches":

Question: Besides Vaseline®, motor oil, and gasoline, what other modern products are petroleum based?

Answer: The list is far longer than you might think, and, in general terms, includes: asphalt; energy products such as butane, propane, coal, gasoline, kerosene, jet fuel, heating oil, and diesel oil; lubricants like oil and grease; petroleum coke; mineral oils; napalm; naphtha; wax; paraffin; mineral wax; plastics; tar; and petrochemicals such as fertilizers, paints, some medicines, detergents, synthetic rubber, vinyl, acrylics, nylon, polyester, and styrofoam.

From "A Note of Inspiration":

Question: Are chemical elements still being discovered today, or have they all already been found?

Answer: New chemical elements are still being discovered. However, it has been many years since a new natural element was last found. New elements are now created in laboratories by forcing extra protons and neutrons into the nucleus of existing atoms.

Question: Is there anything on earth not made from a combination of the known chemical elements?

Answer: No.

From "A Glowing Discovery":

Question: Is the radiation from radioactive elements harmful?

Answer: Yes. It can cause severe tissue burns and many forms of cancer. However, radiation is more quickly absorbed by cancerous cells, which are killed by the radiation, than by healthy tissue. For this reason, radiation is used to treat cancer.

Question: We have all heard of "fluorescence" and "phosphorescence." But what are they and how do they differ?

Answer: Both types of light are caused when a substance absorbs incoming light rays and then re-emits them. Fluorescent substances stop emitting light as soon as they stop receiving incoming light. Phosphorescent substances continue to emit light, or glow, for a while after light has stopped striking them.

From "A Crystal-Clear View of Science":

Question: Why use crystals to study the molecular structure of a compound?

Answer: The molecules in a crystal are all locked in a regular, repeating pattern, and are all aligned the same direction, rather than being randomly oriented. This makes it much easier to examine and understand the shadows cast by individual molecules and atoms.

Question: Why did Dorothy Hodgkin use X-rays to study the structure of a molecule?

Answer: By 1940, X-rays had been known for over 50 years. Equipment was readily available to create and control them. How X-rays interacted with various types of atoms was well-known. X-ray film was also available, inexpensive, and easy to work with. So, X-rays were easy to use, and, because of their small size, they could do the job Dorothy Hodgkin needed them to do.

From "Funny Rubber":

Question: Does science always have to be serious?

Answer: No. Science is a systematic, thorough exploration into the unknown. At times it can be funny, or even silly, and still be careful, good science.

From "An Ounce of Correction":

Question: Since 1954, and the invention of Liquid Paper®, what ways have been discovered to correct typewritten mistakes?

Answer: The list includes: lift-off typewriter ribbon, typewriters with memories, and computers.

From "Sticking to Basics":

Question: How does glue work? What makes it stick?

Answer: It happens at a molecular level. Individual molecules of some liquid and semiliquid substances tend to hold onto each other. These substances are called "cohesive." Liquid mercury, which will ball up and not stick to or even leave a mark on anything, coheres to itself. Molecules of some other substances, however, don't hold to each other, but reach out and lock onto molecules of any other substance. These molecules are called "adhesive." Glues are examples of very strongly adhesive substances. Water is adhesive, but is weakly adhesive.

Question: What won't a Post-it® stick to?

Answer: Try an experiment to see. They won't stick to wet surfaces, or to very rough surfaces like lawn grass or a bumpy shower door. See if you can find common traits in the surfaces they will and will not stick to.

From "The Evolution of a Voyage":

Question: Why couldn't Darwin make the observations necessary to discover his principles of species evolution in England and Europe? Why did he have to go to isolated islands like the Galapagos?

Answer: The key to Darwin's discoveries was seeing how the same species evolved differently in separate, isolated environments. There are no real barriers in Europe to isolate one area from another and let a species evolve differently over many thousands of years.

From "Spontaneous War":

Question: Many of us drink pasteurized milk. What is pasteurization?

Answer: Pasteurization is really sterilization. Pasteurized milk is merely heated to kill microorganisms living in the milk.

Question: Besides discovering the field of microbiology, what other contributions to our health and well-being did Louis Pasteur make?

Answer: Pasteur's contributions to our scientific knowledge span four broad areas. These are: the identification of the role, source, and control of bacteria, and the development of bacteriology; the development of "pasteurization" and its application to the wine, silk, and milk industries; the development of a comprehensive "germ theory"; and the development of successful vaccinations for diseases including anthrax, cholera, and rabies.

From "The Dawn of Blood":

Question: If each being begins as one single cell, how do different cells decide to specialize and turn into different organs, blood cells, hair, or other body parts?

Answer: Each cell contains a complete blueprint, or plan, for the entire organism. This blueprint is written on our DNA and has many millions of individual instructions. As cells multiply, these DNA instructions guide each cell to adapt to its particular function.

Question: Why would anyone care how, and from where, the blood vessels and blood cells are formed?

Answer: There are two general reasons. First, understanding how individual body parts form helps us understand and correct many of the diseases and deficiencies these body parts can have. Second, this knowledge helps us understand how our very complex bodies function, and so how to care for and protect them.

From "Shark Bait":

Question: Are sharks in captivity dangerous?

Answer: Yes, but not nearly as dangerous as you might think. Many species of shark do not tend to attack anything as large as a grown person, and virtually all species will only attack when hungry. Newly captured sharks tend to be disoriented and in mild shock, and so are neither hungry nor prone to attack.

Question: How do sharks find their prey?

Answer: Sharks have an extremely sensitive sense of smell. This can guide them to food over long distances of open water. When a shark gets closer to its prey, it follows vibration patterns in the water. These vibrations can lead a shark to prey hundreds of yards away. Sharks have relatively poor eyesight. Still, they tend to rely on it during actual attacks.

From "Green Pea, Yellow Pea":

Question: Why do geneticists study plants, when we really want to know about heredity in humans?

Answer: There are many good reasons. Here are five. We can't experiment on people; we can on plants. Plants have far fewer genes to track and separate. The reproductive cycles of plants are much shorter, so it is possible to study more generations. Plants can be isolated and carefully followed; humans cannot. Finally, plants can be torn apart, ground up, and analyzed; humans cannot.

From "The Fly Room":

Question: How would you examine 1,000 tiny flies?

Answer: Morgan sprayed anesthetic gas over the flies. It is generally the same kind of gas used to put humans to sleep before surgery.

Question: Name as many traits we inherit through genes as you can.

Answer: The list is very long indeed, and includes every aspect of how you look, your bone structure, and how your body functions.

From "What the Mold Told":

Question: What is mold? Where does it come from, and how does it grow?

Answer: Mold is the fluffy growth of a fungus. Molds tend to grow where there is a good food supply for the fungus, such as food, leather, and fabric, and where the atmosphere is warm and damp.

From "Jumping Genes":

Question: Why did genetic researchers use pea plants, corn plants, and fruit flies to study heredity instead of looking at people?

Answer: Those plants are easy to crossbreed, and to tear apart and study. Flies have a short life cycle, so that many generations may be studied quickly. Simpler organisms also have fewer chromosomes and a simpler genetic makeup.

From "AB or Not AB":

Question: What does it mean to have different blood types? How are they different?

Answer: All blood groups are identical in composition. The only difference is in whether the antibodies in the blood recognize another blood sample as being a foreign body or not. If the antibodies believe the other blood sample is foreign, they will attack the new blood, clotting with it.

From "The Sweet Juice of Success":

Question: Are there other well-known human diseases treated with tissues extracted from animals?

Answer: Yes. The long list of cures provided by animals includes: thyroid medicine, smallpox vaccinations, estrogen, anesthetics, hemorrhoid medicines, and most hormone treatments, among others.

From "Miracle Mold":

Question: Are there other molds we now use to cure or prevent disease?

Answer: Surprisingly few. Normally, Western medicine uses only penicillin and ergotamine, a mold that grows on rye bread and is used to treat migraine headaches.

Question: What molds are we most likely to encounter?

Answer: While we are regularly exposed to many, probably the most common are food molds, such as those found on bread, cheese, or leftovers in the refrigerator, and household molds, like those on shower walls.

From "Skin-Deep Success":

Question: What is the purpose of color pigment in human skin? How did it develop? Why don't we all have the same amount of it?

Answer: Melanin pigment in skin cells blocks harmful solar radiation from reaching the sensitive tissues and organs below. It developed in humans in the same way virtually all species evolutions occur. In exposed areas near the equator, where there are more harmful amounts of solar UV radiation, people with more pigment survived better than people without. Over time, the human species in those areas developed with heavy concentrations of melanin pigment cells. Human populations farther north were never exposed to the same levels of solar UV radiation. So it did not benefit populations in those areas to develop pigment cells.

From "Circles in the Sky":

Question: Does the earth travel in a circle around the sun?

Answer: No. All the planets orbit in ellipses. While Copernicus mistakenly thought the earth traveled in a perfect circle, his work led to Keppler's discovery of elliptical orbits.

Question: Do the planets travel around the sun at a constant speed?

Answer: No. Velocity varies along an elliptical path as the distance from the sun to each planet varies. The closer the earth is to the sun, the faster it travels. Copernicus had no real way of detecting these velocity variations and so thought all planets orbited at constant velocities.

From "The Orbit of Truth":

Question: Galileo was persecuted for his scientific findings. Has that happened at any other time in history?

Answer: Often. New theories threaten old beliefs which most of us are very reluctant to change. Copernicus was hounded for his observations 70 years before

Galileo was condemned. Unfortunately, it still happens today, although the persecution isn't quite as harsh. The scientists who first suggested, in the late 1970s, that mitochondria are independent organisms living symbiotically within our cells were publicly condemned for over a decade before it was proved they were correct. Everyone laughed at the first scientists to suggest, in the late 1980s, that the dinosaurs all died because of a great asteroid collision with earth on what is now the Yucatan Peninsula of Mexico. Now it is the most widely-accepted theory. Everyone dismissed Dr. Linus Pauling as a senile old fool, when he claimed in the early 1980s, that massive amounts of vitamin C could prevent a variety of diseases. Now much research backs his claim.

From "A Gold Medal Speck of Light":

Question: Can you see the differences between planets and stars with the the naked eye?

Answer: No. You need a telescope to see the differences. They do, however, move differently across the sky from night to night. This motion can be tracked by the naked eye for planets closest to earth.

Question: How do comets look different from planets and stars?

Answer: Comets can be distinguished by their pattern of movement across the night sky and by their characteristic tail. Often, however, the tail cannot be seen without a telescope.

From "The Sands of Time":

Question: How fast are mountain ranges pushed up by the shifting plates of the earth's crust?

Answer: Only by small fractions of an inch per year. But a mountain pushed up at a rate of only one-fourth inch per year would rise over 25,000 feet in a million years, which isn't very long in geologic terms.

Question: Have the continents of the earth always been where they now are?

Answer: No. They drift on huge plates in the earth's crust that float on the semiliquid mantle and core. For example, South America used to be joined with Africa, and North America used to be part of Europe. As these continents drifted apart the Atlantic Ocean was formed.

From "Putting the Truth on Ice":

Question: How do glaciers shape the earth's surface?

Answer: Glaciers exert tremendous pressure as they creep slowly across the earth—enough pressure to blast through solid rock and to scoop up hard-packed dirt. With this great pressure, glaciers gouge out long U-shaped valleys, pushing tons of rock and earth ahead of them. Of course, glaciers do this very slowly, over many thousand years.

From "Nutty Science":

Question: Which parts of the peanut did George Washington Carver use to create his many peanut products?

Answer: All parts. He used the meat, the thin skin around the peanut, the shell, and the plant and the roots. Besides using each of these parts whole or ground up, he extracted many separate components from each plant part—oils, fiber, glutens, proteins, fats, juices, and resins. He was able to use each of these in unique and different ways.

Index

About the Author

The only West Point graduate to ever become a professional storyteller, Kendall Haven also holds a master's degree in oceanography and spent six years as a senior research scientist for the United States Department of Energy before finding his true passion for storytelling and a different kind of "truth." He has now performed for more than 250,000 children and adults in 36 states, and has presented workshops to more than 10,000 teachers on the practical, in-class teaching power of storytelling. Haven has won numerous awards both for his story-writing and for his storytelling. And he has become one of the nation's leading advocates for the educational value of storytelling.

Haven has published five audio tapes and two picture books of his original stories, and recently created a three-hour high-adventure radio drama for National Public Radio on the effects of watching television, which has won five major national awards.

Haven has used his writing talent to create stories for many nonprofit organizations including The American Cancer Society, the Institute for Mental Health Initiatives, several California Crisis Centers, the Children's Television Resource and Education Center, one regional hospital, and the Child Abuse Prevention Training Center of California.

He lives with his wife and nephew in the rolling Sonoma County grape vineyards of rural northern California.